A Return to Justice

A Return to Justice

Rethinking Our Approach to Juveniles in the System

Ashley Nellis

ROWMAN & LITTLEFIELD
Lanham • Boulder • New York • London

Published by Rowman & Littlefield
A wholly owned subsidiary of The Rowman & Littlefield Publishing Group, Inc.
4501 Forbes Boulevard, Suite 200, Lanham, Maryland 20706
www.rowman.com

Unit A, Whitacre Mews, 26-34 Stannary Street, London SE11 4AB

British Library Cataloguing in Publication Information Available

Library of Congress Cataloging-in-Publication Data

Nellis, Ashley, author.
A return to justice: rethinking our approach to juveniles in the system/Ashley Nellis.
  pages cm
Includes bibliographical references and index.
ISBN 978-1-4422-2766-8 (cloth: alk. paper) — ISBN 978-1-4422-2767-5 (electronic)
1. Juvenile justice, Administration of—United States. 2. Juvenile delinquency—United States. 3. Juvenile corrections—United States. I. Title.
HV9104.N35 2016
364.360973—dc23   2015023175

♾™ The paper used in this publication meets the minimum requirements of American National Standard for Information Sciences—Permanence of Paper for Printed Library Materials, ANSI/NISO Z39.48-1992.

Printed in the United States of America

In memory of Jerome Miller
1931–2015

Contents

Acknowledgments

This book would not have been possible without the historical wisdom of scholars and advocates who have devoted their life's work to bringing youth justice closer to its original vision. I am grateful to Paolo Annino, Shay Bilchik, Bart Lubow, Liz Ryan, and Mark Soler for sharing their perspectives as well as providing historical materials that greatly assisted with my research. A juvenile justice system suitable for children is within reach because of the perseverance of today's youth advocates who have worked to end policies and practices that put youth, particularly youth of color, in harm's way.

I am grateful for the patience and encouragement of my colleagues at The Sentencing Project. One could not ask for a more supportive environment in which to research and write. I am fortunate to have Marc Mauer as a mentor and friend.

My work is inspired by the children and families whose lives have been touched by the justice system.

Introduction

Ralph Brazel Jr. was raised in low-income neighborhoods in New Jersey by a loving mother who divorced when he and his brother were young. As a teen, he chafed at her restrictions, skipping school and getting into trouble. Against his mother's wishes, he moved to St. Petersburg, first living with his father, who struggled with addiction problems, then with his grandmother. Before long, Brazel got caught up in selling drugs. "I didn't make a lot of money—never saw a thousand dollars of my own—but I was living every day like it was a Friday—going to the beach, go-cart racing, riding in the '72 Cadillac Sedan DeVille given to me by my uncle," he recalls.

At seventeen, Brazel was caught with eighteen grams of crack cocaine. He pled guilty and the state of Florida sentenced him, as a juvenile, to twenty months in state prison for two counts of conspiracy to distribute and manufacture the drug. While he was waiting to go to state prison, the federal government apprehended him for a new drug offense. The earlier charges now became two prior convictions—along with a new sentence in the federal system.

For a nonviolent offense committed as a juvenile, Brazel was sentenced by a federal judge to three life sentences—a lifetime in prison with no possibility of parole. Some 2,500 others are in similar situations in the United States, the only nation in the world that sentences juveniles to life in prison without parole.

In August 2013, days before his fortieth birthday, after having served twenty-two years in prison, Brazel became a free man, thanks in part to a 2010 U.S. Supreme Court decision striking down such life sentences for non-homicide cases. Today he is slowly building his life back.

Ralph Brazel's story is a symbol of the extremes of crime policy that dominated the 1990s in a frenzied political response to address violent crime, much of which was attributed to young black males. Though the impact of these policies on adults and their communities has received much attention, Brazel's story reminds us that children were affected too—from the thousands of youth funneled directly into the adult criminal justice system through legislative changes, to the 2.2 million individuals today who have a parent in prison.

In the minds of most Americans, juvenile crime is a serious problem, and policy makers have historically responded by enacting ever-harsher penalties that incarcerate increasing numbers of young offenders. Harmful youth policies enacted in the 1980s and 1990s in particular set juvenile justice policy and practice back in time, removing the long-standing appreciation of young age as a principal factor in limiting culpability from the court's deliberation and sentencing process.

Many of these youth policies are still in place. At the same time, substantial reforms during the past fifteen years have produced a steady and substantial decline in the number of youth who encounter the juvenile justice system. States are saving millions of dollars annually through redirecting thousands of young people from institutions to treatment in their communities, where they are more appropriately and effectively served. Time and financial investment have been devoted to researching what works to improve youth outcomes. And perhaps most important, substantial *system* reforms have accompanied the expansion of options for offending and at-risk youth. There is now general agreement that so long as outdated policies and practices are in place that have been demonstrated to harm children and fail to produce public safety results, lasting change remains out of reach. With this in mind, various jurisdictions around the country have overhauled their juvenile justice systems and replaced them with a renewed vision for juvenile justice that operates from the inside out.

The system, now more than a century old, has fluctuated significantly in its philosophies and practices about wayward youth. At times it has tried to serve as a compassionate and caring system with a duty to redirect errant youth and provide the support and services lacking in their homes and communities. At other times, the system essentially replicated the congregate care approach apparent in adult prisons and jails, serving as little more than a warehouse for criminal and other unwanted youth. Legal attention to the gaps in procedural protections afforded to youth resulted in substantial improvements to the system during the 1960s and 1970s. Yet in the latter part of the twentieth century, as juvenile crime experienced a troubling rise, the juvenile justice system suffered from accusations of being too soft on crime; in response, it re-created itself as one that would make kids "accountable" through punishment and deterrence. And in recent years, the juvenile justice system reversed course again, recommitting to its initial purpose by incorporating critical developments in science and medicine that confirm what many parents already know: kids are different.

A main objective for this book is to offer an account of the reforms under way within the juvenile justice field while identifying the remaining areas for attention given current political, social, and economic factors at play. Though reforms are challenged within divisive legislatures, much progress has still been made.

To continue the momentum of today's reform movement, it is necessary to appreciate the current environment in the context of what preceded it, and the various forces that have converged to create change. This book tells the story of the contours of juvenile justice through a lens of four eras of juvenile justice. In each of these eras, reforming the system itself was the primary aim, but the definition for what that reform should look like changed substantially. The first of these four eras was defined by the creation of an independent juvenile system (1899–1960) followed by procedural protections for youth (1960s–1985), the tough on crime movement (1985–2000) and, finally, an increased focus on age-appropriate responses that restrict the use of detention in favor of alternatives to incarceration (2000–present).

The prevailing account of juvenile justice's history discusses the emergence of a separate system by a benevolent charity movement to accommodate important developmental differences because of age. Alternate accounts of American juvenile justice history challenge the notion that it emerged solely from a benevolent charity movement engaged in child-saving and citizen-building because this version omits the tremendous influence of deeply divided race relations in America. A less frequently told version takes account of the significant impact of race. Woven throughout the history has been a persistent message to young people of color that they are less worthy of humane treatment and less capable of reform.

The juvenile justice system has changed substantially in many places during the past two decades, to the point where the record number of incarcerated youth has been cut in half. This book assesses the strategies and policies that have produced this unlikely directional shift. Sustained declines in youth crime have helped to create the opportunity for new advances in justice reform, as have advances in adolescent brain science, a nationwide domestic budget crisis, focused advocacy with policy makers and practitioners, and successful public education campaigns that address extreme sanctions for youth such as solitary confinement and life sentences for juveniles. The U.S. Supreme Court has voiced its unfaltering conclusion that children are different from adults in four landmark cases since 2005. The question is how to take advantage of the momentum for juvenile justice reform of the kind that would reorient the juvenile justice system in a permanent way that is designed to succeed in getting wayward youth back on track.

Around the country, practitioners, policy makers, and researchers in the field of criminal justice are turning to the juvenile justice field as a model for reform. Crime has declined steadily for both youth and adults since the mid-1990s, but incarceration on the adult side has not seen nearly the same level of decarceration. In fact, despite modest progress in areas of the adult criminal justice system, the United States remains the world's leading jailer and continues to support a variety of policies and practices that have been clearly demonstrated to harm communities, exceed our abilities to pay for them, and do little to strengthen public safety.

Yet a different story is emerging in the field of juvenile justice. Over the past decade, the size of the juvenile justice system has declined significantly; far fewer youth who are adjudicated delinquent are placed in secure confinement. From a peak of 76,600 committed youth in 1999, the 2013 census count was 35,659 youth, representing a 53.4 percent decline in secure confinement over this period. Growing numbers of states are shuttering their juvenile justice institutions and providing financial incentives to counties to keep youth locally, investing instead in evidence-based interventions. Reforms of juvenile justice systems are occurring in jurisdictions around the nation. A wholesale shift in the tone about juvenile offenders has taken place during the past fifteen years that few would have predicted during the "superpredator" era. Today it is largely accepted that secure confinement of youth, especially in institutions designed for adults, is harmful to youth, communities, and public safety. Since the beginning of the twenty-first century, state legislatures have reversed harmful youth policies that failed to consider the important differences between youth and adults, such as the transfer of juveniles to criminal court.

Despite progress, troubling problems remain. Chronic racial and ethnic disparities persist today throughout the juvenile justice system and accumulate as youth go deeper into the system despite overall declines in youth incarceration. And, the extent to which we can celebrate the reforms in juvenile justice must be tempered by recent events that have drawn national attention. Since 2012, police shootings of several unarmed people have reignited racial tensions, highlighting lingering associations of people of color and criminality. Achieving fairness and equity in the juvenile justice system is also hindered by school discipline trends that have created a school-to-prison pipeline.

While confinement has declined at an unprecedented rate and systems are much more likely to incorporate evidence-based solutions to juvenile delinquency, the conditions for youth who experience incarceration are often substandard. These can include periods of solitary confinement, second-rate treatment and education opportunities, and excessively long periods of confinement. In addition, thousands of youth under the age of eighteen are transferred to the adult system each year despite strong evidence that the juvenile justice system is better suited for their needs. After an encounter with the system, youth face collateral consequences that follow them through life and inhibit their ability to move beyond their mistakes. Finally, the juvenile justice system continues to operate in a silo without collaboration or coordination with neighboring child-serving agencies. As a result, prevention and intervention efforts are too often fragmented.

These problems are significant but not insurmountable. Because of the continuous drops in juvenile crime combined with steadily falling confinement rates, juvenile justice is well positioned to make these adjustments. A question that should remain central as reforms continue is how to guarantee that these improvements will be sustained in the event of a rise in juvenile crime, shifts in the political landscape, or less-restrained fiscal climates.[1] As the light continues to shine on juvenile justice and its many important reforms, it is imperative to consider steps that will make the system both more effective and smaller.

Chapter 1

Visions for Juvenile Justice

[T]he juvenile justice system was created to control and regulate the children of the poor, not to save them.

—Sheldon and Osborne, 1989

Varying historical accounts of the emergence of the modern juvenile justice system help toward an understanding of contemporary mechanisms for responding to juvenile delinquency. The most widely accepted portrayal of America's juvenile justice history is that of a child-saving movement led by social activists, women's organizations, crusading judges, and bar associations seeking better outcomes for wayward youth.[1] The concerns of these groups arose from an awareness of serious, chronic troubles at existing institutions where youth were confined: adult jails and prisons, as well as houses of refuge and reform schools. Reformers wished to remove youth from the negative influence of adults as well as design a new system that would appreciate the unique qualities of youth in developing the appropriate sanction. The components of the early systems for juvenile justice shed light on the separate system that emerged in the twentieth century.

The establishment of the juvenile court in 1899 let to optimism for the treatment of youth. Before that, little regard had been paid to a defendant's young age, amenability for reform, or consequences that accompanied a period of incarceration, stymying a young person's chances to move beyond the crime. For decades earlier, too, children had been mistreated physically and mentally through confinement in the large, fortress-like institutions in which they were incarcerated.

EARLY SYSTEMS OF REFORM

The isolation of offenders from the rest of society is a favored crime solution in American culture for juveniles and adults alike.[2] Historically, institutionalization has been the primary response to misbehavior for juveniles.

The dominant philosophy about misbehaving youth during the nineteenth century was that they had gotten off track through lax parenting and/or environmental temptations, but that they were not inherently deviant.[3] The solution—incarceration—was justified on the basis that it could accomplish several different goals: separation from the negative environment, isolation from negative influences (i.e., peers and adult offenders), moral education and development, and disciplined labor. Aside from separating youth from adults, which was thought to be especially problematic, early systems of reform claimed to offer rehabilitation to those who were believed to be capable of change.[4]

Houses of Refuge

Houses of refuge for children and adolescents appeared in select cities starting in New York in 1824. On the whole, New York's house of refuge was envisaged to provide shelter, reform, education, and training to those who were labeled as troubled youngsters. The purpose of the institution was described by the Society for the Reformation of Juvenile Delinquents, the primary group that advocated for its creation. The description read, in part:

> The design of the proposed institution is, to furnish, in the first place, an asylum, in which boys under a certain age, who become subject to the notice of our police, either as vagrants, or homeless, or charged with petty crimes, may be received, judiciously classed according to their degree of depravity or innocence, put to work at such employments as will tend to encourage industry and ingenuity, taught reading, writing, and arithmetic, and most carefully instructed in the nature of their moral and religious obligations while at the same time, they are subjected to a course of treatment, that will afford a prompt and energetic corrective of their vicious propensities, and hold out every possible inducement to reformation and good conduct.[5]

The Massachusetts House of Refuge allowed for a wide variety of children to be imprisoned, including those convicted of criminal offenses, "as well as all children who live an idle or dissolute life, whose parents are dead, or if living, from drunkenness or other vices, neglect to provide any suitable employment, or exercise any statutory control over said children."[6] Teaching

Protestant work ethics of discipline and hard labor was a primary goal of the nineteenth-century institutions, in addition to "moral training," or methods to "socialize the boys and girls into a 'realistic' acceptance of their place in society."[7] The modes of discipline utilized frequently included brutality.

The desire to reform certain youth took precedence over a duty to determine guilt or even suspicion of delinquent behavior. As a consequence, youth frequently entered institutions without having been convicted or even charged with an offense. Because the system was informal in nature, procedural rights for young defendants were a low priority.[8] When youth encountered the justice system, greater attention was paid to their prospects for change than blameworthiness. Children were sentenced to indeterminate lengths of imprisonment, and release typically did not occur until at least two years of secure confinement had been served.

Houses of refuge were large, fortress-style congregate institutions where as many as one thousand youth resided at a time.[9] A heavy punitive quality dominated early institutions; tales of abuse and neglect were widely circulated. Fostering a sense of self-esteem for the youngsters was far from a priority. New York's house of refuge founders openly voiced their disdain for young inmates, referring to them as "little vagrants" who "should be stopped, reproved, and punished."[10]

Reform Schools

Reform schools emerged during the latter part of the nineteenth century and held a slightly different mission than preexisting houses of refuge. Reform schools were designed to be small, rural, cottage-like homes operated by caring parental figures who served to supervise, train, and educate youth in their care. The first reform school was the Lyman School for Boys[11] established in Massachusetts in 1886; seven years later the Lancaster School for Girls was opened. By 1876, there were fifty-one reform schools around the country, funded through both state and private funds.[12]

Youth convicted of more serious crimes typically remained imprisoned with adults, but some attempts were made to limit this negative exposure. In Illinois, for example, the 1883 law establishing reform institutions read, "persons under 18 shall not be punished by confinement in the penitentiary for any offense except robbery, burglary, or arson; in all other cases where a penitentiary punishment is or shall be provided, such a person under the age of 18 shall be punished by imprisonment in the county jail for any term not exceeding 18 months at the discretion of the court."[13]

As in earlier institutions, the acts that could lead to incarceration were not clearly defined. In Utah, for example, a child could be removed from his home and placed in a reform school for being "incorrigible, vicious, neglected, vagrant, or . . . found frequenting a house of ill fame."[14] In general, though the proposed design for these institutions was envisioned to be a vast improvement over houses of refuge, the two were hardly distinguishable: both were overwhelmingly custodial and oppressive.

Youth of Color

A young person's need and capacity for reform was an important and unique feature of youth reform (though the definition of reform would not meet today's standards) and was a qualifying factor for admission to early youth prisons. Not all youth were determined to be amenable to reform, however. Deep ethnic and racial divisions persisted throughout the nineteenth century and were apparent in early American juvenile justice as well, which ultimately shaped the treatment of children in such a way as to provide two systems of justice: one for youth of color and one for white children.

The placement of white children in facilities specifically reserved for youth began by the mid-nineteenth century, but since black youth were essentially considered irredeemable, they continued to be sent to adult prisons and jails. If they did enter a reform school, a more likely prospect in the South, they were typically segregated from the white population and afforded no opportunities for personal development. Instead, African American youth were typically assigned menial, physically demanding jobs that restricted upward mobility on release. Rehabilitation was believed to be an unattainable goal for black youth, and the racial integration of youth facilities was described as a "haunting" prospect.[15] A superintendent of the Philadelphia House of Refuge, for example, explained that "it would be degrading to the white children to associate them with being given up to public scorn."[16]

For white youth, work typically involved learning a craft that led to apprenticeships after their exit from the institution, such as training to become a skilled artisan. White youth also participated in education, whereas black youth were excluded.[17] In short, white youth were being prepared for life on the outside, while black youth were kept from such opportunities.

Toward the latter part of the nineteenth century, separate houses of refuge opened for African American youth but, still, the daily programming was limited to sharpening one's agricultural skills and the like. According to one account, their days were composed of learning "how to handle a hoe, shovel, and spade; to manage horses, mules, and cattle, to plow, to sow, and to reap."[18] Since the skills they developed proved to be useful traits for institution maintenance, there was little incentive to release African American inmates in a timely manner. Indeed, statistics from this time reveal that black youth were held as long as three years on average while white youth typically stayed half as long.[19]

THE CHILD-SAVING MOVEMENT: "A CHILD'S CASE IS NOT A LEGAL CASE"

The child-saving movement that began at the close of the nineteenth century was signaled by the establishment of Chicago's juvenile court. The first juvenile court aspired to transform the methods and institutions of the previous century. According to an analysis by criminologist Barry Feld, the juvenile court "was driven from the top by a national organization of charity reformers and fueled from the bottom by local civic groups who seized upon it as a safe focus for their varied efforts to do good."[20]

The reform efforts pertaining to young people centered on the notion of citizen-building; of primary concern to many during this time was establishing the obligation of the state to intervene in the lives of needy children with the goal of molding them into productive, successful members of society. Substantial reforms emerged on parallel tracks in the areas of child labor laws, compulsory school attendance laws, and juvenile delinquency. "These three reforms—school, work, and delinquency—constitute the trinity of legal and social construction of childhood. They reflect the central Progressive assumptions that strengthening the nuclear family, shielding the child from adult roles, postponing economic integration, formally educating him or her for upward mobility, and allowing the state to intervene in the event of parental or youthful deviance constituted the ideal way to prepare children for life."[21]

The creation of a separate court for juveniles is recounted by some as an altruistic undertaking by a wide coalition of child-savers, developed from an understanding that children were fundamentally different from adults in ways that rendered them less culpable for their delinquency.[22] The genesis of the first juvenile court came from a recognized need to improve conditions and to discontinue the harmful practice of confining convicted youth with adults.[23] Frederick Wines, a nineteenth-century criminologist, recommended "an entirely separate system of courts for children, in large cities, who commit offenses which would be criminal in adults. We ought to have a 'children's court' in Chicago, and we ought to have a 'children's judge,' who should attend to no other business."

The juvenile justice framers believed that a youth-oriented court could attend to youth in the same spirit as a loving and caring parent rather than the neutral arbiter role that judges played in the adult court system. The goal of judicial decisions in the juvenile system would be to provide the opportunity for reform that would set young delinquents on a better course while keeping their misdeeds confidential. It was seen as very important to prevent the stigma—a common consequence of adult adjudications—that might harm their efforts to move past their encounter with the juvenile justice system. For this reason, court processes and decisions were intended to be private and confidential.

Authority for the nation's first juvenile court, the Cook County Juvenile Court in Illinois, was created through the passage of "An Act for the Treatment and Control of Dependent, Neglected, and Delinquent Children." The law established special, informal rules of procedure, including the deliberate elimination of indictments, pleadings, and jury trials.[24] The juvenile court judge also served as jury and counsel,[25] and the newly established juvenile court was to pursue "child welfare when children were at risk by using the agencies of the state government to ensure that 'the care, custody, and discipline of the child shall approximate . . . that which should be given by its parents.'"[26] Advocates argued that childhood was a time of dependence and risk where supervision was essential for survival. It was evident, however, that many of the youth who encountered the court lacked sufficient parental supervision. When family was identified as providing inadequate guidance and supervision, the state stepped in as a surrogate parent. When the child was identified as at risk, the most appropriate authority to decide his or her best interests was believed to be a public official.[27] Chicago's juvenile court included six probation officers and thirty-six private citizens who voluntarily supervised children on probation. Racial segregation was an integral part of the system: an African American woman was hired, without compensation, to handle black youth who were on probation.[28]

Juvenile justice wards in the first years of the court were considered to be capable of rehabilitation and reform given that they could be separated from "hardened criminals" in the adult system. Though scientific evidence did not yet exist to support their claims, youth were recognized as especially vulnerable to negative influences and not yet fully capable of autonomous decision making.

Contact with the juvenile court system was advised to be brief and informal. It was also designed to be protected with the utmost confidentiality to protect youth from being branded as criminals. Court proceedings were held in private, few records of proceedings were maintained, and attempts were made to conceal disposition decisions from public view.[29] This was a departure from adult court hearings, which were open to the public. The court process for juveniles was situated almost as a medical procedure in which the judge was the doctor. This act of keeping issues private, observers commented, allowed "the judge the closest approach to the conditions under which a physician works."[30]

By many accounts, the first formal juvenile court that developed in Chicago claimed to prioritize rehabilitation, viewing the role of the court as that of a concerned and caring parent rather than a punisher. The court's responsibility was to temporarily intercede and redirect troubled youth toward a better path.[31]

Since punishment was not the goal of the juvenile court, there was no desire to distinguish between criminal and noncriminal acts in designating a child as "delinquent." And because the court was to be guided solely by the child's best interest, "formal processes of fact finding were viewed as unnecessary."[32] In fact, the language of the original Illinois legislation authorized penalties for "pre-delinquent" behavior.[33] Statutory definitions of delinquency elsewhere were broad, including such acts as "vicious or immoral behavior," "incorrigibility," and "profane and indecent language."

Oregon's statutory definition of a juvenile delinquent from this era exemplifies that which was typically found in state laws, a result of the desire to be all-encompassing rather than narrowly defined:

The words "a delinquent child" shall include any child under the age of 16 . . . years who violates any law of this State or any city or village ordinance, or is incorrigible, or who is a persistent truant from school, or who associates with criminals or reputed criminals, or vicious or immoral persons, or who is growing up in idleness or crime, or who frequents, visits, or is found in any disorderly house, bawdy house or house of ill-fame, or any house or place where fornication is enacted, or in any saloon, bar-room, or drinking shop or place, or any place where spirituous liquors are sold at retail or exchanged, or given away, or who patronizes, frequents, visits, or is found in any gaming house, or in any place where any gaming device is or shall be operated.[34]

In his description of the early juvenile court process, sociologist Anthony Platt writes, "A child was not accused of a crime but offered assistance and guidance; intervention in his life was not supposed to carry the stigma of a criminal record; judicial records were not generally available to the press or public, and hearings were conducted in relative privacy; proceedings were informal and due process safeguards were not applicable due to the court's civil jurisdictions."[35]

From its inception, the juvenile court's role in young people's lives differed considerably from the adult criminal justice system in that it maintained virtually unrestrained involvement in the lives of youth. The rehabilitation or treatment model that governed juvenile justice was frequently analogized to a medical model; judges viewed themselves as a type of physician tasked with making a diagnosis, and thus obligated to study the entire life and environment of a child in their courtroom. The symptoms of disease were "poverty, 'unfit families' (i.e., poor families), and 'idleness.'"[36]

A network of activist judges, including Julian Mack and Ben Lindsey, shaped the early juvenile court systems. Judge Julian Mack was an influential social reformer at the turn of the twentieth century who helped start the first juvenile court in Illinois. In his view, "society's role was not to ascertain whether the child was 'guilty' or 'innocent' but 'what is he, how has he become what he is, and what had best be done in his interest and in the interest of the state to save him from a downward career.'"[37] Like others in the movement at the time, Mack believed youth should be brought before a judge after a charge of delinquency to find out whether the child and the state would benefit from his or her custody for an indefinite period of time. Guilt and innocence were irrelevant.[38] Judge Mack's court model was essentially an extension of the preexisting criminal court, but designed to incorporate the young age and attending age-related factors that affect delinquency. His development of the *parens patriae* approach to juvenile justice, wherein the state was likened to a father figure, dominated the juvenile court movement that grew over the next several years.

Judge Ben Lindsey's approach in Denver, Colorado, has also been described as one of the original embodiments of the typical early juvenile courtroom. It was distinct from Judge Mack's design in that Lindsey played a much stronger activist role in the lives of the youth and in the communities where they resided. He extolled the value of community interventions, probation, and, "a juvenile court fueled by optimistic compassion."[39] Judge Lindsey led successful campaigns in seven states to create separate juvenile courts that defined the goal of the juvenile court judge as one who obtained a degree of trust from youth that would allow judicial guidance toward improved behavior.[40]

Whereas the Chicago model was built on the perspective that juvenile court should be an extension of the adult, criminal court but that it should be age-appropriate, Lindsey's courtroom was deliberately absent of procedural rules, instead maintaining an informal atmosphere where the prevailing view was that "a child's case is not a legal case."[41] The Chicago model interpreted the notion of *parens patriae* with "associating the court with authority and control," whereas the Denver model viewed *parens patriae* as a means to free juvenile court judges to "exercise broad discretion."[42] Lindsey wrote,

> We seek to make the child a co-worker with the state for his own salvation, which, of course, in the end, is the salvation of the state; for the child is the state and the state is the child. He is taught, literally, to overcome evil with good. He is taught his duty to society, the meaning of law—why ordinances are passed, and by a system of education, he is taught to know how to help himself, and to make himself honest and industrious.[43]

Lindsey attributed delinquency to faulty parenting and environmental temptations, and argued that parents of delinquent children should be fined and/or penalized when the actions of their children were determined to be the result of insufficient guardianship.[44] Observers of the Lindsey courtroom were not overwhelmingly supportive of his mixing of criminal and non-criminal cases. They criticized his strategy as overly inclusive, expanding the docket to include cases that were not appropriate for juvenile court. In addition, Lindsey's approach was accused of embracing a "willingness to shoulder the failures and leave-overs of every other institution."[45]

By 1917, there was at least one juvenile court in all but three states.[46] But the reality for youth in the newly established juvenile courts fell far short of their lofty ideals. The majority of juvenile court judges and probation officers did not share Lindsey's principles,[47] but neither did they necessarily follow the law established in Illinois. Instead, the courtrooms that emerged around the country over the next few decades were described as "vague and unsystematic in their statutory definitions of juvenile courts, and actual court organization varied from statutory prescriptions."[48] In conflict with the intention to maintain an informal environment and use the courtroom as infrequently as possible, they instead quickly developed procedural rules and heard trivial cases that could have been diverted.

And while some of the juvenile court practices may have somewhat improved, the sorts of cases that were accepted were mostly not serious, and the cases presented to judges continued to be mostly from poor, immigrant families.[49] An analysis of early-era Chicago court hearings found that 80 percent of the defendants came from low-income and working-class backgrounds.[50] Historical offense data from the first ten years of the court show that the alleged offenses for boys included fairly trivial infractions: stealing (50.8 percent), incorrigibility (21.7 percent), disorderly conduct (16.2 percent), malicious mischief (6.5 percent), and "other offenses" (4.8 percent). In 31.4 percent of the female cases, the accused crime was "immorality," which was an undefined sex-related offense.[51]

Youth Confinement in the Early Twentieth Century

Despite the fact that court referrals often were comprised largely of low-level offenses, commitments to juvenile institutions continued to soar: data from 1899 to 1903 in Chicago show that 44.3 percent of the cases heard in juvenile courts resulted in secure confinement to an institution, and only 24.3 percent were diverted to probation. The remaining third were dismissed or discharged informally.[52]

Memphis opened its first juvenile court in 1910, and an analysis of 1,575 cases heard before the court in its early days identified about 80 percent of court cases were noncriminal in nature, including incorrigibility, "bad environment," truancy, running away from home, and other status offenses. Among these, 27 percent of adjudicated youth were committed to the Shelby County Industrial School, orphanages, other state reformatories, adult prisons, or detention homes.[53] The main objective of the separate system for adolescents was to keep youth out of large, congregate care types of institutions to the greatest extent possible, as their negative influences were well documented by this point.[54] Like the reform schools and houses of refuge in the preceding era, however, institutionalization remained the predominant intervention for juvenile delinquency. Despite the creation of new juvenile-only courts, youth secure confinement in the twentieth century did not improve. Youth continued to be held in large, overcrowded, and poorly maintained institutions with minimal programming and where corporal punishment was condoned. Rather than diverting youth from adult facilities, the data suggest that the net was simply widened, resulting in more youth being institutionalized than ever.[55]

By some accounts, youth experiences during this new era were virtually indistinguishable from descriptions of earlier decades.[56] Despite well-meaning intentions that may have stimulated the child-saving movement, on the whole it was not successful in cultivating a reformed justice system for adolescents, nor did it remove young people from adult jails and prisons. According to Anthony Platt, the development of a separate juvenile court ultimately failed to develop a procedurally sound judicial system; rather, "the child savers helped create a system that subjected more and more juveniles to arbitrary and degrading punishments."[57]

Race and Juvenile Justice

Why did problems persist despite multiple attempts to overhaul and reform the system? One explanation lies in the extent to which these institutions remained mechanisms for social control of undesirable populations, namely immigrants and African Americans.[58]

According to race scholar Geoff Ward, the dominant account of the early juvenile justice era is told as if the creation of the juvenile justice system was not impacted by the racially divided country in which it occurred.[59] Class- and race-based inequities in the treatment of youth permeated juvenile delinquency prevention and treatment from its start but were given too little recognition for their capacity to stagnate attempts at reform.[60]

Appreciation of the cultural and societal landscape of the late nineteenth century helps in understanding the environment in which the first juvenile court was created. The migration of families from farm to city as well as the advances and reversals for blacks during the latter part of the nineteenth century inform the nascent juvenile justice years. Between 1866 and 1875 a number of substantial reforms were accomplished, affecting the African American community: slavery was declared unconstitutional, equal protections were extended to blacks, and black men obtained the right to vote. In addition, black citizenship was recognized during this period, and certain protections against discrimination were established. Opportunities for African Americans in the areas of labor and education improved during the Reconstruction period, and representation in government by people of color became a reality.

Despite these gains, when identifying the families that were failing to provide appropriate guardianship and thus requiring intervention, officials focused on low-income people of color. Anthony Platt notes that "[a]lthough the child savers affirmed the value of the home and family as basic institutions of American society, they facilitated the removal of children from 'a home which fails to fulfill its proper function.' . . . In effect, only lower-class families were evaluated as to their competence, whereas the propriety of middle-class families was exempt from investigation and recrimination."[61]

Just as the juvenile justice reformers of the late 1800s did not want to see youth housed with adults, they also did not want white youth housed with children of color.[62] In the early decades of separate juvenile justice systems of the twentieth century, the majority of secure confinement facilities were reserved for white youth.[63] Geoff Ward makes this observation:

> Of course, when the juvenile court was established in 1900, there was no sense that black Americans had any standing within this liberal democracy and, therefore, no sense that black youth had any future as normal, productive citizens. However, black Americans at that time were very invested in these same notions that through concerted effort you can prepare a young person to take a position of influence and leadership within a liberal democracy.[64]

An analysis of juvenile institutions and courts in the nineteenth and early twentieth centuries that incorporates an analysis of the race and ethnicity dynamics leads to a better understanding of the racial divisions that remain a core component of juvenile justice systems. Today's observers note that we have a juvenile justice system that is designed for "other people's children." The meaning behind this is that it is a system designed for predominantly poor youth of color. The next chapter reveals how the decades from 1950 to 1980 were led by youth advocates, social scientists, and policy makers attempting to better understand and respond to environmental barriers that led to minority overinvolvement in delinquency.

CONCLUSION

When the idea of a separate juvenile justice system was first conceived, both delinquency and poverty were considered to be threats of equal measure on the social order.[65] One reviewer notes that "Good ladies of that period were firmly convinced that it was their Christian duty to offer moral uplift mixed with strong instruction in home economics to bring the homes of the poor up to the middle-class hygienic and moral standards of the time."[66] Therefore, what essentially developed was a mix of salvation and repression that attempted to serve the youth in its care.[67]

According to many accounts, the juvenile justice system was seen as an appropriate place to assimilate immigrants and youth from poor neighborhoods as much as it was to reform errant youth.[68] "Despite their rehabilitative rhetoric, however, reformers who created the juvenile court system actually designed it to discriminate—to Americanize immigrant children, to control the poor, and to provide a means with which to distinguish between 'our children' and 'other people's children'—an orientation that persists today."[69]

There exist multiple and sometimes contradictory historical accounts of the nation's formalized juvenile justice system. Combined, they help settle some confusion about racial disparities that permeate the juvenile justice system that is in place today. The popular account of juvenile justice history development as a benevolent institution created from humanitarian origins is largely an account of the history of juvenile justice to benefit white youth and middle-class society. It is clear from this account of the history that the vision of juvenile justice delivering reformed, rehabilitated youth was not a vision intended for poor, nonwhite youth.

Reforms of the early twentieth century vastly altered the handling of youth in the courtroom. The informal atmosphere and careful attention to the best interests of the child were dominant features, representing a wholesale shift in the treatment of children. Yet, conduct that brought a young person to court was unnecessarily broad, many times not even criminal. The institutions to which youth were sent—large, repressive, and lacking in rehabilitation programming—remained largely unchanged. Moreover, the youth who were sent to them had usually been convicted of trivial misdeeds or none at all. One description of the population includes "minor offenders, unsupervised children, and children of immigrant parents," all of whom were viewed as "social victims and appropriate objects of benevolence."[70]

Chapter 2

Improving Safeguards

A person's a person no matter how small.

—Dr. Seuss

The concept that society's primary responsibility is to protect its youngest members is a value that transcends countries across the globe. In theory, the framers of the original juvenile justice system sought to protect vulnerable youth from three potential harms: older offenders, societal stigma, and the assumption that their moral character was fixed. Yet American justice history is awash with evidence that the early systems relied on harsh and sometimes brutal disciplinary practices, isolation, and physical labor as the primary means of correction. In addition, racial disparities continued to dominate the newly created system from its start.

Despite the poor treatment of youth, juvenile courts and institutions in the first half of the twentieth century functioned with minimal controversy or criticism, but important changes emerged during the second half of the twentieth century that have altered the trajectory of juvenile justice.

Three major developments guided juvenile justice reform during the first part of the twentieth century. First, lawmakers expressed interest in exerting a stronger federal role in juvenile justice with the twin goals of providing more equal administration of juvenile justice services and overseeing institutions with reported abuses. Second, state-level reformers experimented with depopulating youth prisons and moving youth to community-based settings closer to home. Third, a series of landmark Supreme Court rulings pertaining to youth justice stressed concerns about the lax procedures for protecting adolescent rights in court and established guidelines for youth.

FEDERALISM IN JUVENILE JUSTICE

From the start, juvenile justice entities have been governed largely by state and local jurisdictions. The federal government stayed out of juvenile justice matters prior to the late 1940s, but a temporary upsurge in juvenile crime at the end of World War II, together with reports of abuse and neglect, elevated concerns and led to a public interest in federal oversight. These concerns prompted calls for extended federal involvement in youth matters. The 1959 Uniform Crime Report, the official source for arrest data compiled and reported by the FBI, stated that "by directly comparing the percentages of the rise in delinquency and the growth in the young population, we find that juvenile arrests have increased two and one-half times as fast."[1]

The progressive reforms of this time were partially due to the joint efforts by federal bodies wishing to play a larger role in juvenile delinquency at the state level. One of the agencies was the Children's Bureau, in existence since 1912 and housed in the current-day U.S. Department of Health and Human Services. The Children's Bureau was responsible for a wide array of youth-centered issues since its inception. It was the sole federal agency responsible for handling juvenile justice at the time, though its concern competed with other challenging issues related to children as well. Specifically, its federal mandate was to "investigate and report . . . on all matters pertaining to the welfare of children and child life among all classes of our people and . . . especially investigate the questions of infant mortality, the birth rate, orphanage, juvenile courts, desertion, dangerous occupations, accidents, and diseases of children, employment, legislation affecting children in the several states and territories."[2]

In the 1950s Congress held a number of hearings on the rising juvenile delinquency rates and considered proposals for solutions on a national scale. But while President Eisenhower issued requests for legislation to aid states in combating juvenile delinquency during the 1950s, no bills advanced during these years.[3] Instead, much of the attention centered on the negative influence that comic books had on delinquency.

The pace of federal juvenile justice reform began to accelerate under the Kennedy administration. Several professional groups helped to bring attention to stories of abuse and neglect, including the Parent Teacher Association,

National Education Association, and the International Association of Chiefs of Police, among others. Concerns about abusive conditions of confinement in the juvenile justice system itself began to surface at this time as well. Stories of suicides and abuse were reported regularly in the media. "Runaways and other troublesome inmates were put in isolation cottages, beaten, or had their knuckles broken."[4] At the same time, concerns mounted about housing youth in adult jails where facilities were described as dirty, overcrowded, and chronically deficient in any education or treatment programming.[5]

Historians point to federal concerns combined with involvement of progressive advocates as explanations for moving youth justice to a new level.[6] For the first time, federal courts began to get involved, marked by a number of class action lawsuits on behalf of youth in confinement alleging poor conditions. Considered the leading case in youth prison conditions, *Morales v. Turman* (1973) was filed by eleven incarcerated youth in Texas. The case highlighted a variety of abuses endured by youth including physical force, corporal punishment, and solitary confinement. The case also illustrated the lack of access to counsel that permeated the institution—of the 2,500 Texas Youth Commission inmates residing in the Mountain View State School for Boys, over one-third had had a court hearing before their commitment during which they were not represented by legal counsel. Twelve percent of the inmates had had neither a hearing nor counsel.[7] Allegations of corporal punishment were also part of the lawsuit. Lawyers for the plaintiffs argued that slapping, punishing, and kicking were regular forms of discipline, as well as "racking," which involved forcing youth to stand against the wall with their hands in their pockets while being "struck a number of times by blows from the fists of correctional officers."[8]

In 1961, a presidentially appointed committee on juvenile delinquency and youth crime was established for the purpose of developing new methods of handling juvenile justice. The focus was to be on pilot testing community-level prevention programs based on developments in the fields of social work and sociology that aimed to understand the root causes of delinquency. Even so, there was still a heavy emphasis on the value of labor as a rehabilitation tool for young delinquents, as it had been during each of the previous reform eras. In a hearing in the Senate Committee on the Judiciary, one witness expressed support for "a planned work program in the home, school, and community which will give children experience in the responsibilities of a job assignment."[9] Though a strong work ethic and development of skills are key to success upon release, youth in the juvenile justice system were predominantly prepared for low-skill, menial labor positions.

Sociological theories dominated academic circles in the 1960s and 1970s, as scholars attempted to understand the origins of crime and delinquency. Explanations for why some youth engaged in crime and others desisted from crime were a central concern to sociologists and criminologists. Many concluded that community-level disparities could explain crime. A dominant theme in this work centered on efforts to understand delinquency through the lens of family, community, and peers. This perspective advanced the view that deciphering appropriate punishments for the young offender was less valuable than understanding salient features of their life experience that explained their delinquency. This, they argued, would prevent juvenile crime. The work of Richard Cloward and Lloyd Ohlin exemplifies this perspective. Cloward and Ohlin attributed youth delinquency to blocked opportunities for legitimate success that were experienced predominantly by low-income youth of color facing structural inequities. They argued for solutions to be obtained through enhanced social programming in local communities. Their "opportunity theory" was the backbone to the programs funded by President Kennedy's Office of Juvenile Delinquency.[10]

Sociological analyses like that of Cloward and Ohlin also greatly influenced the recommendations that developed from President Johnson's Commission on Law Enforcement and the Administration of Justice in 1967; the third chapter was devoted to juvenile delinquency. The commission report blamed juvenile delinquency on structural disparities including urban decay, school failure, large-scale unemployment, and poverty. Family breakdown was another key contributor to the problem of juvenile delinquency. The authors described the "typical" juvenile delinquent as coming from slum neighborhoods that lacked guardianship or structure. Children from single-parent households or those without enough affection in the home were blamed for the majority of juvenile crime, though the authors failed to provide evidence of just how many juvenile offenders came from such households. "More crucial even than the mode of discipline is the degree of parental affection or rejection of the child. Perhaps the most important factor in the lives of many boys who become delinquent is their failure to win the affections of their fathers."[11]

The shortage of sound alternatives to formal adjudication of youth was made clear through the lack of suggestions offered by the members of the commission. The commission argued generally that an overhaul of the juvenile justice system was "America's best hope for reducing crime."[12] Even though the problems besetting youth were accurately blamed on the limited community opportunities available to them, the solutions presented focused on adapting resources to disadvantaged communities rather than offering proposals to improve the structural inequities that contribute to youth crime in the first place. For instance, recommendations included: "help slum children make up for inadequate preschool preparation; deal better with behavior problems" and "relate instructional material to conditions of life in the slums."[13]

Despite troubling assumptions about low-income communities of color and the accompanying suggestions for improvements, a number of observations within the commission's report helped inform federal juvenile justice policy. They also provided a number of concrete areas in need of immediate reform. First, the report noted that one-third of youth in detention never even appeared in court and 40 percent of youth in detention had only been charged with a status offense (actions that would not be considered illegal except for their young age, such as skipping school). This was due in large part to the absence of standards at the time for preadjudicatory detention. The report criticized the arrest and detention of status offenders,[14] and noted that in at least seventeen states, no set criteria for initial detention decisions were specified in the state juvenile code.[15] The commission noted the inherent transience of delinquency among youth and, like the visionaries of the original juvenile justice system, felt that intervention—even with the best of intentions—could very well do more harm than good. "Most juveniles commit trivial offenses, outgrow their delinquencies normally, and do not require formal intervention."[16] Instead the commission recommended diversion from formal processing.

The commission report emphasized the need to provide legal counsel and protections for juveniles when they appeared in court, far from standard practice at the time. Finally, the recommendations also stressed the importance of sealing juvenile records so that they would not affect prospects for rehabilitation.

On the whole, the commission viewed the juvenile justice system as a failure. These recommendations were unique to the time and helped shape future reforms. "Studies conducted by the Commission, legislative inquiries in various states, and reports by informed observers compel the conclusion that the great hopes originally held for the juvenile court have not been fulfilled. It has not succeeded significantly in rehabilitating delinquent youth, in reducing or even stemming the tide of juvenile delinquency, or in bringing justice and compassion to the child offender."[17]

In 1968, one year after the commission report, the Department of Health and Human Services was given the responsibility through the Juvenile Delinquency and Control Act of 1968 to develop a national approach to juvenile delinquency problems that included grants to states for preparation and implementation of comprehensive juvenile delinquency plans. Upon approval, states would receive federal monies to carry out prevention, rehabilitation, training, and research. Between 1968 and 1974, various federal funds were provided to the states to pursue juvenile justice reforms, but it was not until the Juvenile Justice and Delinquency Prevention Act of 1974 was passed that there was a unified, national grant-making agency to address juvenile delinquency within the context of a broader criminal justice and law enforcement model.

Stories of abuse and suicides continued to air in local and national media frequently, and concerns about status offenders in detention spread, along with concerns about youth being kept in adult jails. Finally, youth crime was again experiencing a rise. Between 1960 and 1974, there was a 216 percent increase in violent crime arrests for juveniles.[18] Arrests for violent crimes among juveniles had risen steeply in recent years, which placed more pressure on policy makers to pass a federal grant-making program that would streamline juvenile justice activities and provide technical assistance to the states.

Pressure on lawmakers resulted in a series of federal congressional hearings and debates attempting to establish what, if any, role the federal government should play in regulating the nation's juvenile justice systems. Many years of footwork led up to the creation of the Office of Juvenile Justice and Delinquency Prevention in 1974. A handful of champions for youth had emerged in the 1960s in the Congress, most notably Senator Birch Bayh of Indiana. Senator Bayh, the main architect of the legislation, first introduced the Juvenile Justice and Delinquency Prevention Act on February 8, 1972, and the final bill was signed into law by President Ford on September 7, 1974, with strong majorities in the House and Senate. The act was initially funded at $5 million.

Two components of this historic bill mandated compliance for states to receive federal funding: the deinstitutionalization of status offenders and the separation of youth from adults in jails and lockups by "sight and sound." Six years after the bill's original passage, a third mandate was added, requiring youth to be removed from adult jails unless they were being tried as adults.[19] The original two mandates of the act read,

> In order to receive formula grants under this part, a State shall submit a plan for carrying out its purposes . . . In accordance with regulations established under this title, such plan must . . . provide within two years after submission of the

plan that juveniles who are charged with or who have committed offenses that would not be criminal if committed by an adult, shall not be placed in juvenile detention or correctional facilities, but must be placed in shelter facilities . . . provide that juveniles alleged to be or found to be delinquent shall not be detained or confined in any institution in which they have regular contact with adult persons incarcerated because they have been convicted of a crime or are awaiting trial on criminal charges.[20]

In the first years after passage, states made extraordinary improvements within their juvenile justice systems. In Michigan, for instance, there had been 1,611 status offenders securely detained in jails and youth detention centers for more than twenty-four hours in 1974, but by June 1985 only seventy-two status offenders were being detained in jails and detention centers. Similarly, in June 1981 sixty-three youth were being held in adult jails in Michigan but by June 1985, there were only thirteen.[21]

STATE-LEVEL YOUTH PRISON DEPOPULATION

A popular trend among states during the 1960s and 1970s was to close large-scale reform school–style facilities in favor of small, community-based ones. In this way, the juvenile justice system separated itself from the adult corrections system, which was expanding its carceral state at the time.[22] At the state level during this time, Massachusetts was engaged in unprecedented reforms, which collectively came to be known by some as "radical non-intervention" approaches[23] under the leadership of Jerome Miller, the commissioner of the Massachusetts Department of Youth Services. Though the story of Massachusetts's reforms typically begins with the start of Miller's term as commissioner, Massachusetts had been operating in crisis mode for a number of years prior to his leadership; it underwent seven independent investigations in the years immediately preceding Miller's tenure.[24] One investigation concluded that all sorts of youth in confinement were not serious offenders. Instead many suffered from mental retardation, emotional disturbances, truancy, and parental neglect but were not chronic delinquents.[25]

Jerome Miller was appointed in 1969 to fix the troubled system through diversion tactics. His appointment was as much a symbol of the problem as it was a key to the solution. Though he ended up changing the system substantially, he was not an insider; in fact, he did not have any juvenile justice experience prior to his appointment. Miller did not initially set out to radically change the system. Miller observed that the longer youth were confined in state institutions, the worse their outcomes were upon release regardless of their level of risk upon admission.[26] His initial goals to improve the system were relatively modest: replace the militaristic and hierarchical culture with a small, rehabilitation-centered model.

After encountering substantial resistance to his reform agenda, Miller determined that it would be more effective to close every juvenile facility in the state, and by 1972 this had been accomplished. "As I looked around the department at the superintendents, directors of education, chaplains, planners, and others in leadership roles, I saw that most would be there long after I left. They could outwait and outlast me. I'd made a mistake in concentrating on making the institutions more humane. The idea of closing them seemed less risky."[27] As a result, and despite lack of concrete plans for what to do with the youth after facility closures, the state managed to drop its institutionalized youth population from one thousand to fewer than sixty youth within two years.[28]

In place of the institutions, the state created small, high-security treatment units for the most dangerous youth and prioritized a diverse network of more than seventy small, community-based alternatives for the remainder of previously incarcerated youth. Juvenile crime declined in the following years, and fewer Department of Youth Services clients were transferred to the adult system.[29] Additionally, youth residing in jurisdictions with more community-based programs showed lower rates of recidivism than those without as many community-based opportunities.[30] A decade later, the National Council on Crime and Delinquency compared recidivism across five states and reported that Massachusetts had the lowest rate of all. Moreover, the state was saving an estimated $11 million each year through utilizing private, community-based approaches instead of housing youth in state-run institutions.[31]

Miller's approach was exceptional compared to smaller, piecemeal reforms in other states at the time. His view was that the systems themselves were generating the most problems: most youth correctional systems had become large bureaucracies rather than the small, community-based settings that were envisioned. He observed that "[c]orrectional reform in this country of lawyers and management experts has taken the form of setting minimum standards and ensuring that rules and regulations are well written and properly promulgated and enforced. Ignoring the possibilities of more basic reform, these actions try to mitigate abuse . . . Court decisions have no doubt moderated harsh prison conditions and softened some of the grosser brutalities. The court's involvement, however, has simultaneously served to reinforce reliance on the failed institutional model as our primary correctional response to crime."[32]

Massachusetts experienced fierce resistance to facility closures. Though some employees within the system expressed concerns about public safety, overwhelmingly, concern centered on the economic benefits derived from the institutions' continued presence. The notion of deinstitutionalization disrupted the entrenched belief in the need for the institutions themselves; they had become a fixture in the community and a source of employment for the residents, regardless of a demonstrated lack of need for them. Miller recalled,

> The word "reform" always has a different meaning when a state institution is at stake. As the number of institutions grew, so did their influence in state legislatures, a fact that people routinely ignore. Any proposed change in services to or supervision of those who would otherwise be inmates had to first pass the political test. Innovation had to be accomplished without threatening the institution's stability. In politics, this means the institution must survive. Reform strategies must therefore absorb existing staff, add new institutional staff, and bolster the institutional plant.[33]

During the same period of the 1970s, a handful of other states were experimenting with downscaling their youth prisons. In Utah, following litigation on inhumane conditions, Governor Matheson ordered the closure of most of the state's facilities rather than risk coming under federal receivership. In 1977 the governor appointed a Blue Ribbon Task Force on Criminal Justice whose mandate was to review the entire juvenile justice system. The youth-oriented recommendations of the task force were to remove runaways and other status offenders from confinement, prioritize the least restrictive setting for adjudicated youth, adopt deinstitutionalization as the governing theme of the youth corrections system, rely more on community-based programming and individualized treatment, and develop guidelines for both the commitment and release of adjudicated youth.[34] Utah shifted its priorities toward rehabilitating youth and built two small, high-security, thirty-bed facilities while reallocating funds toward community-based treatment services.[35] As a result of the state's commitment to these recommendations, the number of youth in secure placement declined from 450 in 1976 to 60 by 1985.[36] Subsequent research on youth outcomes indicated that youth graduating from community-based programs experienced relatively low recidivism rates.[37]

Testifying before the House Committee on Education and Labor, the director of the Utah Division of Youth Corrections attributed the impetus for the state's juvenile justice reforms to the support and leadership provided by the Juvenile Justice and Delinquency Prevention Act (JJDPA). "The JJDPA Act set a direction which was instrumental in igniting states into creative thinking and programming for troubled youth. The Utah response to the JJDP initiative has been to become very proactive in the deinstitutionalization movement and in jail removal . . . the impetus of the JJDP Act has been invaluable in strengthening this effort."[38]

Missouri and Vermont also experimented with closing their state youth facilities. Though not closing facilities across the board, a number of states significantly reduced bed capacity in their state facilities during the 1980s and into the early 1990s: Colorado, Louisiana, Indiana, Oklahoma, Maryland, Florida, Georgia, Rhode Island, and New Jersey.

Massachusetts created momentum for many other states to experiment with reducing reliance on incarceration for youth; the juvenile reform movement of the mid-1980s was dominated by a desire to replicate the successes in Massachusetts. Massachusetts had become the gold standard for juvenile justice systems. The JJDPA served as the financial and technical support that states needed to implement similar reforms.

Yet despite advances in some states, the youth decarceration movement was not sustained. Early skeptics of the movement made this observation:

> The claim that the closing down of institutions, and the instituting of new delinquency prevention and reform ignores the historical record. Ever since the 1820s, when the first institutions for reforming delinquents were founded, each "new" approach has been hailed as a sure solution to the problem of delinquency. In time, each has been pronounced a failure. The present and planned programs of diversion away from the juvenile courts, closing correctional institutions, youth service systems, the use of local community facilities, group homes and halfway houses, even "radical non-intervention" are likely to meet the same fate . . . because it has never been the intent of any of these programs to change the conditions that consign poor and working class youths to menial, dead-end jobs and condemn the juvenile justice system to those who refuse to (or cannot) fit into this mold. All of the programs through the years have aimed at control and discipline of the poorer classes; they have tried to resocialize the boys and girls of the poor, working class, and minority groups so they would accept the place capitalism (in its various forms) chose for them.[39]

SUPREME COURT CASES

At the time of the commission's report and amid state experimentation with facility closures, a landmark juvenile justice decision was pending in the U.S. Supreme Court. A few years earlier, fifteen-year-old Gerald ("Jerry") Gault had been taken into custody in Arizona for allegedly making a prank phone call to a neighbor, a claim which Gault always denied. The first legal issue that emerged was that Gault's parents were not notified of their son's arrest. After arriving home to find him missing, they eventually located him at a nearby detention center, where he had been taken by authorities while awaiting adjudication. His parents were not allowed to take him home, so Gault remained at the detention facility for several days before being released; even when he was released, his parents were not provided an explanation for his detention. At his subsequent adjudication hearing, no witnesses were called, no one was sworn in, no transcript was written or recorded, and his accuser was not even present. The court sentenced him to secure confinement at a state facility until the age of twenty-one, or six years.

The Gault case represented a number of growing concerns around the operation of the juvenile court, principally professionalism, privacy, and the protection of individual rights. The concept of privacy as a central tenet for juvenile proceedings was increasingly questioned as concerns surfaced about the procedural protections afforded to youth in the juvenile court system, such as access to legal counsel. Some wondered whether privacy was being used simply as a cloak for secrecy in the courtroom, and whether this was a disadvantage to procedural fairness. Gault's case was eventually heard by the U.S. Supreme Court to clarify the procedural rights of a juvenile defendant. In its opinion, the court underscored the importance of due process for all defendants, regardless of age, emphasizing that it ensured "the primary and indispensable foundation of individual freedom."[40] The justices wrote that had Gault been eighteen years old at the time of his alleged offense, he would have been afforded the same procedural safeguards available to adults, and that age was not a sufficient condition under which these could be denied. They wrote, "Under our Constitution, the condition of being a boy does not justify a kangaroo court."[41] The court also observed that though there are legitimate reasons for treating juveniles and adults differently, young people facing an adjudication of delinquency and incarceration were entitled to certain procedural safeguards under the due process clause of the Fourteenth Amendment.

This case highlighted the informal and often unprofessional atmosphere that had come to dominate the juvenile courts. At the time of the *Gault* ruling, a full quarter of the juvenile court judges nationwide had no law school training.[42]

Over the next decade, the U.S. Supreme Court heard three additional cases pertaining to juvenile justice procedures: *In re Winship, McKeiver v. Pennsylvania,* and *Breed v. Jones. In In re Winship*[43] the court said that conviction in juvenile court required proof beyond a reasonable doubt, rather than the previous lower standard, preponderance of the evidence.

In *McKeiver v. Pennsylvania*[44] the court continued its aim to protect youth when it declined to extend the right to a trial by jury to juveniles. The important separation between juvenile and adult court was emphasized, noting that if the juvenile court was to allow trial by jury, this would essentially eliminate any significant distinction between juvenile and criminal proceedings. "If the formalities of the criminal adjudicative process are to be superimposed upon the juvenile court system, there is little need for its separate existence. Perhaps that ultimate disillusionment will come one day, but for the moment we are disinclined to give impetus to it."[45] Finally, in *Breed v. Jones*[46] the justices ruled that the state cannot criminally re-prosecute a youth in adult court after adjudication of delinquency on the same offense in juvenile court; this would amount to double jeopardy.

To criminologist Barry Feld and others, though the court's intention was to provide more protections as part of its general aim during this period to ensure equal protection and civil rights, this came at a price. The decisions about juvenile justice proceedings had the unintended impact of shifting the focus from the juvenile to the offense, making the court experience nearly identical to the adult criminal court despite attempts to maintain important differences. The cumulative effects of these decisions drew wide criticism from juvenile justice purists, who argued that the informality and discretion of the juvenile system were the qualities that made it appropriate for youth. Feld observes that "By emphasizing some degree of criminal procedural regularity, the Court altered juvenile courts' focus from 'real needs' to 'criminal deeds' and shifted the focus of delinquency proceedings from a social welfare inquiry into a quasi-criminal prosecution."[47]

Chapter 3

Race-Based Reactions to the Rise in Youth Violence

If the only measure of any generation in the United States was the worst acts that any of its members might commit, each new generation would be viewed as an unqualified disaster.

—Franklin E. Zimring

After a period of relative stability in juvenile violence, homicide arrests for youth began to climb beginning in 1985. From 1985 to their peak in 1993, the rate of homicide arrests for individuals under the age of eighteen nearly tripled.[1] In select localities the rise was even more dramatic.[2] Concerns about violence were legitimate, as were concerns about the government's ability to respond effectively.

The direction of American juvenile justice policies underwent a dramatic reversal during the final decade of the twentieth century. Various federal and state policies endorsed and eventually enacted, and then freely utilized, included transferring teens as young as thirteen to adult criminal court, lowering the minimum age at which juveniles could be sentenced to death, applying lifelong prison sentences with no chance for parole, and imposing other so-called "adult crime, adult time" policies.

An understanding of the gravity of the juvenile crime problem, together with possible explanations, helps shape the analysis of a set of especially harsh crime policies that followed. Also of importance is the plethora of unchecked, factual errors that were generated and widely circulated about young people, especially youth of color, and crime. These miscalculations led many to believe that violence was destined to climb to unprecedented levels, and that young African American males were to blame.

33

WILDING AND THE CENTRAL PARK FIVE

One need look no further than the national frenzy that followed the assault and rape of Trisha Meili to observe the conflation of crime, youth, and race taking place during the latter part of the twentieth century. In the spring of 1989 a twenty-eight-year-old, white female investment banker who lived on Manhattan's Upper East Side was assaulted and raped while jogging one evening in New York's Central Park. The crime grabbed headlines for months as prosecutors, politicians, and the media quickly built their case against five young, African American teenagers from Harlem and pinned the crime on them.

The five juveniles who were eventually convicted happened to be in the police station the night of the crime, having been picked up after a night of adolescent mischief, but initially accused of doing nothing illegal. In fact, none of the boys knew anything about the crime for which they would each eventually be convicted. After the interrogation, which lasted from fourteen to thirty hours for each young man, the boys' parents were told that if their children confessed to the crimes, they would be able to go home and could put the incident behind them. All but one confessed on videotape to the crime. The videotaped interrogations were made *after* they were coerced to submit signed confessions the previous night.

The story of the rape of a white woman by a gang of African American teenagers in Central Park became a routine feature of both local and national news. At the time, New York's lawmakers and police were under tremendous pressure to bring violent crime under control, as the city was experiencing a steep rise. It was not only local and state politicians who were demanding a tough response, other powerful figures expressed their outrage as well. Real estate mogul Donald Trump, for instance, paid $85,000 for a series of ads in various New York newspapers calling for the boys to receive the death penalty before they had even been convicted. Though they were spared death sentences, each of the defendants was found guilty and sentenced to a range of five to fifteen years. There is no record of any opposition to the ways the case was handled at the time.

All five convictions were overturned in 2002 when another man's confession was corroborated by DNA evidence. The five men subsequently sued New York City for $250 million in damages and settled at $41 million (equating roughly to $1 million for each year of incarceration) in June 2014.[3]

Rising juvenile crime and its attending hysteria, compounded by the persecution of young black males, provided the sociopolitical atmosphere in which the Central Park Five trial of five innocent young African Americans occurred. But this case was only the most high profile in an environment that transformed the use of juvenile justice.

RISE IN JUVENILE HOMICIDES

After a period of relatively steady crime rates, juvenile crime began a troubling rise in the mid-1980s that did not begin to recede for about a decade. The number of juvenile arrests for murder, forcible rape, robbery, and aggravated assault climbed 64 percent between 1980 and 1994. Though violent and nonviolent crimes both increased during this time, serious violent crimes, especially homicide, accounted for most of the rise. The rate of juvenile homicide arrests increased an astonishing 201.2 percent—from a low point of 6.7 per 100,000 in 1984 to the highest rate, 20.1 per 100,000, in 1993. More homicides were being committed by youth than ever before in American history.

Juvenile violence was not equally distributed and Americans were not, in large part, at high risk of victimization. In fact, when analysis accounts for age, race, community, and weapon-related variables, the cause for the crime rise begins to takes shape. First, the acquisition of handguns by teens accounted for the vast majority of the increase in homicides.[4] Access to handguns was facilitated by expanding gun distribution networks, which made it easier for teenagers to obtain them. In the preceding two decades, there had

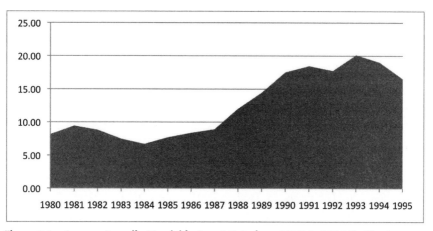

Figure 3.1   Average Juvenile Homicide Arrest Rate from 1970 to 2011 (by Year)

been minimal fluctuation in handgun use among youth arrested for homicide, but starting in 1985 this began to change, with no comparable rise in the number of non-gun homicides.[5]

Age and gender breakdowns also help to better understand the rise in violence. Disaggregation of violent crime statistics by age and gender reveals that males fifteen to nineteen years old were responsible for a 127 percent rise in handgun deaths.[6] In fact, homicide rates among older individuals actually remained relatively stable from 1985 to 1993: firearm deaths declined slightly (1 percent) among twenty-five- to twenty-nine-year-old males, and even more (13 percent) among thirty- to thirty-four-year-old males.[7]

When race is accounted for, the location of the crime spike becomes even more apparent. Specifically, African American youth were responsible for a disproportionately high number of homicides during the period of the juvenile crime rise. Though racial differences in the rate of homicide arrests existed in earlier decades (indeed, the rate of arrests of black youth occurred at approximately five times the arrest rates for white youth for at least the two previous decades),[8] starting in 1985, arrests for murder between black youth and white youth diverged much more starkly. Between 1986 and 1993, the rate of homicide arrests among white youth rose by 40 percent, compared with a 278 percent rise in the arrest rates for African American youth.[9] By 1992, black youth were arrested for homicide at a rate that was more than seven times as high as the arrest rate for white youth.

Deaths from gun-related homicides among adolescents ages twelve to seventeen rose from fewer than 600 victims in 1984 to more than 1,700 victims in 1993.[10] Many Americans were consumed with worries that youth were going to seriously harm or kill adults, especially white adults, but the real victims of this era were young black males. Between 1988 and 1992, a shocking 60 percent of deaths among teenage black males resulted from a firearm injury, compared to 23 percent of deaths for white male teens.[11] In fact, death by shooting was 4.7 times more likely than natural causes for African American young males during the 1980s.[12] Though young black males were much more likely to be the victims of violence, this was not a central point of concern in the national conversation around rising crime.

Finally, not all jurisdictions experienced a similar spike in juvenile violence. Areas of concentrated disadvantage in American communities experienced the greatest levels of violent crime during this era, including inner-city neighborhoods in Houston, Chicago, Detroit, New York City, Philadelphia, Baltimore, San Francisco, Los Angeles, and the District of Columbia.

The War on Drugs

Research on the crime rise of the late 1980s and early 1990s attributes the large rise in violence to the crack epidemic that started to infiltrate many inner-city communities between 1984 and 1985.[13] Crack was enticing to drug users in high-poverty areas because of its low price, and crack distribution was attractive to dealers in these areas because of the frequency with which users purchased it, typically amounting to several deals a day for the typical crack user.[14]

The new market for crack in certain low-income communities demanded the recruitment of new sellers, and youth from disadvantaged neighborhoods made ideal recruits for these positions. First, youth were (erroneously) assumed to be less vulnerable to apprehension and prosecution than adults. Second, risk taking and miscalculation of apprehension are key features of adolescence.[15] Third, youth were less likely to be crack users themselves, making them more reliable employees. And finally, the idea of selling crack was alluring to inner-city youth: life in disadvantaged communities provided few opportunities for upward mobility and little in terms of a satisfying future, but selling crack provided employment, status, and income.

The dominant role that the crack market, combined with the diffusion of handguns to teenagers, played in the shifting crime trends within America's inner cities goes far in explaining the temporary surge in juvenile violence between 1985 and 1993.[16] City-level analyses show a concentrated effect of the crack trade on violence during these years.[17]

Additional explanations about the connection between homicide trends and the illicit drug market point to the "turf battles" that often accompany the entry of a new illegal drug to the market, drug-related robberies of sellers, retributions, and punishments of subordinates for underperforming.[18] The rise in serious juvenile crime is also attributable to economic and social hardships that were felt most strongly in communities of color.[19]

Some of the relationship between youth violence and the drug trade is also explained by the arms race that developed in urban areas where the crack market proliferated.[20] As crack selling spread through increasingly dangerous neighborhoods, violence then took on a life of its own that served to safeguard inner-city living. Youths' fears of violence became a mediating factor that prompted the desire for guns for self-preservation—one survey of 2,508 adolescents in ninety-six randomly selected elementary, middle, and high schools found that one-third of students felt they would die young due to violence.[21] Violence may also have afforded youth with a sense of stature. Criminologists Jeffrey Fagan and Deanna Wilkinson explain it this way:

While gun homicides among adolescents increased rapidly following the onset of the crack crisis of the mid-1980s, it is unclear whether these homicides can be traced to business violence in the drug trade or to other situational and eco-logical forces during that time. In part, the infusion of guns and their diffusion to teenagers may have had broad impacts on fear, motivating gun acquisition as a form of self-defense.[22]

In all, a mix of factors have come to explain the juvenile crime spike. They include the spread of the crack trade in inner cities, the acquisition of handguns by youth, youth living in vulnerable communities that had fallen prey to crime, community disorder as a result of economic and social disad-vantage, gang involvement, and fear of victimization.[23] All of these factors point to the crime rise as a public health crisis that developed out of poverty and addiction, but the "war on drugs" campaign did not portray it as such. In fact, nowhere in the outcry was the rise in youth violence framed as a public health problem or as a problem rooted in structural inequities. Instead, these changes were characterized by some social scientists and commentators as "a fundamental transformation in child development that corroded empathy and morality, spawning a new generation of remorseless youths who were feared to be 'muggers, killers, and thieves.'"[24] Perhaps this characterization was not discredited at the time because the primary victims were low-income African Americans.[25] If it had been the case that the substantial use and sales of crack cocaine were affecting white, middle-class neighborhoods, the approach to remedying the problem would likely have been something other than punitive criminal sanctions. Indeed, a more holistic public health approach would have addressed the underlying addiction, poverty, and structural disadvantages that drove the crime problems during this period. However, as one analyst notes, the responses to the rise in juvenile crime reflected a political process rather than a scientific one.[26]

EXPANDING THE MYTH OF THE YOUTH PREDATOR

Responses to the violent crime rise among juveniles in the late 1980s and early 1990s were made possible by the consistent conclusion by the public, lawmakers, practitioners, opinion leaders and advisors, and even some aca-demic scholars that juvenile crime would continue its unrelenting rise unless drastic actions were taken. The recommended approach to stem violence was to apply severe sanctions on youth that would act as a deterrent and serve to remove some youth from the community permanently. Claims made about juvenile crime and juvenile offenders during this era were often little more than a thinly veiled commentary about youth of color, especially African Americans, and this group received the bulk of the negative consequences resulting from these policies.

Public panic about rising juvenile violence was amplified by the widespread circulation of grossly inaccurate predictions about juvenile violence by a variety of sources—media, policy makers, opinion leaders, and some scholars. By the time most of the rhetoric reached its fever pitch, juvenile violent crime had already started to recede (and has continued to do so for the past twenty years). This downward trend did not affect the public hysteria, since most rhetoric of the time was situated in the claim that, though juvenile violence may experience a temporary plateau, it was guaranteed to rise to unprecedented levels in coming years because of an unavoidable rise in the juvenile population.[27] One often-cited prediction was that there would be an additional 270,000 young violent offenders by the year 2010. This outrageous statistic, cited frequently in the media, included all people under the age of eighteen, including babies.[28]

A poll conducted in 1996 revealed that 84 percent of respondents thought that violent crime had risen in the previous year, but in reality it had dropped, and 81 percent believed that adolescent violence was a major social problem in the United States. Another poll conducted in the early 2000s showed that even though the arrest rates for youth homicide had plunged 69 percent between 1993 and the end of the decade, 62 percent of the American public believed it was still rising.[29] Ironically, few respondents believed crime was a problem in their neighborhoods, suggesting that their estimates were not based on personal experience.

The rise in violent crimes committed by youth was not insignificant, but it was also not arbitrary nor was it equally distributed across American communities. In fact, the risk of death by homicide to the average citizen remained quite low. But this was not the message conveyed to the public, even by those providing the official statistics on homicide arrests. Authors of FBI's annual Uniform Crime Report gave authority to claims that serious violent crime was rampant and largely random; in its 1993 report the authors concluded that "[e]very American now has a realistic chance of murder victimization in view of the random nature that crime has assumed."[30] Even though less than one-third of the homicides involved strangers, violent crime was conveyed to the public as indiscriminate and unpredictable.[31]

At the same time juvenile crime was rising, the strength of the Office of Juvenile Justice and Delinquency Prevention (OJJDP) had been deliberately weakened under the leadership of OJJDP administrator Alfred Regnery, who served from 1983 to 1987. Consequently, the office was not well positioned to respond to the policies that would be advanced in the 1990s under the Clinton administration. Regnery supported President Reagan's position that the OJJDP should be eliminated entirely. As a result, OJJDP suffered numerous threats to its continued existence.[32]

Unlike his two predecessors, Regnery deliberately refocused the work of OJJDP away from its historical emphasis on diversion and procedural protections to enhancing sanctions for serious and violent offenders. He clarified the new role of OJJDP as such: "In essence, we have changed the outlook of the office from one emphasizing the lesser offender and the nonoffender to one emphasizing the serious juvenile offender. We have placed less emphasis on juvenile crime as a social problem and more on juvenile crime as a justice problem."[33] On its face, this shift may not have seemed problematic, but when considered in the context of understanding the impetus behind creating OJJDP, this repurposing of the agency was momentous. In 1984, OJJDP's advisory board, the National Advisory Committee on Juvenile Justice, issued a report recommending a change in direction for the federal agency.[34] Rather than working to divert the category of low-level and at-risk youth from juvenile justice involvement, the committee recommended a tighter focus on the small cohort of serious and violent offenders. The report came to the baffling conclusion that youth of color would benefit from greater attention placed on them, and that the federal juvenile justice office had been directing too much attention on white youth through its concentration on noncriminal status offenders. This, they reasoned, was a *disservice* to youth of color. Youth of color required more attention from the juvenile justice system than they received because of the system's preoccupation with low-level, white offenders. The report criticized the overemphasis on status offenders by stating,

> In brief, OJJDP is piloting the demise of poor and minority youngsters in this nation by pursuing policies and programs that are fostering the development of a separate juvenile justice system: one for the white, middle-income youngsters and one for the minority, low-income youngsters. The principal cause of all this is OJJDP's missionary preoccupation with the deinstitutionalization of status offenders.[35]

Regnery did not equivocate on his thoughts about who was to blame for juvenile crime. While in his post as administrator of the OJJDP, he authored an opinion piece for the Heritage Foundation's journal, *Policy Review*, in which he characterized juvenile offenders in the following way:

Fourteen years old, the boy has already been arrested a dozen times. He dropped out of school years ago and cannot read or write; he has no job skills nor any hope of getting them. He is mostly likely black, possibly Hispanic, born to an unwed teenage mother on welfare, living in public housing or a tenement, and has more than five siblings. A series of men have lived in his mother's house; the boy has not developed a rapport with any, and he has tended to be regarded as a nuisance by the adults. He has been physically abused since early child-hood, and has spent a good deal of time living on the street. His only way of getting anything of value is either by theft or going on welfare. This boy will survive, for most of his life, at the taxpayers' expense.[36]

He surmised that 75 percent of crime was "probably" committed by persons fitting this profile. This conclusion is problematic for at least two reasons. First, as the administrator of the only federal juvenile justice agency, one should (and could) be absolutely certain of the "typical" offender's characteristics. This information is readily available, after all. And in fact, upon examination, it was *not* the case that most crime was being committed by low-income, illiterate, fatherless, black children. In 1986, when this article was written, just over half (52.6 percent) of juvenile violent crime arrests involved African Americans and only about a quarter (26.6 percent) of juvenile property offense arrests involved African Americans.[37]

Leaving aside the sweeping generalizations about offenders, children, and African Americans more broadly, this begs a broader question: why would the adult criminal justice system been deemed appropriate for the boy described here, even if the description *was* accurate? The juvenile justice system had long ago been committed to the idea that youth were especially vulnerable and for that reason should be *retained* in the juvenile system. Regnery and many others in this period rejected this perspective entirely, preferring one that viewed youth who fit this description as so damaged as to not have even a remote chance of reforming their lives.

The Pseudo-Intellectual Analysis

While thoughtful criminological analysis and debunking of the myths about youth were circulated,[38] these were largely ignored by policy makers in favor of claims that a new breed of youthful offender would soon drive violent crime levels to new heights. John DiIulio, one of the main propagators of the myth that a rising wave of juvenile violence was impending, coined the term "superpredator," which was quickly adopted by media and political officials to describe the predicted rise in violence.[39] Consider the following excerpt from *Body Count*, which embodies the standard definition of the superpredator:

> Here is what we believe: America is now home to thickening ranks of juvenile 'super-predators'—radically impulsive, brutally remorseless youngsters, including ever more preteenage boys, who murder, assault, rape, rob, burglarize, deal deadly drugs, join gun-toting gangs, and create serious communal disorders. They do not fear the stigma of arrest, the pains of imprisonment, or the pangs of conscience.[40]

Predictions of rising juvenile violent crime presented by DiIulio and others were baseless and had mathematical errors. For one, promoters of the super-predator perspective who warned of an unprecedented increase in the number of teenagers from 1990 to 2010 failed to account for the steady population decline that occurred between 1975 and 1990. Once this was accounted for, the predicted population of 21.5 million youth was essentially the same as in 1975.

Franklin Zimring emphasized the myriad problems with relying so heavily on arrest data for juveniles, which was a primary source for drawing conclusions on the predicted wave of violence.[41] There are three main reasons why he discouraged relying solely on arrest data for measuring juvenile crime: first, juveniles tend to offend in groups much more so than adults, so one homicide might result in several arrests. This phenomenon is much more common in juvenile crime than among adult offenders. Since a single offense often results in several arrests, the incidence of juvenile crime is artificially inflated when only arrest data are relied on as a measure of the incidence of crime. Another problem with relying on arrest data to inform the frequency of juvenile crime is that it fails to capture the tendency of law enforcement to initially overcharge, which can also misrepresent the true incidence of homicide. And finally, the widespread use of plea bargains distorts the incidence of juvenile crimes even further, as many offenders are convicted of offenses other than those for which they were initially arrested and charged. As a result of these problems with arrest data, Zimring noted, "The only conclusion that can be drawn from the data with any confidence is that there was no consistent pattern of youth arrests for violent crime from 1980–1996."

Lawmakers, too, contributed to the discourse around juvenile crime at the time, relying on media and pop culture news rather than academic research to inform their policy decisions. Legislators were not swayed by scholarly evidence. As a result, terms like "superpredator" made their way into state legislation as if they described an actual phenomenon rather than an invented myth. New Mexico senator Pete Domenici introduced a Juvenile Justice Modernization Act in 1996, which aimed to "update laws to deal with the 'superpredator,' the increasingly violent juvenile criminal."[42] In radio addresses during his presidential campaign, Bob Dole used the word "superpredator" and mentioned the alarming projections of juvenile violence in his speeches.[43]

The state of Florida became ground zero for the political rhetoric around the surge in violent juvenile crime. Republican U.S. representative Bill McCollum represented the Eleventh District of Florida, comprising most of Orlando, and was the chair of the House Subcommittee on Crime in the U.S. House of Representatives' Committee on the Judiciary in the mid-1990s. McCollum was one of the most vocal policy makers advancing the super-predator myth and pushed for federal legislation that would greatly stiffen penalties for juvenile offenders.[44] His bill mandated, among other things, the creation of an Armed Violent Youth Predator Apprehension program that would require the designation of at least one U.S. attorney to prosecute "armed violent youth predators" who were defined as individuals under 18 with at least one violent criminal conviction.[45] The task force would develop "strategies for removing armed violent youth predators from the streets." The rationale for this was to impose "severe punishment" because of its purported deterrent value. In his testimony before the House Subcommittee on Early Childhood, Youth, and Families in 1996, Representative McCollum said:

> In recent years, overall crime rates have seen a modest decline—nevertheless, this general decline masks an unprecedented surge in youth violence that has only begun to gather momentum. Today's drop in crime is only the calm before the coming storm . . . Now here is that really bad news: This nation will soon have more teenagers than it has had in decades. In the final years of this decade and throughout the next, America will experience an "echo boom"—a population surge made up of the children of today's aging baby boomers. Today's enormous cohort of five year olds will be tomorrow's teenagers . . . More of these youths will come from fatherless homes than ever before, at the same time that youth drug use is taking a sharp turn for the worse. *Put these demographic facts together and brace yourself for the coming generation of "super-predators."*[46]

MEDIA DISTORTIONS ABOUT YOUTH VIOLENCE

Three-quarters of the public say that they form their opinions about crime from the news.[47] Unfortunately, the picture of crime presented by the media was grossly distorted in the direction of sensationalizing violent crimes, minimizing the prevalence of nonviolent crimes, and attributing the bulk of crime to African Americans. Media stories not only exaggerated the amount of crime during this decade but also joined in mischaracterization of its perpetrators as animals. Juvenile offenders were described as moving in "wolf packs," for instance. The skewed presentation of crime by certain media outlets left the public unaware of significant fluctuations in the crime rate. The media focus on juvenile crime was particularly acute in the 1990s and did not recede even once the crime rate started to fall, leaving the public unaware that it had, in fact, started to fall. During this time, the media expanded the descriptions of juvenile offenders through terms carelessly used by some: Northeastern University criminologist James Fox summarized his erroneous predictions for the volume of future homicides as a "bloodbath"; this description was quickly adopted and used by the media because of its shock value. Similarly, a 1999 cover in *Time* magazine read, "Teenage Time Bomb."

Media reports are the primary source of information about crime frequency and seriousness, and since the media tends to focus disproportionately on violent crime, it is not surprising that the public believed that violent crime was a very real problem long after it had started to fall. During the 1990s, nearly half of the news coverage about young people focused on crime and violence, with far less attention paid to other important child-related topics like education and schools, poverty, child care, and child welfare matters.[48] Numerous print journals covered teen violence as their lead story, including *Time, Newsweek, Ladies' Home Journal, U.S. News and World Report,* and *People.*[49] According to one observer, "The daily look-alike headlines and familiar stories have helped to perpetuate a sense of futility and doom. Progress toward a solution for the escalating epidemic is stalled by a notion that violence is inevitable, a notion that the media have seldom questioned. As long as a phenomenon is considered inevitable, not much progress can be made toward a solution."[50]

Media stories not only exaggerated the amount of crime during this decade but also joined in the mischaracterization of its perpetrators as animals. The vast majority of stories about crime focused on minority youth. Media-reinforced messages that youth of color commit the most crime had substantial and long-lasting consequences for people of color.

Just as now, policy makers were obligated to listen to and consult with their constituents, even if their constituents had been misguided.[51]

The grave warnings about juvenile crime continuing its historic rise turned out to be entirely false: James Fox's prediction of a 40 percent increase in violent crime turned into a 67 percent decline. Franklin Zimring notes that "In less than a decade, future superpredators had become pioneer leaders in the great American crime decline."[52] This decline was largely attributable to restrictions made on handgun availability, changes in policing strategies, and the decline of the crack market.[53] Alfred Blumstein, one of the nation's preeminent criminologists of the twenty-first century, concluded that "the growth in homicide committed by young people was more attributable to the weapons they used than to the emergence of an inadequately socialized cohort of 'super-predators' as some observers claimed."[54] Suggestions that crime declined because of the punitive sanctions that followed (discussed in the following chapter) are discredited in the light of available research.[55]

As noted elsewhere in this book, juvenile crime rates underwent a dramatic reduction beginning in 1993. Some point to the policies of the tough on crime era as a reason for this reduction. Bill McCollum, one of the most prominent lawmakers promoting the superpredator myth, is an example: "Florida, like 40 other states, purposefully confronted its juvenile violent crime problem . . . These deliberative and focused strategies worked; violent crime rates plummeted from their 1990s highs . . . serious and violent offenses by juveniles ages 12–17 declined 61 percent from 1993 to 2005 nationwide."[56] Careful analysis fails to find a causal relationship between stiffer punishments for youth—specifically transfer—and the juvenile crime decline, however.[57] For instance, Jeffrey Fagan studied transferred youth and compared crime outcomes to youth in a neighboring state who were not transferred; his results revealed that transferred youth were 39 percent more likely to be rearrested than those who were retained in the juvenile court system.[58] Franklin Zimring and Stephen Rushin produced a retrospective look at crime trends for teenagers affected by transfer laws in comparison to those in the neighboring eighteen-to-twenty-four age group, one that was unaffected by the transfer laws but exhibited similar offending patterns during the late 1980s and early 1990s. Their results also indicate that the transfer laws did little to exert a deterrent effect on adolescent crime.

Some criminologists attempted to clarify misinformation about juvenile delinquency in hopes of restoring rationality to policy proposals, but their messages did not reach nearly far enough. Franklin Zimring, for instance, published a series of analyses on the juvenile violence problem of the 1980s and early 1990s. Jerome Skolnick, another leading criminologist at the time, encouraged his colleagues to be more unrestricted and vocal about their findings regarding juvenile violence, reminding them of the obligation to "bring evidence and reasoned discussion" to debates about crime and "inform the public about 'alternatives and payoffs.'"[59] However, with few exceptions, the academic community was largely silent in the matter of responding to the false claims and gross miscalculations of this period.

The facts presented by Zimring and others, mostly in academic publications not widely read by the general public or policy makers, did not have nearly the same reach as the claims in popular media that a new and especially dangerous breed of young offender was on its way. If they had, the public would have learned that the dire assessment of juvenile violence was distorted and that predictions of future violence were baseless.

Chapter 4

From Rehabilitation to Retribution

And I ask you to mount a full-scale assault on juvenile crime, with legislation that declares war on gangs, with new prosecutors and tougher penalties; extends the Brady bill so violent teen criminals will not be able to buy handguns; requires child safety locks on handguns to prevent unauthorized use; and helps to keep our schools open after hours, on weekends, and in the summer, so our young people will have someplace to go and something to say yes to.

—President Clinton, State of the Union Address, 1997

At the time that President Clinton made the above statement, serious juvenile crime was experiencing its fourth consecutive year of decline, though this fact was not considered in the growing number of harsh policies being mounted against youth. At both the state and federal levels, the 1990s were dominated by punitive youth violence policies widely endorsed despite warnings about their ill effects on both juveniles, and public safety. These included broadening the death penalty for juveniles, expanding mandatory minimum sentencing policies, transferring thousands of youth to the adult criminal court system, funding military-style boot camps, passing habitual offender laws, and reversing policies that previously sealed or expunged juvenile delinquency records.

Despite the localized nature of violence during this period, punitive crime policies were applied broadly across American communities. The preferred tool for addressing crime was "accountability," which, as it turned out, equated to retribution and incapacitation. Neither retribution nor incapacitation was part of the juvenile justice framework neither in its original design nor in practice for its first century, but a number of coinciding elements converged to shift the focus of public safety responses almost exclusively to the offender's actions in the last decade of the twentieth century. President Clinton's notorious crime bill of 1994, though mostly targeted at changes to the adult criminal justice system, also implemented punitive sanctions for juveniles that surpassed anything enacted at the federal level before or since. At the state level, the tone of juvenile justice policies was similarly punitive, taking the focus off adolescent vulnerabilities and placing it solely on exacting punishment for crime.

Recall that the 1970s marked a time in which root causes for juvenile delinquency were seriously examined through scholarly research, with many concluding that structural inequalities were to blame. Some policy makers and practitioners alike searched for solutions that used incarceration as a last resort because they recognized the collateral damage caused by it. This perspective guided the writing and passage of the Juvenile Justice and Delinquency Prevention Act (JJDPA), as discussed in chapter 2. These reforms were short-lived, however. During the juvenile crime rise of the 1980s, there was a growing distrust in the juvenile justice system as well as an increasingly dominant news frame that depicted juvenile delinquents as menacing black, inner-city youth. Indeed, the groundwork for the policy proposals that followed was laid by stark changes to public depictions about those responsible for crime. The justice system was repurposed toward one that would hold kids "accountable" through punishment and incapacitation, deterring other youth who might be considering breaking the law themselves. While race had always played a distinctive role in juvenile justice structure and administration, the last decade of the twentieth century marked an overt adoption of the notion that demography predestined certain youth to violence and little could be done to avoid it other than incarceration.

The legislative actions directed against at-risk and offending adolescents during this decade unraveled the progressive juvenile justice accomplishments of the preceding years, altering the course of juvenile justice away from striving toward a system that fostered humane, age-appropriate interventions for youth while still holding them liable for their crimes. Instead, policies that enhanced sanctions for adolescents based solely on their crimes were favored, similar to the tone and responses of the adult system.

The response to the juvenile crime rise amounted to twin assaults on juvenile justice: the criticism of the juvenile justice system itself for failing to serve its purpose, and the assault on a new category of offender: the superpredator. It is helpful to examine the rhetoric that emerged around the notion of eliminating the juvenile justice system, as well as the characterization of juvenile offenders, in order to understand shortcomings of today's system. These two developments in the last part of the twentieth century had a particularly troubling impact on African American youth.

ASSAULT ON THE JUVENILE JUSTICE SYSTEM

Widespread criticisms of the effectiveness of the juvenile justice system by liberals and conservatives alike led many to issue grave concerns about the juvenile justice system, ultimately questioning whether it should be abolished altogether.[1] A CNN poll of the general public in 1989 reported that 88 percent of respondents thought that teenage violence was a bigger problem than in the past (which was true), and 70 percent of the respondents felt that the courts' leniency was part of the problem.[2] Various constituents—academics, policy makers, the public, and even the administrator of the Office of Juvenile Justice and Delinquency Prevention (OJJDP) at the time—fought actively to dismantle the juvenile justice system. Officials within the system were skeptical of the system as well: almost half of the judges polled in a survey released by the *National Law Journal* believed that the juvenile justice system was failing.[3] The Los Angeles County district attorney was quoted as saying, "We need to throw out our entire juvenile justice system."[4]

Conservatives blamed the juvenile justice system itself for failing to handle the volume and type of youth who encountered it. They criticized juvenile courts for diverting most youth from the system (a positive trait of the system by today's standards) instead of being adjudicated and confined. The daily operation of the juvenile court system was interpreted by some as being too limited in its handling of youth. The vast majority of cases were assumed to be released without any formal processing. Some complained, "Nowhere does the revolving door of justice spin faster than in the juvenile court system. Nearly one-quarter of all juvenile arrests are dismissed immediately and only 10 percent result in the detention of the offender."[5]

A related complaint was that among the relatively few youth who were incarcerated in the juvenile system, their sentences were far too short. In many states, it was generally the policy that youth were released at the age of eighteen if not before. Many assumed that short stays in youth detention facilities were the only option, but in truth youth can be retained in the system until age eighteen, twenty-one, or even twenty-four in some states under blended sentencing mechanisms. With proper and intensive programming, a convincing argument can be made that the juvenile justice system ought to be able to rehabilitate most young offenders over a span of a few months or years.

The juvenile system was accused of being too soft, treating serious crimes as "trivial indiscretions," and thus needed to be eliminated, sending all youth to criminal court instead. [6] In addition, conservative abolitionists pointed to the recent volume of scholarly research that discredited the rehabilitative objectives of the justice system, finding them unattainable. [7]

Though focused on the adult system, the conclusion that "nothing works" famously advanced by social scientist Robert Martinson had rippling effects on the juvenile justice system, whose focus on rehabilitation had always been its defining feature. It is worth noting that the claims that rehabilitation did not work were somewhat problematic for at least two reasons. First, though rehabilitation was the goal of corrections in theory, in practice it was much less apparent. So research conducted by Martinson and others was not truly measuring rehabilitation. Second, Martinson's research itself suffered numerous methodological shortcomings, which he eventually admitted to in a follow-up commentary to his research.

Another widely circulated claim was that the juvenile justice system was ill-equipped to handle superpredator youth, as these youth did not exist when the original system was established at the turn of the twentieth century. As discussed in detail in chapter 2, the impetus for creating the JJDPA and the OJJDP in the first instance was to divert youth from the juvenile justice system whenever possible, as the harms associated with youth incarceration had been clearly demonstrated. When OJJDP was established in 1974, nearly 40 percent of youth were being detained because of a status offense. The JJDPA was not designed to address serious juvenile crime as its primary mission, as this was already being handled through established state and federal statutes. The purpose of the JJDPA was to divert unnecessary cases from the juvenile justice system.

Progressive juvenile justice reformers catalogued insurmountable problems with the juvenile justice system as well. This group recognized that the rehabilitative ideal had never materialized as designed. Some felt that the procedural rights of the 1960s and 1970s line of cases from the Supreme Court consequentially limited the flexibility of juvenile justice systems to engage in rehabilitation and use discretion. In order to comply with the rulings, juvenile courts became more administrative, bureaucratic, and less able to consider individual circumstances that accompanied one's delinquent act. In short, it became more like the adult court.

Another argument revolved around fairness. Some studies that compared sanctions of youth who were transferred to the adult system to those retained in the juvenile system suggested that the severity of youth sentences in the adult system depended on the crime. With the exception of serious offenses, transferring a case did not lead to greater certainty or severity of sanctions; instead, these sentences tended to be shorter than those adjudicated in juvenile court.[8] Of the transferred cases, only about 30 percent were serious charges, a contradiction to the "adult crime, adult time" premise on which advocacy for transfer was built. On the other end of the spectrum, cases transferred to adult court for serious crimes received significantly *longer* sentences than similar cases heard in juvenile court. These disparate outcomes raised concerns about equal justice: "some youths experience dramatically different consequences than do other offenders simply because of the disjunction between two separate criminal justice systems."[9]

Arguments in favor of stricter sanctions, transferring more cases to the adult system, and removing confidentiality protections around youth records dominated policy conversations at both the federal and state levels. Advocates for pushing juveniles out of the juvenile justice system and into the adult system pointed out that many youth had already shown that the juvenile system could not fix them, as evidenced by their extensive juvenile records. Therefore, the adult system was the only viable system for them. The reality, longtime legal and academic scholar Paolo Annino writes, is that a significant proportion of youth had never even spent a day in the juvenile justice system, making it impossible to determine whether the system had been a failure: he identified 43 percent of the 1,100 Florida youth under sixteen years old serving sentences in adult prisons in 2000 for whom this was the case.[10]

To Barry Feld, one of the foremost advocates in favor of eliminating the juvenile court, and others, the juvenile court as a separate entity had become conceptually problematic as well as a failure in terms of its implementation. In the decades since *In re Gault* and *McKeiver*, over a quarter of the states had revised their juvenile codes to reflect a legislative purpose less focused on rehabilitation and intervention in the child's "best interest" and more so on the value of public safety, punishment, and accountability.[11] Concepts like restitution, community service, and fines were now viewed as reasonable sanctions, but these would have been rejected in earlier decades as violating the fundamental principles of the system.[12] To many, the judicial decisions, legislative changes, and bureaucratic layers added to the juvenile justice system in the last half of the twentieth century had transformed it from "a nominally rehabilitative social welfare agency into a scaled-down, second class criminal court for young people."[13]

A number of influential decision makers, researchers, and practitioners concluded that the one-hundred-year experiment with a separate, youth-oriented juvenile justice system had failed and proposed that it be abandoned. Instead, all cases should be tried in the adult court, and to show that adolescence mattered, young age should be applied to rulings as an important, mitigating factor.[14]

THE FEDERAL-LEVEL PUSH TO GET TOUGH ON KIDS

After Bill Clinton became president in 1993, both his administration and the Congress soon initiated broad punitive crime policies, the consequences of which continue to be felt today.[15] President Clinton's appointment for attorney general was Janet Reno, who was, by most accounts, a staunch child advocate. A strong supporter of early prevention and intervention programs like Head Start, Nurse-Family Partnership, and other science-based approaches, Reno spoke frequently about the need to intervene early in the lives of disadvantaged youth as a primary crime control strategy.

Attorney General Reno brought only one member of her Florida-based staff to join her office in Washington, DC, state prosecutor Shay Bilchik. Bilchik, who became the administrator for OJJDP in 1994 (and served until 2000), had been her chief aide at the Dade County State Attorney's Office in Miami, Florida. Here he had led the agency's juvenile justice work and had been responsible for handling hundreds of juvenile cases. Bilchik was immersed in the daily work of coping with rising juvenile violence in one of the nation's largest cities.

Florida had become ground zero for juvenile transfer because of the vast number of youth who were placed in the adult criminal courts. Together Reno and Bilchik had crafted and implemented a system by which select youth could be tried as adults; replication efforts in other counties around the state broadened the applicability and use of transfer. In the first year after the state enacted a transfer law, more than half of the nation's transfers occurred in Florida.

Bilchik's views about waivers to adult court were an important point of discussion during his Senate confirmation hearings. Unlike many public officials at the time, Bilchik maintained a relatively modest stance on transfer and did not openly support statutory mechanisms that removed discretion from the decision to waive a young person to criminal court. "I think that many States have already revised their codes and built in flexibility for transfer of juveniles to criminal courts, for enhanced punishment for juvenile offenders, extended jurisdiction for juvenile offenders for more serious offenses. I think those are all steps that need to be taken in some instances to allow us the flexibility within which to work for each individual offender. So I would not advocate, for example, an absolute rule that a particular category of offense must be treated as an adult offender."[16] He did, however, support prosecutorial waiver, a practice that has received much criticism for its misuse and its tendency to result in racially and ethnically biased outcomes.

The 1994 Crime Bill

In 1994, Congress passed the Violent Crime Control and Law Enforcement Act, the largest and most expensive ($30 billion) crime package in U.S. history. The main components of the bill that pertained to youth included lowering the age for adult prosecution from fifteen to thirteen years old for individuals charged with certain federal offenses,[17] establishing firearm possession for juveniles as a federal offense, and the tripling of maximum penalties for employing youth to distribute drugs on or near a protected zone (i.e., schools, playgrounds, arcades, and youth centers).[18] In addition, $150 million was authorized in formula and competitive grant monies to state agencies to fund military-style boot camps, some of which supported juvenile boot camps.

The bill contained $9 billion in prison construction funds and numerous harsh sentencing provisions that accelerated mass incarceration and deepened racial disparities.[19] While the centerpiece of the prevention portion of the bill was dedicated to youth violence prevention, the enacted legislation greatly reduced prevention efforts both in language and in authorization levels.[20]

STATE-LEVEL JUVENILE JUSTICE POLICIES

The transcript below represents part of the Texas gubernatorial debate on October 21, 1994, between Governor Ann Richards and George W. Bush.[21] It illustrates the competition among political candidates at the time over who could be tougher on juvenile crime. During the debate one audience member asked, "What do you plan to do to reduce crime and, also, not only reduce the crime but the punishment of criminals? And not just strictly incarceration." Bush's response typifies the popular rhetoric of the time:

The core of crime in Texas is the juvenile justice problem. I think we ought to try 14 year old[s] as adults, down to 14 years old. To help our gang task force members fight crime. I know we need to expand the determinate sentencing statutes in the state of Texas. We need to have boot camps, reform schools, and detention centers. We should expand the Texas Youth Commission by 1,500 beds. We [ought to] unseal juvenile records so that teachers, educators, and law enforcement officials know full well who they're dealing with. We need to say to our children, "We love you, but we understand in Texas that discipline and love go hand in hand." There must be a consequence for bad behavior in our state if we expect to have a peaceful world in the state of Texas.

Another question posed at the debate was: "Given the fact that we have seen more heinous crimes committed by juveniles, as in the case of the five Houston gang members who killed those—brutally killed—those two women, are you in favor tonight to say that you would support lowering the capital punishment age for juveniles from 17?" Though governor Ann Richards emphasized the importance of considering the rehabilitative characteristics of adolescence in her remarks, she ultimately concluded that some adolescents were not capable of reform: "The question is whether or not you are dealing with someone at the age of 14, 15, 16, 17—that has some opportunity for some life afterwards. I think some can and I think that there are some, very frankly, that deserve exactly what occurs to them and that is capital punishment."

Both candidates were asked whether they would sign a bill that would bring capital punishment down to thirteen years old. When asked directly, Richards responded, "I really don't know. I'd have to see a bill like that. And I'd have to hear from law enforcement officers. That's who I always turn to and ask." Bush's response was clear: "I would seriously consider a bill down to 14 years old."

Debates like the above were typical for the time. Like Texas, Florida used a "tough love" approach to juvenile crime, encapsulated in its 2000 juvenile crime bill. The architect of the legislation was Governor Jeb Bush. Ironically, only one component of the bill improved services for youth (through it enhanced the education services for youth in the department of juvenile justice); the remaining components of the bill promised to send more youth into the adult system where they would not be able to reap the benefits of those services. Also part of the package was a reorganization of the juvenile justice system to make it more like the adult correction system, new mechanisms for transferring youth to adult court, and weapon enhancements that resulted in mandatory minimum sentences applied to juveniles as young as fourteen years old for certain offenses.[22] About the bill, Governor Bush said, "There is no great joy in sending a young person to prison for life. But it will create a healthy deterrent that people know the rules of the game have changed."[23] In reality, little evidence exists to show that young people knew about these statutory changes, negating the possibility for them to serve a deterrent value.

The juvenile crime policies that developed from the rhetoric of the tough on crime era represented a stark reversal from the original juvenile justice ideals that had stood for nearly a century. These ideals, and modest success in achieving some of them, were discarded in the tough on crime era in favor of juvenile sanctions that focused exclusively on the offense rather than the individual. In specific, enacted state juvenile policies focused on transfer, expanding the juvenile death penalty, easing confidentiality laws, removing judicial discretion through the imposition of determinate sentencing schemes and extended jurisdiction (i.e., blended sentences), and supporting "innovative" new approaches like boot camps. State-level policy makers felt pressure to be tougher on juvenile crime as the public's victimization fears continued to rise. With accountability and retribution as the new goals for responding to violent youth, the adult criminal justice system was seen as a more appropriate fit for the day's offenders. Consultation with experts in crime reduction and public safety was not part of the process.[24]

Moreover, many states revised their juvenile codes to "explicitly endorse the aims of punishment, accountability, and protection of public safety."[25] By 1991, thirty-nine state codes had incorporated statements of philosophy in their juvenile codes, and two-thirds of these statements supported punishment in some way; one-third claimed punishment as the sole aim of the juvenile justice system. This was a profound shift from even three years earlier, when less than a quarter of the states considered punishment to be a goal of the juvenile system.[26]

Support for even tougher punishments strengthened whenever individual incidents drew national attention. Nine international tourists were killed by teenagers in Florida during an eleven-month period between 1992 and 1993; one of the shooters was fourteen years old at the time. These incidents raised alarm over juvenile crime even higher in Florida, since tourism was a main driver of the state's economy.

Juvenile Transfer to Adult Court

There were 6,800 judicially ordered transfers of youth to criminal court in 1987; by 1994 this number rose to 11,700, representing a 73 percent increase in only five years.[27] It is estimated that many more juveniles were transferred through legislative and prosecutorial transfer mechanisms, though data on these two modes of transfer are not routinely collected.[28]

Across the country laws were enacted to permit or expand juvenile transfer. Between 1992 and 1995, forty-one states created or modified their transfer provisions, and by the end of the twentieth century youth were either allowed or mandated by law to be tried in adult court in every state.[29] Legislative statutes in thirty-two states lowered the age of eligibility in the juvenile justice system or expanded the category of offenses excluded from juvenile jurisdiction; some states did both. The Department of Justice estimates that 176,000 youth were transferred to criminal court through lowered age statutes in 1991 alone.[30]

The scope of transfer practices and policies is important not only because of the sheer number of youth placed in the adult system, but because transfer represents a sharp departure from the philosophical underpinnings of the juvenile justice system.[31]

Florida was at the center of the nation's zeal to transfer youth out of the juvenile justice system. Between 1994 and 1995, Florida prosecutors sent more than seven thousand cases to adult court through direct file,[32] nearly as many youth as the rest of the nation combined. The rate at which youth were transferred using prosecutorial waiver, also known as direct file, was staggering. In 1980, fewer than 3 percent of the state's forty-three thousand juvenile delinquency filings in Florida were transferred to criminal court; half of these were through prosecutorial waiver. By 1993, nearly 9 percent of the fifty-seven thousand juvenile delinquency cases were transferred; 93 percent of the time the prosecutor initiated the transfer. Florida's especially high rate of transferring youth and expansion of the ways youth could be transferred makes it illustrative of the shift in policy and practice around juvenile sentencing in the 1990s. Crime severity was not the sole driver of juvenile transfers; misdemeanors comprised over 15 percent of the overall number of transferred cases. In Illinois, 40 percent of 334 transferred cases examined that used prosecutorial waiver represented charges that did not involve a serious felony.[33]

Florida has allowed juvenile transfer to adult court since 1951, and judges have had the discretion to waive juveniles charged with a felony as young as fourteen years old since this time. Over time, the state has enacted a variety of ways by which a young person could be transferred to the adult court, the most significant expansion of the state transfer statute beginning in 1994. Today youth as young as fourteen years old can be transferred to the adult system in multiple ways: prosecutorial waiver (i.e., direct file); statutory exclusion for certain offenses; and judicial waiver. Florida also has a "once an adult always an adult" statute in place, which requires the transfer of juveniles who were previously sentenced as adults.[34]

Boot Camps and "Scared Straight"

The Clinton administration was a strong proponent of boot camps as an innovative alternative to costly incarceration and a demonstration of the administration's commitment to being tough on crime. One Clinton aide was quoted as saying, "Boot camps done right reduce prison overcrowding and, more importantly, ensure that young offenders don't get off scot-free."[35] Through the 1994 crime bill, $150 million in federal dollars was allocated to fund boot camp programs around the nation. Attorney General Reno noted, "Boot camps are another innovation that can make a difference. Though not a cure-all, boot camps with strong aftercare components can and do help young offenders get onto the right track by providing a quasi-military program similar to military basic training."[36] However, there was not any research to support this claim.

Juvenile boot camps, first opened in Louisiana in 1985, came into vogue as a popular intervention approach for sanctioning juvenile offenders during the mid-1990s. Their cost-effectiveness compared to traditional incarceration was enticing to policy makers as they promised lower recidivism rates.[37] By 1999 boot camps were operating in nearly every state. The Department of Justice reported that 3,811 individuals were in boot camps in the country in 1997.[38] In many ways, boot camps were the most popular in Louisiana, Georgia, Arizona, Maryland, North Dakota, Colorado, Oregon, and Utah. They were characterized by a military-style environment that emphasized strict obedience, physical labor, and repetitive drills and were appealing to states aiming to get tougher on juvenile crime. Boot camps were reminiscent of the training and reform schools of the pre-juvenile justice reform era, and support for them marked a clear divergence from the rehabilitation-based approach to juvenile crime. Instead of instilling pro-social values and empathy among participants as a way to lower reoffending rates, boot camps were governed by demeaning and aggressive tactics that aimed to break youth down in order to rebuild their character.[39] They were popular because of their mix of strict discipline combined with behavioral training that harnessed "peer pressure and group spirit," both of which were assumed, though not demonstrated, to have a reformative effect on wayward youth.[40]

Not long after they became a fixture in juvenile justice interventions, instances of abuse and wrongful death began to emerge. In 1999, fourteen-year-old Gina Score was sentenced to a state-operated boot camp in South Dakota for having stolen a Beanie Baby. On her fifth day at the boot camp, Score was ordered to complete a 2.6-mile run in the hot sun despite the fact that she was substantially overweight and did not exercise regularly. During the run she showed obvious signs of heatstroke, including frothing at the mouth, gasping for breath, fainting, and twitching. She was denied water and mocked by the correctional staff as "faking it" instead of being assessed medically. After three hours of ridicule while she lay in the dirt essentially motionless, she was taken by ambulance but died on the way to the hospital.[41]

The U.S. Department of Justice investigated reports of abuse in Georgia's boot camps in 1997, three years after the state passed a comprehensive juvenile justice package that stiffened penalties for juveniles, enhanced juvenile transfer, and funded boot camps. Despite some reservations voiced about the effectiveness of boot camps, Georgia's governor, Zell Miller, claimed, "Nobody can tell me from some ivory tower that you take a kid, kick him in the rear end, and it doesn't do any good."[42] The Department of Justice's investigation revealed that children in Georgia's boot camps were being forced to crawl on their hands and knees to lunch, clean floors with their T-shirts, and run in the summer heat in excess of ninety-five degrees while carrying car tires.[43]

Boot camps were marketed as providing lower incidences of recidivism compared to traditional youth incarceration approaches, but research failed to demonstrate this.[44] The internationally renowned criminology consortium, Campbell Collaborative, for instance conducted a meta-analysis of forty-three boot camp studies in 2005 and found no discernible impact on recidivism.[45] Based on his extensive research in this area, criminologist Francis Cullen concludes:

Amazingly, millions of dollars were spent to implement boot camps without any thought given to the existing criminological technology on program effectiveness. No one involved in the boot camp movement seemed to question the amorphous, if not ridiculous, notion that offender change involved "breaking people down" and then "building them back up"—whatever that means. No one asked what known predictors of recidivism the program was targeting. No one wondered whether such a program, which involved threatening confrontations and punishment in the name of discipline, was a "responsive" treatment for the population to which it was directed—low-risk offenders. No one paused to consult the literature showing that military service has, at best, a modest and complex impact on criminal propensities, with no evidence that boot camps per se have any ameliorative effects.[46]

Life without Parole Sentences for Adolescents

Lionel Tate is the youngest person ever to receive a life sentence with no parole (LWOP). In 1999, at the age of twelve, he was arrested and subsequently convicted in 2001 of killing his six-year-old playmate, resulting from horseplay between the two boys. At trial proceedings, Tate turned down a plea that would have resulted in three years in a juvenile detention facility followed by ten years of probation. At trial, Tate was convicted by a jury of first-degree murder under the state's felony murder rule, which includes certain acts of child abuse resulting in death and does not require demonstration of intent. Florida law required a mandatory sentence of life without the possibility of parole for first-degree murder convictions.

In 2004, Tate successfully appealed his case and was even joined in the request for appeal by the state prosecution. His LWOP sentence was overturned by a state appellate court for failure to determine mental competency at his original trial, and he was then placed on house arrest for one year and sentenced to ten years on probation. He continued to have run-ins with the law that escalated in severity; Tate is currently in prison serving a thirty-year sentence.

Tate's case is but one of thousands of juveniles who were subjected to mandatory life sentences upon conviction. The combination of the expansion of transfer laws, mandatory life sentences, and a temporary spike in youth violence resulted in a rapid rise in the use of juvenile life without parole sentences in the mid-1990s.

Juvenile life without parole (JLWOP) only becomes a sentencing option once an individual is transferred to the adult system, and in some states, this sentence is mandatory upon conviction without regard to age. The majority of JLWOP sentences applied in recent decades occur in the twenty-nine states where the sentence is mandatory. The use of JLWOP when discretion is allowed is minimal: between 2005 and 2010, seventy-three JLWOP sentences were imposed in states where discretion is allowed. Comparison to mandatory JLWOP sentences shows that during the same period more than five times as many (370) JLWOP sentences were applied in states where the sentence is mandatory. The graph below illustrates that the majority of the growth in JLWOP sentences over the years is attributed to the states where the sentence is mandatory upon conviction.[47]

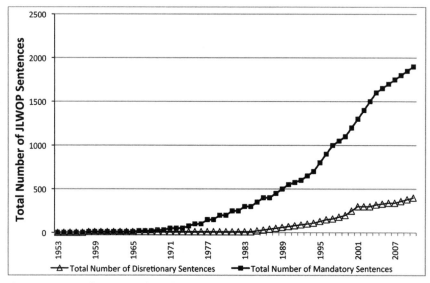

Figure 4.1   Mandatory vs. Discretionary JLWOP Sentences 1953–2010

Putting aside the departure from the philosophical origins of the juvenile justice system, the policies endorsed in the "tough on crime" era and discussed in the preceding pages failed to account for the true causes of the rise in violence. A more reasonable policy response would have situated the violent crime rise in a public health paradigm that it truly was, with children as the victims rather than the perpetrators. In this model, a more effective juvenile crime policy response would have been to provide intensive early prevention and community-based interventions to youth in neighborhoods that were witnessing and experiencing the perils of drug infestation, easy access to handguns, and rapidly diminishing opportunities for upward mobility. Some of these policies are still in place today.

Chapter 5

Collateral Consequences of Youth Encounters with the Law

You can trace it way back to an early youthful offense that resulted not in us helping them, not in us intervening to empower them—but in taking children and abandoning them and saying, "You made this mistake, and we're going to punish you, and, by the way, that punishment is going to continue every day of your life.

—U.S. Senator Cory Booker

For the 1.2 million young people who are processed through juvenile courts each year, the acquisition of a juvenile record limits opportunities that would otherwise support their efforts to stay free of crime. Today, after an encounter with the justice system, a young person may face school reenrollment challenges, barriers to employment, restrictions in accessing public benefits, homelessness, and potential placement on a national or state offender registry.[1] Additional collateral consequences include social stigma by peers, disruption to normal adolescent development, and even evidence of higher recidivism as a result of encounters with the juvenile justice system.[2] While voting rights are not lost for juveniles adjudicated delinquent in the juvenile justice system, an adult conviction brings with it disenfranchisement from many state and federal elections.[3] This means that in some cases, a young person might lose his or her right to vote even before reaching legal voting age. Collateral consequences of justice system involvement begin to accrue at the point of arrest, regardless of whether charges are subsequently applied or a conviction results.

Most young people do not learn about collateral consequences until they encounter them. As is the case with adult defendants,[4] there are virtually no requirements to inform a young person of the barriers they could face as a result of their involvement in the system, or means of accessing expungement or sealing opportunities. Added to this is the issue of reduced competence because of one's young age that comes into play when trying to understand the court process, implications of taking a plea bargain, or fully appreciating the long-term consequences of courtroom decisions.[5]

The aftereffects of formal intervention with the justice system are greater for youth of color than for whites.[6] This is in part because of the bias that youth experience in the juvenile justice system and in part due to structural factors in American culture that make it more difficult for people of color, even those without a record, to achieve equal access to education, employment, housing, and other goals.

As discussed in detail in earlier chapters, the creation of the juvenile system was premised on the belief that, more so than adult offenders, young people deserve a fresh start. Jane Addams, one of the original visionaries of the American juvenile justice system, noted that the goal of the system should be "to understand the growing child and a sincere effort to find ways for securing his orderly development in normal society."[7] The system acknowledged that youth are in a key developmental period of life that could explain, though not excuse, their behavior. Confidentiality of court proceedings, it was argued, was the key to moving beyond one's misdeed.[8] The founders recognized that the developmental period of adolescence held great capacity for reform. Emphasis was placed on correcting misbehavior and minimizing disruptions in the transition to adulthood for young people who break the law.

The retention and use of juvenile records conflicts with a body of knowledge that finds that delinquency does not necessarily foretell future criminality. Adolescents are undergoing key developmental changes that make them prone to risky behavior, more likely to fail to foresee consequences, and more susceptible to peer pressure.[9] These features are characteristics of adolescence rather than predictors of adult offending; for these reasons, records should be kept private.

Key U.S. Supreme Court rulings regarding juvenile court procedures during the 1960s and 1970s aimed to preserve the original intentions of the justice system as they affected collateral consequences while at the same time affording necessary procedural protections. In *In re Gault*, first discussed in chapter 2, the court acknowledged that though applying legal safeguards to juvenile hearings would make the juvenile court more analogous to the adult court, the importance of protecting youth from being labeled as criminal remained the priority. Keeping legal matters private protected youth from disqualifications associated with being labeled as criminal. The distinction between "criminal" and "delinquent" was essential in shielding youth from the collateral punishments associated with a criminal conviction. The court said,

> It is also emphasized that, in practically all jurisdictions, statutes provide that an adjudication of the child as delinquent shall not operate as a civil disability or disqualify him for civil service appointment. There is no reason why application of due process requirements should interfere with such provisions.[10]

The justices further argued that allowing the public to attend a juvenile court hearing would invite unnecessary disclosure and with it a host of collateral consequences, regardless of case outcome. This reasoning confirmed the approach of the founding principles of the juvenile justice system: the majority of youth mature out of their misdeeds and may be harmed by the secondary stigma of making court matters public. The justices believed that a young person's past should not be used to foreclose future opportunities and thus cautioned against opening juvenile courts to the public. "The juvenile justice planners envisaged a system that would practically immunize juveniles from crimes in an effort to save them from youthful indiscretions and stigmas due to criminal charges or convictions."[11]

The cautions of the Supreme Court did not survive the shifts in the political landscape toward a more punitive, accountability focus on responses to crime during the 1990s. Calls for greater transparency within the system during this time led to policies that opened juvenile records to schools, employers, the media, and in some cases the public at large. In states such as Pennsylvania, for example, juvenile court hearings are open to the public for serious charges.[12]

ACCESS TO RECORDS

Loss of confidence in the system's ability to rehabilitate was accompanied by doubts about the value of keeping juvenile records confidential. That is, since the system was not going to be able to effectively reform the individual, some reasoned that the public had a right to know their various criminal offenses and thus protect themselves.[13] Many states altered or abandoned their confidentiality statutes in the 1990s during the tough on crime era.[14] Today agencies enter into agreements to share delinquency data, school data, mental and behavioral health data, and family data freely. The need to protect society has justified policies surrounding school expulsion, employment barriers, public housing bans, and placement on offender registries. The impact of juvenile justice encounters now being used to disqualify young people from services and opportunities runs counter to the underlying philosophy of the juvenile court system.

Information sharing about adjudicated juveniles has become easy and encouraged, as rules surrounding youth privacy and confidentiality have loosened based on a rationale of public safety. While information sharing is a useful tool to keep track of youth across systems, the lack of discretion with which sensitive information is released has often outweighed this usefulness.

A common assumption is that the records of those who are processed in the juvenile justice system are automatically destroyed once they turn eighteen, but this is often not the case. The laws governing whether a juvenile record is sealed (not accessible by public or private entities) or expunged (completely destroyed) vary tremendously from state to state.[15] A recent nationwide report card on the availability of juvenile record data ranked states according to the degree to which they keep records confidential.[16] In the two lowest-performing states, Idaho and Arizona, there are no restrictions on juvenile records; they are freely available to anyone. Even though this degree of access is not standard practice, the report found that every other state allowed some level of access to juvenile records by agencies outside the court. In about half of the states, adjudications for offenses that would be felonies if committed by an adult are not eligible for record expungement.[17] This means that, regardless of age at offense, a felony committed as a juvenile will stay on one's record forever, creating permanent roadblocks to employment, housing, and education.

Even though a record may be statutorily required to be expunged, record destruction is not guaranteed. Record destruction sometimes means the files are kept in a separate file still accessible by specified parties through a court order.[18] Only five states (Indiana, Maryland, Missouri, Oregon, and Wisconsin) allow for complete record sealing and expungement for a juvenile adjudication.[19]

Once eligible for record expungement, individuals often must complete a complicated application process even if they had been arrested but found not guilty of the offense. The application process in North Carolina, for instance, entails submitting all of the following: an affidavit by the petitioner stating that he or she has stayed out of trouble since the adjudication and has not had any subsequent delinquent adjudications or convictions; a verified affidavit of two adults who are unrelated to the petitioner substantiating that the petitioner has exhibited positive behavior; and a statement determining whether the petitioner was adjudicated delinquent or undisciplined.[20] In addition, young people cannot apply for their records to be expunged until they are eighteen years old and eighteen months have passed since the adjudication. By this time, most have already experienced the negative consequences of having a record.

The Internet creates an easy way to search someone's criminal record if it is not completely expunged. For a small fee, a criminal record can be obtained almost instantly. In Washington State, for example, records of arrest within the past year, regardless of whether the arrest resulted in adjudication, are available on the Internet by the Washington State Patrol without restriction.[21] Since information on the Internet is permanent, even offenses that were committed decades ago can appear. Many private companies now exist to obtain and publish criminal and juvenile justice information originating with police and court records for use by potential employers, schools, and even potential neighbors or home buyers.[22] And while record expungement or sealing is possible for many cases that are retained in the juvenile justice system, it is not an option once a juvenile has been transferred to the adult system. Juveniles transferred to criminal court and processed as if they were adults are not protected from any restrictions on record expungement that do not already apply to adults. According to findings from an American Bar Association study, juveniles transferred to the adult system are exposed to potentially 38,000 collateral consequences nationwide, including deportation, disenfranchisement, imposition of licensure restrictions, loss of public benefits, and severe employment barriers.[23]

As discussed below, dissemination of records to an array of interested individuals blocks opportunities for youth to move beyond their misdeeds by accessing supportive institutions and services to help them stay free of crime.

EDUCATION

Young people who attend school are much less likely to commit crime both in the short term and in the long term,[24] but students who drop out are approximately three times as likely to end up incarcerated.[25] Conversely, youth who are touched by the juvenile justice system are much more likely to stop pursuing their education voluntarily or get "pushed out" by policies that restrict enrollment based on a record of adjudication. Evidence suggests that even the first encounter—the point of arrest—can have lasting impact on a juvenile's education.[26]

Schools have been granted unparalleled access to juvenile records. Most schools are alerted when a student has been arrested outside of school and in most cases, a school can apply its own disciplinary measures including suspension, expulsion, or placement in an alternative school.[27]

As discussed in the next chapter in greater detail, as of 2001 changes to the Elementary and Secondary Education Act, public schools are held accountable for the percentage of their students who attain proficient scores.[28] Schools face intense pressure under the No Child Left Behind Act to produce passing scores on standardized performance tests. The financial repercussions for being classified as an underperforming district are so high that schools have an incentive to exclude low-performing students.[29] Since those who are involved in the juvenile justice system typically perform far below the national average,[30] these youth are particularly vulnerable to school push out policies.

When youth return to school after a juvenile justice placement, they are less likely to recidivate.[31] And yet more than 66 percent of youth who leave secure placement do not return to school upon release.[32] Much of this mismatch can be explained by the disruption caused by juvenile justice involvement and the wide range of barriers that make it difficult for young people to resume their education upon release, especially policies that automatically expel a student who has been in secure care or those that require transfer of the student to an alternative school setting.

One way to improve the odds of returning to school upon release, and thereby lower the odds of reoffending, is to provide high-quality education to youth during their incarceration. Youth with a GED or high school diploma earned during a residential placement generally have lower rates of rearrest compared to those without these accomplishments.[33] One recent empirical study of education during confinement revealed that students who earned an above-average number of credits during their incarceration were 68 percent more likely to return to school upon reentry to their communities than those who fell below the average number of credits earned. In addition, longer terms of incarceration were associated with greater odds of dropping out of school, all other factors being equal. And finally, the study found that those who returned to school after placement were 26.4 percent less likely to be rearrested within one year and 15.3 percent less likely to be rearrested after two years.[34] Quality of education while youth are living in residential placement centers, then, appears to be highly indicative of education completion and recidivism upon release.

Yet education is a low priority in many facilities.[35] Between 1978 and 2008 at least fifty-one class-action lawsuits were filed against states concerning education services for youth in correctional facilities.[36] While federal and state laws exist to set education requirements in place, the extent to which facilities comply with these laws is not publicly available.[37]

EMPLOYMENT

Individuals who are employed are less likely to commit crime,[38] yet when youth seek employment, they may be turned away if a criminal or delinquent history is revealed. Though many job applications ask about one's convictions, which would not require a young person to reveal an adjudication of juvenile delinquency, they sometimes ask whether the individual has ever been arrested. In these cases, a juvenile applicant would be required to reveal his or her arrest. In some states, such as Pennsylvania, Montana, and Washington, regardless of whether an application asks about one's prior arrests or convictions, a potential employer can call the local police department and ask whether there is an arrest record.[39] Surveys of the post-incarceration employment application process find that having a criminal record places job seekers in a very undesirable position.[40]

Moreover, the months or years spent out of the labor force while in detention place youth who would otherwise be entering the labor force at a distinct disadvantage in finding a job. The time youth spend in confinement is generally not spent in preparation for employment, despite the protection employment serves against future offending. In many residential treatment settings, vocational programming designed to prepare young people for a job upon release is not accompanied by any industry certification, or associated with high-growth jobs in the communities where the youth would be returning.[41]

Completion of education is also closely related to securing employment. The consequences of not finishing school were reinforced by findings in a Northeastern University study.[42] The economists found that, in 2008, fewer than half (45.7 percent) of the nation's high school dropouts were employed and nearly 10 percent of young high school dropouts were in a correctional institution; for high school graduates, this figure was 2.8 percent.

Employers are often wary of hiring someone who could put their company or organization at risk; for some places of employment, like those that deal with children or the elderly, it may be wise to disqualify candidates with certain convictions or adjudications. Yet the public safety value of the indiscriminate practice of background checks has not been established. In fact, criminologists who study the impact of criminal records on future offending find that after a crime-free period of six years, offenders display virtually no difference in offending risk compared to those who never committed a crime.[43]

EVICTION AND HOMELESSNESS

Many youth reentering their communities from out-of-home placement struggle to achieve housing stability.[44] Factors contributing to high mobility and residential displacement can include severe and unresolved conflicts with parents, abuse from parents, homeless parents, absence of a rental history, income levels insufficient to afford market rate rent, criminal history, and deficits in independent living skills. Some youth return to supportive homes, while many do not. The communities to which youth return are also often rife with problems. Sometimes it is best to remove youth from high-crime neighborhoods. Adult offenders returning to their communities will have more autonomy in their housing decisions, but youth may not.

Family reunification after a juvenile placement is certainly ideal, but this may not make sense in situations where the child would be placed at risk. Because facilities often fail to work with the family during a young person's incarceration, they may be unaware that he or she could be returning to a family with chemical dependency, physical or sexual abuse, or criminal activity. Two separate studies found that one in four youth released from foster care, a group home, or juvenile detention center spent their first night either in a shelter or on the street.[45] If adolescents become homeless after discharge from secure placement, they run a higher risk of returning to the juvenile justice system on a new offense.

In 1996 under the Clinton administration, the U.S. Congress passed a federal law that drastically broadened eviction policies governing low-income housing. The National Affordable Housing Act required eviction for "[a]ny criminal activity that threatens the health, safety, or right to peaceful enjoyment of the premises by other tenants or drug related criminal activity on or off such premises, engaged in by a public housing tenant, any member of the tenant's household, or any guest or other person under the tenant's control."[46] The policy also rendered evicted family members ineligible for public housing for at least three years following the eviction. In 2002, the issue went to the Supreme Court in *Department of Housing and Urban Development v. Rucker*, where it was affirmed that residents could lawfully be evicted from public housing based on the offenses of their relatives.[47]

Because of this law, a juvenile conviction might result in an eviction of an entire family. In fact, in a 2002 study of Chicago it was determined that a quarter of the so-called "one-strike" evictions resulted from a juvenile conviction.[48]

The work of a juvenile's defense attorney becomes more complicated when a conviction can also affect housing for family members, as in the case of a potential eviction. It might seem appropriate to turn to the defendant's parents for instruction on the best interests of the child, but not if they are influenced by potential collateral consequences that would be imposed on them as well.[49]

PLACEMENT ON A NATIONAL OR STATE REGISTRY

Every state maintains some type of law that mandates the registration of sex offenders in a searchable database and requires notification each time an offender changes residence.[50] In many jurisdictions, this information is publicly available, and individuals remain on the registry for the rest of their lives. Offender registries are designed to track the whereabouts of persons who have been convicted of certain offenses. Though most registries pertain to persons convicted of sex offenses, some states maintain registries for people convicted of certain violent or drug crimes. Juveniles are typically not listed on registries other than sex offender registries, however.

In many states laws also exist that require offenders to inform the community that they are a registered sex offender directly through distribution of flyers or notices on community bulletin boards. The high volume of sex offender laws that have passed since the 1990s was precipitated by highly sensationalized crimes rather than the development of specialized knowledge about how to prevent, respond to, and reduce repeat sex offenses. While the stated purpose of sex offender laws is to inform interested parties of strangers in their midst who have been convicted of a sex offense, the fact is that over 96 percent of sex offenses are committed by a victim's relative,[51] rendering victims unaided by these laws.

As the knowledge base about sex offenders develops, it has become increasingly clear that placement on a sex offender registry is especially harmful to young people, ineffective at accomplishing its intended purpose, and wasteful of taxpayer resources. Nevertheless, over half of the states require juveniles to be placed on a sex offender registry, and the remainder are either silent about the inclusion of juveniles or include juveniles once transferred to the adult system. New Mexico is the only state that specifically excludes juveniles from sex offender laws.[52]

The dangers of sex offender registries are especially real for juveniles who are adjudicated delinquent for sexual offenses. Juveniles who engage in such offenses are especially amenable to treatment and frequently exhibit low reoffending rates, particularly in relation to other crimes.[53] In addition, juveniles convicted of sex offenses are sometimes caught in a situation where a sexual act occurred consensually, but one of the parties is below the statutory age of consent. The law does not account for this and potentially requires that the "offender" must register as a sex offender. Youth who are already under the close scrutiny of the juvenile justice system are the most likely to fall under this scenario.

Most states have adopted strict requirements for young people convicted of sex offenses. For instance, individuals as young as eleven years old are required to be placed on North Carolina's sex offender registry if convicted of committing or attempting to commit first-degree rape, second-degree rape, first-degree sexual offense, or second-degree sexual offense.[54] Registry information is circulated to various statewide databases and retained until the individual reaches the age of criminal majority.

In Michigan, more than 8 percent of the state's sex offender registry is comprised of juveniles, some as young as nine years old.[55] According to state law, identified sex offenders must stay on the registry for at least twenty-five years and for life under some circumstances. Unlike some states that restrict sex offender registries to particular sex crimes, Michigan law dictates that all sexual offenses are required to be registered, though their placement is on a nonpublic registry only available to law enforcement. And illogically, unless the case is transferred to the adult court, the juvenile cannot petition the court to avoid being placed on the sex offender registry, putting him or her in a bind about which option is worse.[56]

In 2006, the U.S. Congress enacted the Adam Walsh Act to strengthen the federal response to sex offenders. It was the first time in U.S. history that federal law required children fourteen years old and over who have been adjudicated delinquent for certain sex-related offenses to be placed on a national sex offender registry for as much as twenty-five years to life.

Title I of the act pertains to the Sex Offender Registry and Notification system, or SORNA, which sets national standards for sex offender registration and notification. It has received much criticism, especially for the mandatory inclusion of children.[57] Once a person has been added to the registry, they face strict limitations on where they can live, attend school, and work. Anytime a registrant changes residency, they must notify the authorities and update their registration; failure to do so promptly can and frequently does result in incarceration. The registry is accessible by Internet searches, though it is typically placed on a protected website not accessible by the general public. States that do not amend their laws to comply with the act face a 10 percent withholding of their federal Justice Assistance Grant funds.

Despite the law's intent to make children and the community safer, it does the opposite. Young people face social stigma and branding as predators, housing bans, and exclusion from schools as a result of placement on the registry. Registration may also foreclose opportunities for obtaining much-needed treatment. It is widely established that one's attachment to the community, engagement in school, and stable housing are predictors of delinquency; those who are presented with these sorts of challenges may thus be more inclined to continue delinquent behavior. In addition, the entire family may be treated like pariahs if it is revealed that their child is on the federal sex offender registry.

In 2014, the Juvenile Law Center successfully argued these points in its claim that Pennsylvania's juvenile sex offender requirements, enacted to be in compliance with the federal SORNA law, were unconstitutional. In Pennsylvania, the juvenile sex offender law required automatic registration, removing the judge's discretion to consider one's amenability for rehabilitation. In its ruling the court determined that the law violates a youth's "fundamental right to reputation and creates an irrebuttable presumption of dangerousness."[58] Given the breadth of empirical studies that show that young people convicted of sex offenses are uniquely amenable to reform, the court reasoned that mandatory placement on a sex offender registry violated their due process rights by presuming that they presented a high probability of committing additional sexual offenses.

STIGMA

Self-report data reveal that most who encounter the juvenile justice system continue to be punished by the collateral consequences that accompany that first contact. A growing area of scholarly focus lies in identifying the influence of an initial juvenile justice contact on subsequent offending and/or subsequent arrest. A number of research studies now come to the counter-intuitive conclusion that youth are more likely to be arrested subsequently as a result of an initial encounter with the justice system.[59] In other words, the system that is designed to help young people desist from future criminal activity may actually propel them further down a delinquent path.

One possible explanation for the system's role in causing future offending stems from the notion that when youth are labeled as criminals from their first point of contact, this influences subsequent offending. Easy access to public records through Internet or cross-system information sharing assigns juveniles with a label as a deviant. More recent analyses suggest that the recidivism of a youth may come about precisely as a result of the delinquent label. Conversely, future delinquency could be reduced if the label was not applied.

Two paths have been established to show how initial contact with the system can lead to additional contact. First, after an initial arrest, the offender may come to view himself or herself as a delinquent, begin to associate with others in that category, and subsequently turn to future offending.[60] A second path suggests that, following the initial encounter with the juvenile justice system, society imposes a deviant label through the collateral consequences it imposes. These, in turn, narrow a youth's options and point him or her further down a delinquent path. More recent analyses identify society's marginalization of youth as a mediator between initial contact and later offending.[61] This sequence of "cumulative disadvantage" explains a scenario where an initial act of juvenile delinquency results in being labeled as a criminal, which in turn leads to social, educational, and employment-related marginalization. This marginalization is subsequently associated with an increased propensity to commit crime.[62]

Recent studies examine the role of a youth's first arrest on so-called "secondary sanctioning" by measuring the likelihood of subsequent arrest independent from subsequent offending. In one study, researchers aimed to separate the role of internalized deviant labeling from labels that society imposes on youth. Relying on a longitudinal data set of thousands of Chicago-area youth over a forty-five-month period, Liberman, Kirk, and Kim reviewed survey data and official arrest record data from more than a thousand youth to determine that arrest is associated with subsequent offending, especially violent offending, as well as with future arrests. Perhaps more important, though, they identified independent effects of arrest on future, self-reported offending compared with its impact on future formal sanctions that were imposed, suggesting that an initial arrest "seems to increase subsequent law enforcement responses to those youth compared with other youth who offend at a comparable level but have managed to evade a first arrest."[63] That is, the role of a first arrest on subsequent arrests goes above and beyond the reoffending pattern. The authors attribute this to the labels imposed on youth by external forces rather than due to internal labeling.

RACE AND COLLATERAL SANCTIONS

The playing field is not equal for whites and nonwhites from the start, but once an arrest or conviction is added (which is more likely to be the case for minorities), access to structured opportunities (e.g., education, housing, and employment) is even more likely to be blocked. Significant challenges exist for people of color who have a criminal record. Devah Pager's work in this area finds that race has such a defining role that a white person with a record is more likely to be hired for a job than an African American person without a record.[64] Sampson and Laub's work has also found that the consequences of formal intervention are greater for nonwhite youth because of the structural disadvantages that permeate American society.[65]

Because juvenile justice officials are more likely to apprehend, charge, convict, and incarcerate youth of color than white youth despite similarities in offense, one study tested the possibility that disadvantaged youth experience the effects of their encounters with the law to a greater extent than other youth, as defined by employment and education outcomes. Bernburg and Krohn assessed the outcomes of 529 randomly selected youth from age 13 until they turned 22 years old using panel data obtained from the distinguished Rochester Youth Development Study data set. Their findings show strong empirical support for the influence of official law enforcement intervention during adolescence on later criminality, through reduced education and employment opportunities. They find that reduced participation in education and labor among those with initial juvenile justice system contact raised the odds for criminal activity in later years. They also find that these effects are significantly stronger for African American males and those from low-income backgrounds.[66]

IMPLICATIONS FOR POLICY

In 2011, 1.5 million juveniles were arrested[67] and 1.2 million were processed through the juvenile court system.[68] Each year an additional 250,000 cases are processed in the adult court.[69] Approximately 200,000 young people under the age of 25 exit formal custody from one of the more than 2,500 juvenile residential placement facilities[70] and an estimated 10,000 people under 25 leave prison or jail every year.[71]

The barriers discussed in this chapter exemplify additional ways in which the treatment of juveniles has drifted off course from the founding vision for juvenile justice. Access to records, registries, and community notification laws label a young person as a danger to society—a predator—sometimes for the rest of their lives. U.S. Senator Cory Booker (D-NJ) has taken a serious interest in revising federal statutes that continue to punish individuals after their exit from the justice system. He notes the unreasonable expectations on our nation's youth upon reentry after involvement with the harmful and often abusive atmosphere within the justice system.

> Then you throw them back on our streets. And you tell them, "We're not going to help you get a job. You want a roof over your head? Forget it. In fact, if we catch you trespassing on public housing authority property, we're going to take action against you. You're going to get a Pell Grant, try to better yourself through education? Sorry, you're banned from getting a Pell Grant." What do people do when they feel trapped and cornered by society? What I saw in my city was people getting more and more caught up in criminal activity.[72]

Some appellate courts have also reviewed the wisdom of preserving juvenile records. The Wisconsin Supreme Court ruled in favor of juvenile record expungement in 2014. In *State v. Hemp*, the court decided that expungement should occur automatically if statutory conditions are met; young defendants are no longer required to apply for expungement after completing their sentence. More importantly, the court clarified that expungement erases the conviction rather than just the court record. Expungement, the court said, "offers young offenders a fresh start without the burden of a criminal record and a second chance at becoming law-abiding and productive members of the community . . . indeed, expungement allows offenders to present themselves to the world—including future employers—unmarked by past wrongdoing."[73]

Informed defense attorneys are mindful that their clients may not understand the process and will need to be provided with age-appropriate explanations to calculate the impact of their decisions in the court proceeding. For this reason, the role of a competent juvenile defender to translate the potential consequences of a conviction so that the young person can understand has become critical. The collateral consequences of a juvenile conviction should not be an afterthought.

> A juvenile adjudication of guilt has far more drastic consequences than existed just 10 years ago, and both lawyers and their juvenile clients need to be aware of these effects—even if the disposition consists only of probation and includes no active period of incarceration. Some of these consequences may not be apparent for a number of years, but their possibility should be anticipated, fully considered, and planned for, wherever possible.[74]

A reformed policy agenda around collateral consequences would support juvenile justice systems that are focused on rehabilitation and reentry services, connecting young people with meaningful opportunities for self-sufficiency and community integration. At the same time, keeping delinquency matters confined to the justice system so that outside systems and agencies do not impose additional punishments for delinquent and criminally convicted youth supports youth and protects the communities to which they return.

Chapter 6

Shifting Climate for Reform

Juvenile justice is undergoing a sea change of reform, led by a combination of factors that have altered both the size and operation of juvenile justice considerably over the past twenty years. Many states and localities now seek age-appropriate, safety-conscious solutions to juvenile delinquency that meet the twin goals of accountability and effective treatment consistent with an understanding of the capacity for reform.[1] After several decades of getting "tough" on youth, the field has now shifted dramatically. What does this look like, and how did it come about? The current state of juvenile justice is heavily influenced by important contributions from academic and medical research that urges localities to abandon policies and practices that treat juveniles as if they were adults, and instead uses evidence-based interventions that are sustainable, child-oriented, and promote public safety. At the same time, sizable declines in juvenile crime have created opportunities to test new approaches to youth development, including diversion from formal custody and raising the age of juvenile jurisdiction.

In addition, local and state systems of juvenile justice are experimenting with smaller, less custodial institutions for youth that keep them closer to their communities. Akin to the original vision for juvenile justice at the turn of the twentieth century, many of today's juvenile justice systems are oriented toward individualized care, rehabilitation, and reintegration. A wealth of empirical data now supports the claim that both youth and public safety are harmed by incarcerating young people in large, congregate-style institutions that are frequently characterized by abuse as well as by substandard education, mental health, and vocational programming.[2]

Dire predictions from the 1990s of a new wave of juvenile offender—the "superpredator" —never materialized. In fact, just the opposite occurred: between 2002 and 2011 there was a 31 percent drop in juvenile arrests;[3] between the peak year of 1997 and 2011, courts reported a 34 percent decline in juvenile cases; between 1996 and 2011, juvenile delinquency adjudications experienced a 38 percent drop;[4] and between 1999 and 2011, there was a 44 percent decline in the number of youth confined in secure facilities.[5] With only four exceptions, every state in the country lowered its population of committed youth between 1997 and 2011.[6]

The overall use of transfer of juveniles to criminal courts designed for adults has declined substantially as well: there has been a 60.6 percent drop in the use of transfer from 1994 to 2011.[7] Between 2002 and 2011, the number of cases judicially waived to criminal court has been cut by 34 percent from 8,200 to 5,400. As a result, there are far fewer individuals under the age of 18 held in adult jails or sentenced to adult prisons.[8] Between 2005 and 2013, 23 states have passed 40 legislative bills to reduce the use of transfer to criminal court and eliminate the practice of housing youth in adult prisons and jails.[9]

CHANGING THE NARRATIVE ABOUT YOUTH

A new research-based policy framework about adolescents has emerged that discredits earlier, erroneous conclusions about young individuals' inclination toward crime.[10] The National Academy of Science's *Reforming Juvenile Justice* presents a portrait of youth that illustrates today's dominant view that delinquency is part of adolescence for some youth and that most who engage in delinquency will outgrow it with minimal intervention.

> [R]egardless of how serious delinquents are defined, they constitute a very small proportion of the overall delinquent population. They do commit many offenses, but most of their offenses are relatively minor and there are extraordinarily few chronic violent offenders. The vast majority of youth who are arrested or referred to juvenile court are not serious delinquents, and half of them appear in the system only once.[11]

Supreme Court jurisprudence during the past decade has been heavily influenced by the established science on adolescent development; this framework accepts as a fact that youth wrongdoing that violates the law occurs at the stage of human development defined by risk taking and poor judgment. As this stage passes, so does proclivity for delinquent behavior.[12] This "kids are different" perspective has dominated three landmark Supreme Court rulings in favor of age-appropriate responses toward young people who commit serious crime.

Adolescent Brain Research and the Rise of "Kids Are Different"

The "adult crime, adult time" philosophy for juvenile justice that governed the latter part of the twentieth century was a significant departure from the established view that adolescents required a separate justice system that acknowledged that young people who break the law are potentially less blameworthy than adults. Instead, the prevailing view in this period was that the juvenile system had coddled young offenders through lenient sanctions. Confidence in the potential for rehabilitation of an offender—juvenile or adult—had all but vanished by the end of the 1980s because of scathing criticisms on the effectiveness of rehabilitation on crime reduction.

At the same time, medical and psychosocial studies on the development of the adolescent brain began to emerge during the 1980s that now bear greatly on the level of youth culpability as well as the appropriateness of adult sentencing regimes.[13] The John D. and Catherine T. MacArthur Foundation made a substantial investment in research on the topic of adolescent brain development beginning in 1997 through the establishment of the Research Network on Adolescent Development and Juvenile Justice (ADJJ). Foundation funding facilitated a network of interdisciplinary experts to collaborate on long-term research in order to answer rising questions about juvenile justice and adolescent development. The network has produced eight books and monographs and over two hundred articles in peer-reviewed journals and books.

The ADJJ network focused on three broad areas in its research on adolescents: competence, culpability, and capacity for change. In particular, researchers examined whether deficits in any or all of these should be considered mitigating factors in criminal liability and, by extension, in sentencing. To clarify what is meant by the term "mitigation," which some have interpreted to mean that punishment is withheld,[14] they explain that "unlike excuse, which calls for a binary judgment—guilty or not guilty—*mitigation* places culpability of a guilty actor somewhere on a continuum of criminal culpability and, by extension, a continuum of punishment."[15]

The network's research on the competence, culpability, and rehabilitative potential of delinquent youth was led by Laurence Steinberg, an internationally renowned expert on the study of adolescence, and Elizabeth Scott, a legal scholar at Columbia University. Competence refers to the ability of a young person to understand the judicial process and to meaningfully participate in one's defense in an adult setting. Similar to those with serious mental illnesses or certain intellectual disabilities, whose competence to stand trial must be established, Steinberg and colleagues argued that young age should also be considered as a preexisting impairment from a legal standpoint. Young people are more vulnerable to pressures by authority figures such as police and legal counsel. In a criminal court environment this may translate into taking legal advice (such as accepting a plea offer) without being capable of fully comprehending the long-term implications of such decisions. Because of the fact that most juveniles would be deemed incompetent to stand trial based on age-related factors, and that the usual "remedies" for incompetence (e.g., medication) would not be available for juveniles, Steinberg and his associates recommend a categorical exclusion of juveniles from the adult court system.

The aim of the MacArthur-funded research on the second area, culpability, considers whether one's early stage of life impacts decision making in such a way that it renders adolescents less blameworthy for their wrongdoing. The research identified the unique influence of negative peer pressure to which young people frequently succumb.[16] Substantial pressure (e.g., duress), amplified by young age, could force a defendant to carry out a criminal act that he or she might not if not in the adolescent stage of development.

Research on culpability shows that though cognitive abilities are nearly identical between youth and adults by one's mid-teens, emotional, cognitive, and psychosocial maturity is not fully complete until much later. Specifically, short-sightedness is a key characteristic of youth; adolescents routinely fail to appreciate the consequences of their actions because they are developmentally behind their adult counterparts. The research also showed that young people are predisposed to take risks with anticipated rewards but neglect to weigh the potential consequences. This rational balancing of pros and cons does not become a regular feature in decision making until adulthood.[17] This important difference is a factor in culpability because youth are somewhat handicapped in their abilities to refrain from impulsive actions and foresee negative outcomes because of the stage of adolescent brain development.

The third focus of the network's research was whether one's bad acts represent a significant departure from his or her usual behavior, a mitigating factor that is sometimes used with adult defendants. If so, this could mitigate the severity of the punishment imposed.[18] For young people, they argued, the prospects for reform are greater than for a mature adult. Recall that the juvenile justice system was created on the premise that individuals are uniquely capable of modifying their character while they are young. With the right guidance, the framers of the early court advised that a young person could move beyond his misdeeds to lead a law-abiding life.

Neuroscientists from Harvard Medical School, the National Institute of Mental Health, and UCLA's School of Medicine produced analysis of the prefrontal cortex of the human brain that provides a better understanding of why teenagers sometimes act irrationally. Their studies lend additional support to the critical importance of adolescent brain development. Using magnetic resonance imaging, medical researchers relied on longitudinal data to identify an important growth spurt in the brain that begins during adolescence, one that had not previously been detected. The prefrontal cortex, the chief executive decision-making part of the brain, does not finish its development until well into one's twenties.[19] Because of this stage of maturation, adolescents do not have the physiological abilities that adults have to control their impulses, exercise judgment, or fully appreciate the consequences of their actions.

The overall conclusion developed from the comprehensive research on adolescent development by Steinberg and colleagues is that children are not simply miniature adults; they are fundamentally different in ways that pertain to how they should be treated in the courtroom and what sanctions are appropriate. Over the past decade, the term "kids are different" has become a signal that this established science now substantiates what parents of teenagers already know. Because of the important contributions described in the research on adolescent development, we now know that the vast majority of young people who commit crime mature out of their misbehavior with minimal interventions.

The empirical documentation of the important differences between adolescents and adults has been an essential component in reversing the punitive trends of the previous decades. The most notable evidence of this lies in its extensive use in four key U.S. Supreme Court cases pertaining to juveniles over the past ten years.

In 2005, The U.S. Supreme Court struck down the use of the death penalty for juveniles in *Roper v. Simmons.* Seventy-two individuals affected by the ruling were on death row at the time.[20] The court relied heavily on the ADJJ research network findings surrounding culpability, which pointed to critical differences between children and adults. The justices reasoned that "[j]uveniles are more vulnerable or susceptible to negative influences and outside pressures, including peer pressure . . . Their own vulnerability and comparative lack of control over their immediate surroundings means juveniles have a greater claim than adults to be forgiven for failing to escape negative influences in their whole environment."[21]

Capacity for reform was a second justification for their ruling. Justice Kennedy, writing for the majority, emphasized that one's character is not fixed in adolescence but is still undergoing change and maturation: "[a] lack of maturity and an underdeveloped sense of responsibility are found in youth more often than in adults and are more understandable among the young."[22] The transience of adolescence swayed the justices in their ruling. "A child's character is not 'well formed' as an adult's; his traits are 'less fixed' and his actions less likely to be 'evidence of irretrievable depravity' . . . From a moral standpoint, it would be misguided to equate the failings of a minor with those of an adult, for a great possibility exists that a minor's character deficiencies will be reformed."[23]

In 2010, the Supreme Court again considered the constitutional appropriateness of criminal sanctions applied to juveniles. In *Graham v. Florida*, a case in which a teenager had been sentenced to life in prison with no opportunity for parole (LWOP) for an armed burglary, the court reiterated its position that juveniles are less deserving of blame for crimes, even some serious crimes. This was especially true, in their view, of nonhomicide offenses. "It follows that, compared to an adult murderer, a juvenile offender who did not kill or intend to kill has a twice diminished moral culpability."[24] The court also relied on the established science regarding the rehabilitative prospects for youth, and concluded that LWOP "foreswears altogether the rehabilitative ideal."[25]

In 2011 the U.S. Supreme Court heard the case of *J. D. B. v. North Carolina*.[26] The plaintiff was a thirteen-year-old special education student who had been accused of two robberies and questioned at school by law enforcement. He eventually confessed to the crimes, but since he had not been read his Miranda rights before the questioning, his defense counsel argued that the confession should be suppressed. The trial court countered that since it was not a formal police interrogation, Miranda rights were not necessary beforehand. It was relevant to the case that the defendant was removed by a school resource officer in front of his classmates to participate in the questioning, and that he was encouraged to "do the right thing" by his assistant principal. He was also warned during the questioning that he might be removed from his home and placed in detention. Lawyers for J. D. B. argued that any of these factors could place pressure on a young person to confess to a crime even if he had not committed it.[27]

The case hinged on the issue of competence. In specific, due to his adolescent stage of maturity, the plaintiff believed that he was being interrogated by the police even though he was not. He therefore should have been read his Miranda rights. Justice Sotomayor wrote the opinion and relied heavily on established precedent based on ADJJ research findings that age is a key factor to consider in youth entanglements with the law. The court wrote, "to hold . . . that a child's age is never relevant to whether a suspect has been taken into custody—and thus to ignore the very real differences between children and adults—would be to deny children the full scope of the procedural safeguards that Miranda guarantees to adults."

In 2012, *Miller v. Alabama* considered a case in which plaintiff Evan Miller received a mandatory sentence of life without parole for a homicide committed when he was fourteen years old. The court noted the extreme difficulty in "distinguishing at this early age between the 'juvenile offender whose crime reflects unfortunate yet transient immaturity, and the rare juvenile offender whose crime reflects irreparable corruption.'" In this way, the court recognized the established evidence on capacity for reform: one's character is not fixed in childhood or adolescence. The court also incorporated important evidence about Miller's lack of sufficient competence during trial, writing that the mandatory LWOP sentence "neglects the circumstances of the homicide offense, including . . . the way familial and peer pressures may have affected him. Indeed, it ignores that he might have been charged and convicted of a lesser offense if not for incompetence associated with youth—for example, his inability to deal with police officers or prosecutors (including on a plea agreement) or his incapacity to assist his own attorneys."

The contributions of the ADJJ research network are responsible for shifting the narrative about childhood and adolescence toward one that depicts youth as less blameworthy, less competent, and more capable of reform than previously considered. This new narrative, rooted in science, was critical to the opinions of the Supreme Court in its four juvenile justice rulings over the past decade, but the view that "kids are different" has had spillover effects to broader juvenile justice reforms as well.

IDENTIFICATION OF BEST PRACTICES

Beginning in 1996, Colorado's Blueprints for Healthy Youth Development (formerly Blueprints for Violence Prevention) produced some of the first nationally recognized evaluations of juvenile delinquency prevention and intervention programming. The "Blueprints" evaluations were the first of their kind to subject programs to rigorous, experimental study.[28] Through its high standard of program effectiveness, by which programs needed to establish significantly positive and sustained results on youth, as well as replicability to other sites, a series of model programs were established including the now widely used Multisystemic Therapy (MST), Functional Family Therapy, LifeSkills, and Nurse-Family Partnership. Model programs have also been determined as ready for widespread replication. Evaluations incorporating cost-benefit analysis have shown such programs to be vastly less costly than tradition incarceration interventions. For instance, the estimated cost savings to taxpayers for using MST instead of secure confinement is $22,096 per youth.[29]

Blueprints also set the standard for determining interventions that are not effective, or are counter-effective and cause harm to youth and the community through reduced public safety. Two examples of such programs are boot camps and Scared Straight; both interventions were lauded by policy makers and implemented widely because adolescents' anticipated success made intuitive sense, but empirical study of program outcomes proved that these interventions are not helpful in reducing juvenile delinquency and caused harm to youth. An important lesson is derived from this: critiques of juvenile justice interventions are important to obtain *before* widespread implementation, regardless of the popularity of a certain approach.

The federally funded and highly popular DARE (Drug Abuse Resistance Education) program, designed to prevent substance use among adolescents, is another example. DARE first started in one site in Los Angeles, California, but the idea of police officers teaching grade school and high school students about the dangers of substance use quickly spread. By 1998, 25 million students in 300,000 U.S. schools in all fifty states took DARE classes that used 33,000 police officers. Scientific study of the program showed weak or reverse effects: in many localities, students were *more* likely to use drugs after having participated in the class. The Department of Justice identified more than thirty evaluations that demonstrated the ineffectiveness of this popular intervention.[30] It was subsequently redesigned, but an evaluation in 2010 of the so-called "New DARE" program showed mixed results.[31]

In addition to Blueprints, a wide selection of youth interventions have now undergone rigorous academic study to determine effectiveness. Those with the best results include intensive aftercare services for youth as well as components that actively incorporate the child's family, community, school, and peer group. State legislatures are eager to invest in prevention and intervention programs for youth that have been demonstrated to be effective. In fact, eighteen states currently have statutes that support a commitment to evidence-based programs and practices specifically in juvenile justice, and another twenty-eight states have agency administrative regulations that require evidence-based practices in some way.[32] The Washington State Institute for Public Policy (WSIPP) is a leading model. In 2012, the state passed legislation that required that "prevention and intervention services delivered to children and juveniles in the areas of mental health, child welfare, and juvenile justice be primarily evidence-based and research-based." The bill places authority on the WSIPP and University of Washington's Evidence-Based Practice Institute to "publish descriptive definitions and prepare an inventory of evidence-based, research-based, and promising practices and services, and to periodically update the inventory as more practices are identified." As a result of this statute, the two entities now regularly update and produce an inventory of effective interventions for youth. The WSIPP maintains a similar set of research-based cost-benefit analyses based on an economic forecasting model it first developed in 1997. Its "Return on Investment: Evidence-Based Options to Improve Statewide Outcomes" report, funded in part by the MacArthur Foundation, is routinely updated and serves as a resource nationally for states seeking alternatives to secure confinement.

Just as important, some evaluations reveal interventions that have been shown not to work, such as boot camps, shock incarceration, and long imprisonment sentences.[33] In 2013, an internationally renowned research collective, the Campbell Collaborative, published a comprehensive meta-analysis of nine randomized controlled trials studying the effectiveness of boot camp programs, a popular intervention promoted by Janet Reno as "innovative" in its approach to reducing juvenile crimes. The Campbell Collaborative research disputes any suggestion of program effectiveness: in fact, it finds that boot camp–style programs do more harm than good in that they increase delinquency when compared to no intervention at all.[34] Aside from this finding, numerous stories of death by abuse and neglect have led many states, though not all, to abandon boot camps. Similar findings are observed in studies of similar youth awareness or wilderness programs that operate under the same principle of deterring potential offenders through exposure to harsh conditions.[35]

The search for and identification of research-based interventions for youth is a major contributor to the reforms that have taken place in juvenile justice systems across the country over the past two decades. State legislatures in Florida, North Carolina, Pennsylvania, and Washington have enacted policies that require funded programs to be evaluated for effectiveness, and in North Carolina, Oregon, Tennessee, and Washington, the state requires the use of evidence-based interventions. Ohio set aside $2.8 million in its state budget in 2010 and $4 million in 2011 exclusively for evidence-based programs.[36]

SMALLER SYSTEMS, BETTER CARE

A current trend in juvenile justice reform work among practitioners, advocates, and a growing number of lawmakers is to downsize juvenile justice and emphasize local, individualized care. A wealth of evidence now points to successful outcomes when youth are kept closer to home rather than sent to state correctional facilities and residential treatment centers. Smaller systems of care have become popular among lawmakers looking to save resources, particularly in light of the 2009 economic recession.[37]

The administration of juvenile justice is locally operated in many places; more than half the states have a decentralized juvenile justice system.[38] This means their governance is local, and administrative decisions are not made at the state level. This gives local jurisdictions flexibility to adapt reforms to their area, but it can also lead to separate and sometimes conflicting policies, practices, and goals. In decentralized systems, localities often bear the cost of community-level care, but when youth are sent to state-level care, the cost is paid for by the state.[39] Counties, often working under limited budgets, sometimes choose the more affordable option even though evidence shows that large systems of congregate care can be harmful to youth and are associated with increased recidivism.[40] Incarcerating youth interrupts normal adolescent development; it is vital to society and to youth to limit this intervention to those who represent a threat to public safety. Longitudinal research on juvenile offenders shows that for many youth, incarceration is not an appropriate intervention and that it does not reduce recidivism.[41] For some, it is actually associated with greater recidivism.[42]

In the past few decades, some states have completely changed the structure of their juvenile justice systems through statewide reforms initiated and/or supported by the legislature. There are a number of documented successes across the country in adopting this approach, including statewide reforms in Pennsylvania, California, Wisconsin, Ohio, Missouri, and Illinois.[43]

Missouri

The "Missouri Model" that emerged in the later part of the twentieth century has become the national standard in juvenile justice administration. Transformation of Missouri's juvenile justice system began in the early 1960s with the establishment of the W. E. Sears Youth Bluff facility, a small individualized-care facility that aimed to replace the state's two large congregate care–type facilities. With the creation of a congressionally mandated Youth Services

Advisory Panel in 1987, Missouri developed the capacity to secure ample funds and now operates thirty-two small, dormitory-style residential treatment centers throughout the state. The bipartisan board is considered to have been the catalyst for establishing this model of intervention for youth adjudicated for serious crimes.[44] The cost of confinement per youth in Missouri is $61,064 annually, far lower than many other states.[45] Missouri uses a therapeutic treatment model that relies on objective, validated risk and needs assessments to determine the best approach for each individual child. Within facilities, the Missouri Model emphasizes positive youth development, wraparound services that commence upon youth admission to the facility, and intensive individual and small-group counseling. It operates its decentralized residential treatment centers using a restorative rehabilitation modality. As a result of the state's commitment to this approach, there are consistently low rates of recidivism; the 2014 annual report showed that only 13 percent of commitments recidivated within one year of release. Because of its sustained success and child-oriented treatment model, Missouri is held as the standard against which many other initiatives are compared. Over the past several years, hundreds of officials from thirty states have visited Missouri to learn more about the so-called "gold standard" for juvenile justice.[46]

While rigorous analyses of Missouri's system have yet to be conducted that would confirm the claims of success,[47] there are enough indicators, such as consistently low recidivism among those released from the system, to suggest that the Missouri Model is indeed working well.

Ohio

Like most states, Ohio witnessed a sharp increase in its juvenile justice population during the late 1980s and early 1990s in response to a corresponding increase in youth crime. By 1992, Ohio's incarcerated youth population reached 3,770 juveniles, reflecting a 40 percent increase from just 13 years earlier.[48] Due to fiscal constraints in their counties, local judges reported a limited ability to place adjudicated youth in local programs. Instead, and to avoid costs to their county, judges frequently sentenced low-level, nonviolent youth to the state's Department of Youth Services (DYS). Until 1994, there was no cost to the county for sending youth to state confinement. By 1992, Ohio's juvenile institutions were operating at 180 percent of capacity.[49]

Yet in the midst of the national movement to stiffen youth sanctions, Ohio was one of the first states to initiate juvenile justice reforms that prioritized keeping eligible delinquent youth in community-based programs rather than sentencing them to the state's overcrowded juvenile corrections system. This approach was viewed as fiscally responsible as well as protective of public safety.[50] The state was able to accomplish this through financial incentives and sanctions combined with multiple, rigorous evaluations over the years.

In 1993 the state legislature passed legislation (HB 152) authorizing a pilot phase of RECLAIM (Reasoned and Equitable Community and Local Alternatives to the Incarceration of Minors) Ohio in nine counties. RECLAIM Ohio is a funding initiative that supports local court efforts to develop or contract with a diverse array of community-based disposition alternatives for youth who are adjudicated delinquent. The program's stated goals are (1) to empower local judges with more options than placement in DYS and (2) to improve the Department of Youth Services' ability to treat offenders under their care.[51]

Under RECLAIM Ohio, the state imposes county-level costs for each youth sentenced to state-level confinement, which serves as a disincentive to send youth to the state.[52] Instead, RECLAIM empowers local judges with more disposition options than they had prior to this initiative. Previously, local judges were often hamstrung by limited local program availability and fiscal limitations that restricted their ability to place youth locally. Because of these limitations, judges frequently sentenced low-level, nonviolent youth to state commitment, where they incurred no financial cost.

After the pilot phase of RECLAIM Ohio was complete, researchers at the University of Cincinnati conducted an independent evaluation that showed highly favorable results: among them, state commitments dropped by 43 percent,[53] and only 20 percent of youth who completed RECLAIM-funded programs recidivated over a 2.5-to-3.5-year period, compared with 53 percent among juveniles released from DYS.[54] In addition, evaluators found that the quality of the intervention was correlated with recidivism rates such that interventions that were of higher quality and more evidence based were associated with lower recidivism rates.[55] As a result of these findings, in 1995 RECLAIM-funded programs were implemented statewide in all eighty-eight counties; the program has received state funding each year since and continues to be monitored for effectiveness.

Ohio's initiative has had no adverse effects on public safety. In fact, the state's juvenile arrest rate for violent crimes dropped by 74 percent from 1995 to 2010.[56] In addition, evaluators of the RECLAIM-funded initiatives found that while youth convicted of serious offenses were better served in DYS facilities, low- and medium-risk youth had worse outcomes (e.g., higher recidivism rates) when placed in state institutions rather than sentenced to local programming.[57] Research showed that moderate-risk youth had lower instances of recidivism when served in the community (22 percent) versus being incarcerated (55 percent).[58]

The annual cost of incarcerating a youth in one of Ohio's state-run DYS facilities is $202,502.[59] The impetus for the RECLAIM Ohio initiative was to offset these high costs by incentivizing the retention of some delinquent youth in their original jurisdiction rather than sending them to state institutions.[60] A 2005 cost-benefit analysis of RECLAIM Ohio showed that for every dollar spent on a RECLAIM-funded local program, the state saved $11 to $45 in commitment and processing costs.[61]

Since RECLAIM Ohio has been implemented, the state has closed four state juvenile facilities in large part because of reduced admissions to the DYS. The total cost savings because of these closures exceed $50 million in operational costs.[62] The number of youth in state secure care has plummeted: whereas in 1992, 2,600 youth were incarcerated, in 2013 this number dropped to 510.

Ohio stands out as a national model for juvenile justice reform because of a long-standing, well-documented commitment to respond to delinquent youth with community-based interventions rather than incarceration when appropriate. In addition, the state is notable because of its enactment of progressive, research-based juvenile justice legislation; reliance on evidence-based strategies to inform policy; engagement in multiple, rigorous independent evaluations by academic researchers; and, most recently, the adoption of statewide risk and needs assessment tools to guide the decisions about the most effective responses for youth who break the law.

SUPPORT FROM INDEPENDENT FOUNDATIONS

Resources provided to local communities from private foundations during and since the mid-1990s have been a substantial driver of juvenile justice reforms. It is unlikely that the scale of the decline in juvenile incarceration, nor the pace of reforms more broadly, would have been possible in their absence. Two foundations in particular, the Annie E. Casey Foundation and the MacArthur Foundation, have made considerable investments in jurisdictions around the country that have contributed to the juvenile justice reform movement.

MacArthur's Models for Change

The MacArthur Foundation launched its Models for Change (MFC) initiative in 2004 in order to expand the successful reforms that developed out of its Research Network on Adolescent Development and Juvenile Justice (discussed earlier in this chapter). Though some doubted the effectiveness of supporting research as a path to juvenile justice reform, the Supreme Court's heavy reliance on the ADJJ findings inspired the foundation to seek new ways to reform juvenile justice through a developmental approach.[63]

The work initially focused on improving juvenile justice in Pennsylvania; over the ensuing years the MacArthur Foundation invested $100 million in various juvenile justice reforms across thirty-five states. The MFC framework supports areas of reform that are selected in partnership with the communities they fund after determining the component of their systems in most need of improvement. Over the years the selected areas have included aftercare, community-based detention alternatives, improved services for crossover youth, growing the evidence base for juvenile justice interventions, improving juvenile indigent defense, providing better mental health assistance to delinquent youth, and reducing racial and ethnic disparities. Jurisdictions work with a broad array of researchers, legal scholars, lawmakers, topic experts, advocates, parents, and youth to create and pursue location-specific reform agendas.

The Louisiana MFC experience exemplifies the contribution that the MacArthur investment made in transforming its juvenile justice system. In the 1990s, Louisiana incarcerated more youth per capita than any other state, with over two thousand youth being held in secure confinement at the end of the twentieth century. In addition, its juvenile correctional systems were riddled with problems of abuse and neglect. Human Rights Watch documented a series of human rights violations occurring at all four of the state's youth prisons.[64] A separate Department of Justice investigation revealed alarming accounts of abuse from the young inmates themselves. The DOJ findings letter to the governor read, in part:

> [A]lmost each of the more than 100 children we interviewed spoke of being hit and/or kicked by officers and seeing other children being hit and/or kicked by officers. Children reported being assaulted by officers for such minor offenses as talking, not running fast enough, and not walking in line. . . . a juvenile at Tallulah described how a guard punched, choked and hit him on the head with a radio for failing to put his tee shirt on properly. When the child "balled up" on the ground to signal that he was not fighting back, the officer kicked him in the face and head and maced him.[65]

In 2003, the state passed sweeping juvenile justice reform legislation, Act 1225, that established statewide standards for detention, aimed at eliminating abuses in confinement. At the start of the MFC initiative in Louisiana in 2006, the project staff embarked on a statewide effort to implement evidence-based interventions throughout the juvenile justice system. The proportion of youth accessing evidence-based interventions more than doubled between 2006 and 2010; at the same time juvenile arrests have dropped by 43 percent.[66]

Annie E. Casey's Juvenile Detention Alternatives Initiative

Annie E. Casey's Juvenile Detention Alternatives Initiative (JDAI) formally began in 1992 as a multimillion-dollar, five-site, five-year pilot trial targeted at two specific goals: reduced reliance on pre-trial juvenile detention and implementation of broad, system-level juvenile justice changes. JDAI is now operating in almost two hundred sites across the country, representing forty states and Washington, DC.

Unlike the MFC framework, which covers a range of juvenile justice reform efforts, the JDAI model works with sites exclusively toward the goal of identifying alternatives to detention. The framers of the initiative recognized that a reformed system would need to send far fewer youth to detention. Annie E. Casey's initiative was also designed to stimulate system-level reforms. At the start of its investment, juvenile justice systems were generally overcrowded, managed by poorly trained staff, devoid of data-driven assessments and decisions, and largely entrenched in a process that prioritized incarceration over community-based alternatives. In selecting sites for foundation support, jurisdictions commit to a variety of broad, system-level reforms from increased collaboration to data-driven decision making.

Similar to Jerry Miller's efforts in Massachusetts (described in detail in chapter 2), this level of commitment to system-level change has sometimes proved to be the greatest challenge and hampered reforms in some sites. One evaluator of the initiative has noted that a "difficult educational process had to take place within the juvenile justice system, because JDAI required a crucial switch of focus from the behavior of kids to the behavior of adults who deal with them."[67]

Despite some resistance to reform in places, the average length of stay and overall detention population are both down significantly in JDAI sites across the country. Among seventy-eight sites that were studied in the late 2000s, the average detention population in JDAI jurisdictions had dropped 35 percent compared to pre-JDAI data in the same locations. This has had a positive impact on deep-end commitments as well, since detention is associated with an increased chance of being sent to a state facility or other residential treatment center. According to data provided by Annie E. Casey, there has been a 23 percent drop in the population of youth in state secure care in JDAI sites.[68] Average length of stay in detention has also been shortened considerably: of seventy sites in which detailed data were provided in a recent analysis, thirty-nine (or 56 percent) of the jurisdictions had reduced the average length of stay in detention.[69]

The activities of each JDAI site are anchored in the data, and collaboration across government and community organizations is vital to particular site success. The JDAI model also relies on the use of objective admissions criteria by staff to guide the decision of whether to detain a youth.

CONCLUSION

If we relied only on the error-ridden predictions of the 1990s for juvenile crime, the current state of juvenile justice would be unrecognizable. Juvenile crime is at its lowest point in thirty years, and investments in large-scale juvenile institutions are being eschewed in favor of community-based solutions that are child oriented and effective. Adolescent brain research, the development of a strong evidence base for preventing and responding to juvenile delinquency, and strong and sustained foundational support are all part of what has contributed to the widespread juvenile justice reforms evidenced today.

While adult prisons and jails have also experienced declines over this period, these have been nowhere near as dramatic or as consistent across stages of the system, nor across the states, than what is being witnessed in juvenile justice systems. Indeed, mass incarceration continues to be a significant problem, and the United States remains the worldwide leader in incarceration. Its heavy use of mandatory minimum sentencing, a phenomenon largely confined to the adult system, is a major contributor to the persistently high prison population despite sizable declines in crime. Yet across each decision point in the juvenile system, far fewer youth are being funneled through the system without adverse effects on public safety.

Chapter 7

Policing America's Schools

*[I]t is doubtful that any child may reasonably be expected to succeed
in life if he is denied the opportunity to an education.*

—Brown v. Board of Education

Nationwide, more than 70 percent of students involved in school-based
arrests or law enforcement referrals are either black or Hispanic according
to U.S. Department of Education data. The criminalization of misconduct at
school, now widely known as the school-to-prison pipeline, has its origins in
the mandatory minimum policies that became popular in the 1980s. Initially,
federal policies were widely adopted to remove discretion from school
administrators and apply stiff penalties for certain conduct on school campuses. Over a period of two decades, states and local school districts adopted
similar "zero tolerance" policies with an ever-expanding list of criminal and
noncriminal behaviors. A cluster of school shootings during the late 1990s
led to even more so-called "zero tolerance" protocols adopted in the name of
school safety. Intentionally or not, while many had the aim of creating safer
schools, they have instead exacerbated the disparate treatment of students of
color in the education system. The elementary and secondary school experience has shifted in ways that push certain students out and funnel them
directly to the justice system.

FEDERAL POLICIES THAT HAVE ALTERED EDUCATION

Gun-Free Schools Act

Though the nation's deadliest school shootings were yet to come, sufficient alarm about youth violence generally during the 1990s spilled over to concerns about school safety as well. In 1994, the National School Safety Center reported that more than 100,000 students were bringing firearms to school every day.[1] Mandatory minimum punishments became a popular crime policy in the 1980s;[2] policy makers embraced determinate sentencing schemes to counter allegations that judicial leniency, short sentences, and rewards for inmates like "good-time" were causing rises in crime. Despite a lack of evidence that sentence length is an effective deterrent against crime, mandatory sentencing carried over to federal policies on school campuses as well, first appearing in the Gun-Free Schools Act (GFSA) of 1994, which passed with unanimous consent[3] and received broad support by an array of child-serving groups, including the National Education Association, the American Association of School Administrators, the National School Boards Association, and the American Academy of Pediatrics.[4] The GFSA was the nation's first school-based zero tolerance law and represents the first major evidence of the shift away from the traditional discretionary student discipline framework to a crime control model.[5]

The act established as a federal crime bringing or using a firearm within one thousand feet of a public, private, or parochial school or school-affiliated event. The law, still in place, also requires that states receiving federal funds under the Elementary and Secondary Education Act pass "zero tolerance" policies for students "determined to have brought a weapon to school."[6] States are required to establish a minimum one-year expulsion policy for public school students who violate the law, "requiring referral to the criminal justice or juvenile justice delinquency system of any student who brings a firearm or weapon to . . . school."[7] Each violation carries a potential five-year prison sentence and a fine of up to $5,000. A student can still be subject to the provisions of the act even if he or she is found not guilty of the offense, and schools have the authority to terminate all educational services to a person who violates this act. States were given one year to implement these reforms or face a penalty of losing federal education aid.

Under the law, states are required to report the number of students expelled each year, the number of expulsions that were modified under required-IDEA compliance, and the number of expelled students referred to an alternative school or program. Annual data produced by the Department of Education from 1997 to 2011 show that an average of 2,750 students are expelled each year under the GFSA.[8] Thousands more are expelled under various state-based zero tolerance statutes.

Firm responses to true public safety threats are warranted. But zero tolerance policies have since expanded to include non-firearm offenses and even to routine discipline problems.[9] In New Mexico, for example, the board of education banned toy guns and toy knives, establishing a one-year expulsion and automatic referral to law enforcement as a consequence for violating the policy.[10] In Oregon, a twelve-year-old student was expelled after bringing a miniature Swiss Army knife to school.[11]

In some states, boards of education broadened zero tolerance policies to go far beyond bringing a gun to school, to include behaviors such as "school disruption, truancy, and refusal to obey teachers and administrators."[12] In fact, by the 1996–1997 academic year, 91 percent of schools reported such policies in place for contraband *other* than firearms; for instance, 87 percent of schools reported zero tolerance policies for alcohol. In New Jersey, the scope of the GFSA was expanded to include students convicted of using a firearm in the commission of a crime even if it was off school property, anywhere in the state. In Missouri, schools can suspend or expel students who have been charged with but not convicted of a felony.[13] And in North Carolina, a student who is charged but not adjudicated delinquent can be suspended or expelled from school, even if the offense is alleged to have occurred off school grounds.[14]

As discussed in the previous chapter, expelled and suspended students are much more likely to drop out of school, which greatly increases their likelihood of committing crime.[15] One strategy to mitigate this outcome is to place expelled and suspended students in alternative schools. These are designed for students who have been identified as having a learning disability, experiencing emotional troubles, or those who are under the supervision of the juvenile justice system. Though states are permitted under the GFSA to place expelled youth in alternate schools, only twenty-six states actually require this. In an additional eighteen states, an option exists for school districts to take this step, but it is not required.[16] The most recent U.S. Department of Education report on the implementation of the GFSA notes that only 25.9 percent of expelled students were placed in alternative education settings.[17]

Even in states where alternative education is possible, these facilities are often substandard, described by some as "no more than holding pens for children considered to be troublemakers. Students attending those schools are mistreated and denied adequate instruction, thus exacerbating issues of alienation, hostility, and low academic performance."[18] Consider this description provided by a student at an alternative school:

> When we get off the school bus . . . there's two officers standing there and you walk through in a line. You walk through with your hands behind your back . . . Then you go through metal detectors and you have to take your shoes off first. You take your shoes off and roll your pants up and you walk through. They'll take you to the side . . . and make you open your socks and see if you have anything taped to your legs inside. Then she'll pat you up and down. The girls, they have to lift their bras up and shake and stuff, to make sure there's nothing in there .If you have a weave in your hair, they'll feel it to make sure there's nothing hidden in there.[19]

Zero tolerance approaches to discipline nearly doubled the number of students suspended annually between 1974 and 2000, from 1.7 million to 3.1 million, despite the fact that the total number of students in elementary and high schools did not fluctuate during this time.[20] The greatest impact of mandatory expulsion policies has fallen on nonwhite students. The impact of these policies has been most damaging for youth of color. African American youth are suspended at three times the rate of white youth and are 3.5 times more likely to be expelled than white youth, despite evidence that African American youth do not engage in misconduct more frequently than white students.[21]

The racial impact of school suspension and expulsion policies has elevated them as serious civil rights issues. In response to this observation, one legal scholar notes, "Given this country's history of school segregation and other legally sanctioned discrimination against students of color, the conscious decision to deny educational opportunity to those expelled, a group disproportionately composed of nonwhite students, should not be accepted in the absence of strong justification."[22]

Concerns about the impact of excessive school discipline on blacks and Latinos are not new. The American education system has been troubled with racial tension and disparate treatment since its start. And as far back as the 1970s, advocates raised concerns about the potential for school discipline to lead to juvenile justice involvement. A prestigious Senate subcommittee, the Senate Subcommittee to Investigate Juvenile Delinquency, issued its concerns in a 1977 congressional report:

> It would appear therefore that the exclusion of students as a disciplinary strategy, should be carefully controlled so as not to cause more harm than good to the orderly structure of the school. While some students who pose a threat to

the safety of other members of the school property must obviously be excluded from schools, we should be aware that suspension of students for somewhat trivial offenses such as smoking or tardiness might very well be a policy of diminishing beneficial returns.[23]

The report also provides data pointing to racial disparities in discipline practices, noting with concern that during the 1973–1974 school year "African American students comprised 27 percent of the total student population among responding districts, but 42 percent of the total number of suspensions."[24]

The zero tolerance policies in the Gun-Free Schools Act were intended to deter school violence, but empirical support of this effect remains lacking.[25] In fact, well-documented *negative* consequences of zero tolerance policies abound. Zero tolerance policies have led to a broad adoption of suspension and expulsion as the primary responses to misbehavior. In turn, high rates of suspension are correlated with increased disruptive behavior, poorer grades, and higher incidences of school dropout.[26] Zero tolerance policies engendered a feeling of danger in schools, encouraging more police and security hardware on campuses, which has been found to be associated with a greater sense of school disorder.[27]

School safety was and still is a matter of great importance, but there was not sufficient evidence that children were not already safe at most schools across America when the act was originally passed; students today are still safer at school than anywhere else. In schools where safety is a concern, effective interventions include restorative justice and prevention strategies. All agree that schools must do whatever necessary to provide a safe learning environment for children, but controversy has emerged from zero tolerance policies and the strategies used to achieve those results, particularly zero tolerance.

No Child Left Behind

When President George W. Bush signed the No Child Left Behind Act into law in 2002,[28] a broad coalition of advocates celebrated its potential for education reform.[29] Its intended goals were to raise achievement across all students and to close the achievement gaps for the most vulnerable students: those with disabilities, new English learners, students of color, and those living in poverty. To achieve these goals, the bill directed states to focus on improving test scores, providing more school choices to parents, and raising the standards for teacher candidates. In order to receive federal funding, schools were required to make "adequate yearly progress" on a number of criteria with a heavy concentration on standardized test scores, or risk losing federal funds. Holding schools accountable for student performance was an admirable goal, but the structure of the act left untouched the massive disparities in school funding and resources. "The biggest problem with the Act is that it mistakes measuring schools for fixing them."[30]

With its heavy focus on standardized testing and attendant high-stakes consequences, many schools have attempted to meet the performance standards of the act by pushing out lower-performing students.[31] Schools have done this in a number of ways, including assigning students to alternative schools, encouraging degree completion though the GED, removing them from attendance records, misusing exclusionary school discipline mechanisms like suspension and expulsion, and arrest in school.[32] It turns out that Texas, the so-called model state, "boosted test scores in part by keeping many students out of the testing count and making tens of thousands disappear from school altogether. The 'disappeared' are mostly students of color."[33]

In the absence of federal policy disallowing it, some states have enacted laws that create clear obstacles for youth attempting to reenroll in high school upon reentry from secure detention. And in many instances schoolwork completed by youth in detention is not counted by the school toward credit completion. In 2002, the Pennsylvania legislature amended its school code to permit Philadelphia public schools to exclude youth who had been in secure placement or who were on probation from returning to the regular classroom. Instead, these youth were to be enrolled in an alternative education setting. However, in 2005, the state Supreme Court in Pennsylvania ruled this to be unconstitutional.[34] Students in Pennsylvania can now be placed in alternative schools only after an individualized assessment of their education needs has been conducted; they cannot be categorically excluded from public schools.

High school graduation rates, a principal target of the act, have not improved, but suspension rates now stand at an all-time high. Most of the suspensions are experienced by students of color. Between the 2002–2003 and 2006–2007 school years, expulsions declined by 2 percent for white students but increased by 33 percent for African American students and 6 percent for Latino students.[35] Those students who drop out or are pushed out are more likely to enter the juvenile justice system, thus contributing to the school-to-prison pipeline.

School pushout policies that result in suspension, expulsion, or placement in alternative education settings are problematic from a civil rights perspective because of their disproportionate impact on students of color. They are also problematic from the perspective of education policy. State-level analyses find that students who are frequently suspended from school perform poorly on standardized tests because of their time away from school. Though the causal relationship is difficult to pinpoint, it is plausible that time away from the class-room amounts to fewer opportunities to develop basic academic skills that are necessary on standardized exams.[36] One study in Texas examined the impact of suspension and expulsion practices on grade retention and high school dropout, including its economic impact on the state.[37] Their findings include an estimate of $76 million in costs to the state due to grade retentions as well as $750 million to $1.35 billion in increased costs and lost wages because of school dropout during the lifetime of the individuals in their study.[38]

SCHOOL SHOOTINGS

Over the course of a nineteen-month period between October 1997 and May 1999, America experienced seven high-profile school shootings.[39] The most notorious of them occurred at Columbine High School in Littleton, Colorado, on April 20, 1999, during which alienated students Dylan Klebold and Eric Harris opened fire on their schoolmates, killing thirteen people and injuring twenty-one before taking their own lives. News of the Columbine shootings was the third most followed story of the entire decade.[40]

The 1999 shooting at Columbine became enmeshed in the national con-versation about juvenile crime. "Columbine is the most cited school shooting in the United States, is widely referred to throughout the world, and has for some become a synonym for several crises, including gangs, youthful rebellion, institutional failure of schools, as well as crises in families and government."[41]

Reporters and lawmakers alike began to conflate the occasional school shootings with the earlier rise in youth violence, and such comments domi-nated the political rhetoric in the immediate aftermath of a school shooting. Some factually wrong comments even made their way into congressional leg-islation: the language of U.S. Senate Bill 254 introduced in 1999 read, in part, "Congress finds that juveniles between the ages of 10 and 14 are committing an increasing number of murders and other serious crimes . . . the tragedy at Jonesboro, Arkansas is, unfortunately, an all too common occurrence in the United States."[42] In reality, neither of these statements was true. By 1999, youth homicides had been declining for six years already and school shoot-ings, though tragic, were still quite rare.

The location of most high-profile school shootings in small, mostly white suburbs caught the attention of those who were not normally fearful of school crime. The violence of this tragedy was particularly resonant with so-called "middle America" because of the crime's location in a small, middle-class suburb with a landscape familiar to many. Many American adults could relate to having a child in school, immediately alerting them to the possibility that their own children might not be safe.[43] Parents in communities similar to Littleton internalized the event, reasoning that if it could happen in small-town America, communities that were otherwise very safe, it could happen in their neighborhood schools as well. A public poll after Columbine reported that 71 percent thought it was "likely" that school shooting could happen in their community following the shooting, despite the reality that schools remained one of the safest places for children to be. Detailed media coverage of school shootings such as Columbine also elevated concerns[44] because they tended to distort the prevalence of these events.[45] In his comments on the evening of the tragedy, President Clinton remarked, "Perhaps now America would wake up to the dimensions of this challenge if it could happen in a place like Littleton."[46] Americans had been learning about youth violence from the media in previous years, but it was mostly attributed to low-income, inner-city communities, distant from much of the country's daily experience.

School shootings grab national headlines instantly. Despite the twenty-four-hour news coverage of school shootings, the reality is that schools are very safe places and shootings are extremely rare. Fewer than 2 percent of all homicides of school-age children occur at schools. During the 2010–2011 academic year, there were eleven reported homicides of children at school.[47] In fact, children are better protected from violent crime when they are in school than anywhere else. Despite these facts, school safety policies around the country have nearly always tightened following single, high-profile school shootings. Because of its prominent role, heavy surveillance of students and schools in the following years was viewed as a necessary precaution against future Columbines.

The Power of the Gun Lobby

There was never a better time to promote gun control than in the months after the Columbine shooting. At the federal level, a major juvenile justice bill was making its way through the Senate (S.254) that aimed to respond to concerns about juvenile crime.[48] Nearly seven hundred pages long when introduced, the Violent and Repeat Juvenile Offender Accountability and Rehabilitation Act of 1999 covered a broad array of topics related to juvenile crime. It sought to reauthorize a weakened version of the Juvenile Justice and Delinquency Prevention Act, lower the age at which youth could be tried in the federal system to fourteen years old, require that juveniles sentenced in the federal system would not be eligible for parole release, require that juvenile felony records be maintained and shared broadly, and introduce a new incentive program for states to implement systems of graduated sanctions called the Juvenile Accountability Block Grant program. Senate Bill 254 was authorized at $1 billion annually for the next five years toward juvenile justice prevention and treatment.

Senate Bill 254 became the primary federal response to the shootings in Littleton. More than fifty amendments[49] were added to the bill, including at least seven gun control measures.[50] Provisions were quickly added to close loopholes in gun laws and limit the availability of guns, as well as shift the focus toward media violence (i.e., video games) as a likely explanation for school shootings, despite a lack of empirical support for the influence of media violence on actual violence.[51] New school security measures were added as well. The bill passed in the Senate on a 73-25 vote just one month after the Columbine shooting.

Ultimately, however, the juvenile justice bill did not pass. Many believe that the power of the small but highly organized gun lobby to defeat the bill explains why things returned to the status quo despite the public outcry and flurry of activity in the aftermath of Columbine. The same analysis has been offered to explain the failure of meaningful gun law reforms after the tragic school shooting at Sandy Hook elementary school in December 2012.

Despite failure to pass federal legislation to address young people's ability to obtain guns, schools around the country quickly took action after Columbine at the state and local levels, including modifying codes of conduct to impose even more zero tolerance rules and punishments; enhancing physical security mechanisms; and adding a new line of defense against potential violent intruders: police in schools. In fact, the Columbine shootings justified the pursuit of a broad array of policies that contributed to today's high-security school environment.[52]

Physical Surveillance

Efforts to secure schools accelerated significantly in the aftermath of this series of school shootings. Both physical safety measures and personnel-related safety measures expanded tremendously. A national survey of school safety reported that 92 percent of schools now keep doors locked during school hours; 61.1 percent use security cameras; 22.9 percent use drug-sniffing dogs to conduct random drug sweeps; and 12 percent also randomly conduct sweeps for contraband. Some school districts have implemented webcams and others require students to carry "radio frequency identification tags" so they can be monitored.[53]

States and cities around the country have greatly expanded security measures in schools. In 2007, the Cleveland public school system, composed of 111 schools, was approved for a $3.7 million investment in metal detectors and X-ray scanners in each school, 50 full-time armed security guards, and 150 part-time security guards.[54]

Research on the value of such investments suggests that no effect or even a negative effect may result from heavy security systems in schools.[55] It is important to consider the extent to which enhanced security features are effective, because if they simply promote a false sense of safety, this contributes to "a dangerous environment directly as well as indirectly by diverting money and resources away from preventative measures that do work."[56] In a large study of student safety, researchers used national, randomized data from nearly seven thousand surveys of students aged twelve to nineteen years old to examine the relationship between physical security measures and perceptions of student safety. They determined that increased use of physical and personnel-based security measures were associated with heightened perceptions of school disorder.[57]

The physical appearance of many schools, marked by locked doors, metal detectors, barbed wire, and security cameras, has transformed them into the look and feel of prisons and jails.[58] This may create a self-fulfilling prophecy for low-income, inner-city students of color, who may easily incorporate the prison experience as part of their future. School discipline has transformed elementary and secondary schools into a criminal justice paradigm. "The carceral atmosphere of schools and the constant presence of armed guards in uniform in their lobbies, corridors, cafeteria and playground of their establishment habituates the children of the hyperghetto to the demeanor, tactics, and interactive style of the correctional officers many of them are bound to encounter shortly after their school days are over."[59] In one alternative school, students report being required to walk through the halls with their hands behind their backs.[60]

Police in Schools

The presence of law enforcement in schools dates back to the mid-1950s.[61] Federal support for police in schools was first provided to the states through the 1994 Violent Crime Control and Law Enforcement Act's creation of the

Community Oriented Policing Services. In recent decades there has been a rapid proliferation of police officers in schools, commonly known as school resource officers. Between the 1996–1997 and 2007–2008 school years, the number of public high schools with full-time police officers and security guards tripled. Two out of every three schools now have a full-time law enforcement presence,[62] and more than twenty thousand law enforcement officers are stationed in schools,[63] a rise from only about one hundred during the 1970s. Forty-two percent of schools have a full- or part-time security guard, school resource officer, or sworn law enforcement officer on staff, and 28 percent of schools report that their security guard carries a firearm.[64]

SCHOOL-TO-PRISON PIPELINE

The combination of federal policies and reactions to school shootings has created what is now known as the school-to-prison pipeline, which consequently helps to explain the increased incidence of youth of color in particular being handed over to law enforcement for behavioral infractions at school. This trend has worsened racial and ethnic disparities in the justice system. The use of zero tolerance, mandatory regimens in both education policy and juvenile justice policy, has caused wide criticism from civil rights, education, and public safety angles.

The philosophical underpinnings of accountability-based juvenile justice policy and education policy are the same, but there is no indication they have improved either public safety or education outcomes. What is very clear, however, is that these policies are responsible for the expanded reach of the juvenile justice system. Zero tolerance policies modeled after the Gun-Free Schools Act have replaced traditional school discipline with a crime control model. Policies have expanded policies such that low-level behavioral infractions that used to be handled by appropriate school personnel are now often rerouted to law enforcement, widening the system's net to include noncriminal, highly subjective behaviors such as insubordination. This process has had an especially troubling impact on students from low-income communities of color.

MODELS FOR REFORMS

In 2012, The U.S. Department of Justice filed a lawsuit against the city of Meridian, Mississippi, for systematic actions that amounted to operating a school-to-prison pipeline through arresting and suspending students as young as ten years old for infractions as trivial as wearing the wrong-colored socks.[65] Among the specific complaints in the lawsuit were handcuffing and arresting students in school, and often incarcerating them for more than forty-eight hours before a hearing to establish probable cause. In addition, students who admitted to formal charges did so without having their Miranda rights read to them or being given the opportunity to waive this right. Finally, students were not provided meaningful legal representation during the juvenile justice process.[66]

In March of 2013, the city of Meridian and the Department of Justice came to an agreement that the jurisdiction would eliminate police intervention for issues that "can safely and appropriately be handled under school disciplinary procedures." The behaviors that historically resulted in arrests, but would no longer be allowed to, included "disorderly conduct, disturbance/disruption of schools or public assembly, loitering, trespass, profanity, dress code violations, and fighting that does not involve physical injury or weapon."[67] In addition, the school district agreed to refrain from releasing information regarding a student's school discipline record to the police, juvenile court, juvenile detention center, or state correctional facilities unless under court order to do so or as required by state law. The reforms agreed to in the settlement led the Department of Justice's civil rights division to call Meridian a potential model for tackling the national problem of excessive punishment of students of color.[68]

Progress is evident elsewhere as well. In 2012, the Colorado state legislature passed House Bill 1345, the Smart School Discipline Law, after years of tireless advocacy for school discipline reform by state and national organizations. Written into the law is a formal acknowledgment of the existence of the school-to-prison pipeline in the state: "the use of inflexible 'zero tolerance' policies as a means of addressing disciplinary practices in schools has resulted in unnecessary expulsions, out-of-school suspensions, and referrals to law enforcement agencies," and a call for an end to the inappropriate use of criminal and juvenile justice systems to handle "minor misbehavior that is typical for a student based on his or her developmental stage."

To improve troubled discipline practices through the state's schools, the law requires that all 178 public school districts implement "proportionate discipline" or graduated sanctions to reduce school suspensions, expulsions, and referrals to the police from school. In addition, it requires implementation of evidence-based prevention strategies, restorative justice practices, peer mediation, and mental health counseling to divert youth from the school-to-prison pipeline and keep them in school. Third, the law requires systematic data collection and data reporting on school-based arrests, tickets, and referrals to juvenile court. And finally, the law mandates that school-based law enforcement officers are properly trained on appropriate disciplinary practices for vulnerable populations such as students of color, LGBT students, and those with disabilities. In addition to passing the Smart School Discipline Law, the Denver school district entered into an intergovernmental agreement with the Denver Police Department to revise and limit the role of police in schools. In addition, a Code of Conduct was adopted in all 187 districts, which restricts the use of out-of-school suspensions, expulsions, and arrests. Following implementation of these reforms, there have been significant changes. In just the first year there were declines in out-of-school suspensions by 10 percent, expulsions by 25 percent, and referrals to law enforcement by 9 percent.[69]

Broward County is home to the nation's seventh-largest school district; significant racial disparities in school discipline policies have been documented for a number of years. During the 2011–2012 school year, black students comprised more than two-thirds of all suspensions despite the fact that they represented only 40 percent of the student population. In addition, 85 percent of the district's 82,000 suspensions during the 2011–2012 school year were for minor infractions.

In 2013, the Broward County Public Schools announced a comprehensive plan, the Cooperative Agreement on School Discipline, which was agreed to by a broad group of interested parties including the local NAACP chapter, a school board member, a public defender, the local sheriff, and a state prosecutor, among others. Together they outlined a new set of non-arrest procedures for handling low-level misdemeanors at school such as trespassing, harassment, and alcohol- and marijuana-related incidents. Instead of the traditional law enforcement response, officials are urged to encourage counseling, mentoring, and relying on graduated sanctions that could result in an arrest only after the fifth incident. Again, it is too early to see meaningful changes in disciplinary reports, but the collaboration across important allies is a critical first step in dismantling the school-to-prison pipeline.

Chapter 8

Impediments to Lasting Change

There can be no keener revelation of a society's soul than the way in which it treats its children.

—Nelson Mandela

The juvenile justice system has attempted to reinvent itself multiple times over its relatively short history. During each era of reform, serious efforts have been thwarted by such complications as temporary rises in juvenile crime, fear-based political rhetoric that has influenced juvenile justice policy making, racially tinged perceptions about juvenile delinquency, and single national events that have been interpreted as everyday threats. The present moment in juvenile justice has the potential to truly transform how the United States responds to children who break the law, but certain obstacles remain that limit this potential.

Chapter 6 documented a variety of improvements in juvenile justice systems nationwide over the past fifteen years. Most important, the public policies around juveniles who commit delinquent behavior have begun to acknowledge that adolescents are not simply little adults; there are important psychosocial developments during development to adulthood that help to explain delinquent behavior. Additionally, claims about superpredators are no longer taken seriously by lawmakers, media, parents, or practitioners. Third, the U.S. Supreme Court's recent attention to juvenile sentencing has been valuable in scaling back the impact of the tough on crime era on juveniles through eliminating the death penalty and certain sentences of life without parole for individuals under eighteen years old. In addition, states have reduced their reliance on secure placement, policy makers and practitioners are taking seriously the medical findings that adolescent brains are not yet fully developed, and evidence-based interventions are being utilized more frequently with promising results. Many of the advances in juvenile justice would not have been possible without the substantial long-term support provided by private foundations and the Office of Juvenile Justice and Delinquency Prevention.

Sustained reforms are impeded by remaining problems, some of which have vexed the juvenile justice system from the start. A number of changes must be made before the original mission of the juvenile justice system becomes a reality and truly is suitable for children. Among these are the following: persistent racial and ethnic disparities; continued placement of adjudicated delinquent youth in large, congregate care institutions; substandard and, at times, abusive conditions of confinement (including solitary confinement); transfer to adult criminal court and prison; and a lack of coordination across multiple child-serving systems.

RACIAL AND ETHNIC DISPARITIES

Major racial and ethnic disparities exist across the juvenile justice system from the point of entry to the point of secure placement. Despite unprecedented declines in the overall population of youth in the system, there has not been nearly the same impact of reforms for youth of color, especially African American youth. Racial and ethnic disparities continue to plague juvenile justice system reform efforts. While the proportion of white youth who were determined to be delinquent declined from 67 percent to 64 percent between 2002 and 2011, the proportion of delinquency cases for black youth increased from 30 percent to 33 percent over this same period.[1] Racial disparities accumulate through the system such that African Americans represent 33 percent of cases referred to the court, 38 percent of those detained, 60 percent of those for whom an intake decision is made,[2] and 39.8 percent of those placed in a secure confinement facility.[3] African American youth comprise 62 percent of the youth prosecuted in the adult justice system and are nine times more likely than white youth to receive an adult prison sentence.[4]

Among cases waived to the adult system, black youth used to represent a smaller proportion: in 1985, slightly more than one-third (36.4 percent) of waived individuals were African American, but in 2011, 42 percent of waived cases were African American.[5] In its 2013 comprehensive report on the state of juvenile justice, the National Research Council of the National Academies draws the conclusion that many solutions have been attempted to lower over-involvement of youth of color in the juvenile justice system, but by and large, they have not been demonstrated as effective.[6]

The significant decline in the population of juvenile justice institutions has been driven by the decarceration of white youth. African American youth continue to be arrested and confined at rates that are five times greater than white youth, and in some states, black youth are confined at rates as high as 14 times greater than their white counterparts. Consider the case of New York: from 2000 to 2008, the number of juveniles in residential facilities fell by 26 percent nationally, and by more than 30 percent in New York State. Racial and ethnic disparities, however, persist. Though African American and Latino youth comprise only 44 percent of the state's youth population, they represent more than 80 percent of placements in New York's juvenile institutional facilities. This phenomenon, in conjunction with other disturbing characteristics of the juvenile justice system, motivated the state's two most recent governors to insist on systemic change.[7]

Despite the federal mandate within the Juvenile Justice and Delinquency Prevention Act to address racial disparity in state juvenile justice systems, states have failed to make meaningful progress. And despite numerous investments in local jurisdictions and substantial technical assistance, most communities continue to operate systems that unfairly involve youth of color while white youth are diverted.

Hundreds of research analyses have carefully documented the presence and location of racial disparities within particular juvenile justice systems; these studies generally conclude that overrepresentation of youth of color in the system is owed to a mix of factors broadly defined as either differential offending (i.e., youth of color commit more of certain types of crime) or differential enforcement (law enforcement, judges, probation officers, and others make decisions that move youth of color into the system while diverting white youth away from it).[8] Rarely do these studies incorporate the important measures of structural disadvantage and social class that are also likely to explain much of the disparity.[9]

Multilevel studies that allow differential outcomes across individual courts rather than combining all courts in an analysis may also provide key information about the exact causes and locations of racial and ethnic disparity. In a study of Missouri courts by Bray, Sample, and Kempf-Leonard, the researchers used advanced hierarchical linear modeling techniques to find that individual circuits varied considerably in the decision of whom to detain and whom to divert. These decisions fell along racial lines, causing the researchers to conclude that courts were creating a system of "justice by geography."[10]

Implicit and explicit bias by officials in the system accounts for persistent disparities as well. A perception of juvenile justice that is designed for "other people's children" has persevered through the years.[11] Public opinion research shows that much of the punitive sentiment toward lawbreakers can be explained by race-based presumptions about who is responsible for crime.[12] Results from a 2014 telephone survey that was nationally representative suggest that whites' support for harsh punishments is influenced by the perceived demographic makeup of the juvenile offender population. Specifically, whites who associate juvenile crime with African Americans are less likely to support rehabilitation.[13]

A second empirical study on this topic measured perceptions about appropriate sanctions for delinquent youth. Results revealed, again, that the association of youth crime with African Americans is a predictor in favoring more punitive policies. In particular, researchers examined white respondents' level of support for seven different youth policy proposals ranging from trying more youth in the criminal justice system to taking away television privileges for incarcerated youth. Results find that whites who think that African Americans commit more juvenile crime or more violent crime, as well as those who express resentment toward blacks generally, are more likely to support punitive juvenile justice policies.[14]

Bias among practitioners also influences outcomes for youth. Bridges and Steen found that even when gender, age, prior offenses, and crime seriousness were the same, probation officers characterized black youth as more culpable, dangerous, lacking remorse, and presenting a greater overall threat to public safety than white youth. These descriptions influenced their assessment of youth risk of reoffending as well as the recommended punishments.[15]

Identifying the causes of disparity is important, but studies that identify racial and ethnic disparity do little to ameliorate disparities in the absence of concerted action that follows. Longtime racial justice advocate James Bell sees states and jurisdictions as stuck in the question of determining why racial disparity exists at the expense of implementing reform. "There has been a lot of motion but little movement in the last two decades," he notes, and observes that those in a position to make a difference "are unmotivated to do so."[16]

Select strategies to reduce racial and ethnic disparities in some jurisdictions have been evaluated, though insufficiently, and show preliminary evidence of success.[17] Among these is the regular reporting of data pertaining to racial and ethnic makeup of youth at each decision point in the system; this keeps jurisdictions accountable for disparities and attentive to positive or negative changes. Another positive intervention is the modification of policies and practices to reduce biased decision making. A promising policy in this regard is racial impact statements, tools for policy makers to use in assessing the potential of a policy to have disparate effects on youth of color *prior* to enactment or implementation of the policy. Similar to fiscal impact statements, these tools help lawmakers to identify unintended consequences while still able to modify their legislation or policy. Racial impact statements consider the reality that it is much more difficult to undo problematic legislation than it is to address unwarranted effects before they are adopted. Once enacted, the work of creating fair justice policies through racial impact statements can be guided by a number of agencies, including sentencing commissions, budget and fiscal agencies, and departments of corrections.[18] Racial impact statements have been implemented in three states (Iowa, Connecticut, and Oregon) and introduced in another six states (Arkansas, Florida, Maryland, Mississippi, Texas, and Wisconsin) between 2009 and 2014. Thus far, implementation of these policies has been confined to the adult criminal justice system but could be applied to juvenile justice systems as well.

CLOSING STATE INSTITUTIONS

There has been a substantial downsizing of juvenile institutions across the country. Fifty-four percent fewer youth were committed to state and residential facilities in 2013 than in 1999, when commitments were at their highest level. Between 2000 and 2012, the number of public facilities decreased 16 percent, and 49 percent fewer youth were held in them. Large institutions, typically holding more than 200 youth, accounted for 50 percent of the decline in incarcerated youth.[19] Yet the 2012 national census of juvenile

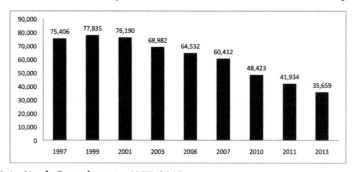

Figure 8.1 Youth Commitments, 1977–2013

facilities reports that one-third of incarcerated youth were still being held in state correctional facilities, while the remaining youth were being held in private facilities (31 percent) or state-operated local facilities (36 percent).[20] Given the long history of harms associated with state correctional facilities for youth, the pace of decarceration efforts is too slow.

Problematic institutions that harken back to the early "house of refuge" days continue to operate and are funded through state budgets. Houses of refuge and reform schools are today's youth correctional institutions; the treatment within them frequently remains the same.[21] And though occasional crises and scandals grab state or national headlines, the proposed remedy is usually to fix these institutions rather than close them. Investigations of juvenile reform schools have been ongoing for as long as the juvenile justice system has existed, and despite many reforms in other areas of juvenile justice, the complaints issued in these investigations are strikingly similar across time. The most tragic of these is that of the Arthur G. Dozier School for Boys.

The first investigation of the Florida Industrial School for Boys (later named the Arthur G. Dozier School for Boys) facility in Florida was in 1903, only three years after it opened. Investigators discovered that boys were kept in leg irons and abused repeatedly by staff. Despite ongoing reports of beatings, sexual assaults, and even murders by the institution's employees over the following one hundred years, the reform school was not closed until 2011. A U.S. Department of Justice investigation of the North Florida Youth Development Center (which comprises both the Dozier school and the Jackson Juvenile Offender Center) documented the following:

> [that] juveniles were subjected to excessive use of force by state; that youth were subjected to lengthy and unnecessary isolation; that youth were deprived of necessary medical and mental health care, including adequate suicide prevention measures; that youth were subjected to punitive measures in violation of their due process rights, such as extensions of their confinement at the facility and, when both facilities were in use, punitive transfers to the more restrictive facility; that youth were denied rehabilitative services; and that youth were subjected to unsafe and unsanitary facility conditions.[22]

At least ninety-six boys died at the facility since it first opened: Eight burned to death in 1914 while locked inside a dormitory. Another twenty or more reportedly died from influenza and pneumonia. One boy was killed by his peers while locked inside a seven-by-ten-foot cell for multiple days with eight other boys.[23] Another died, according to school records, during a tonsillectomy.[24]

As long as large institutions continue to be in operation, the modern juvenile justice ideals cannot be fully realized, as their presence undermines the philosophical underpinnings of a humane system that is appropriate for children and adolescents.

CONDITIONS OF CONFINEMENT

The conditions of confinement in residential placements, especially those in large, congregate-style facilities, continue to face allegations of abuse and neglect. Over the past forty years, nearly sixty lawsuits have been filed across the country requiring a court-ordered remedy because of documented abuse or otherwise grossly substandard conditions in juvenile institutions.[25]

Some of the problematic conditions of confinement include the use of mechanical restraints, locking youth in rooms for staff convenience or as punishment, extended periods of solitary confinement, improper responses to suicidal youth, hogtying, physical or sexual abuse by staff or other inmates, and injury or death while in custody. 2012 survey data from a one-day census of 1,985 juvenile facilities reveal that 78 percent of facilities sometimes lock youth in their room (i.e., cell) when they are out of control and 23 percent sometimes place youth in locked rooms when they are determined to be suicidal. Mechanical restraints (i.e., handcuffs, leg cuffs, waistbands, leather straps, restraining chairs, straitjackets, or other mechanical devices) are used in 23 percent of juvenile residential facilities, and in 22 percent of facilities, solitary confinement for four or more hours is utilized as a form of punishment.[26]

Conditions of confinement are a serious concern among juvenile litigators and advocacy groups. The MacArthur Foundation's Models for Change initiative, discussed in chapter 6, has devoted attention and resources to developing a national standard for acceptable conditions in confinement. These standards are provided in the *Juvenile Detention Facility Assessment: 2014 Update* and offer detailed suggestions by advocates, litigators, researchers, and practitioners with decades of experience in operating juvenile justice systems.[27] They have yet to become part of the federal mandate in the Juvenile Justice and Delinquency Prevention Act despite efforts by advocacy groups to have them incorporated.

Solitary Confinement

The United Nations considers solitary confinement, the practice of isolating an inmate in a small cell for twenty-two hours a day or more, a form of torture. The Attorney General's National Task Force on Children Exposed to Violence—a task force focused largely on the relationships between trauma and delinquency—has also condemned the use of solitary confinement.[28] In its 2012 report, the authors write, "Nowhere is the damaging impact of incarceration on vulnerable children more obvious than when it involves solitary confinement." The American Friends Service Committee describes solitary confinement as "no touch torture."[29] The American Academy of Child and Adolescent Psychiatry issued a public statement in 2012 condemning the practice and noting that the majority of suicides that occur in juvenile facilities happen when the youth is in solitary confinement.[30] Yet on any given day, thousands of youth are kept in solitary confinement in juvenile and adult prisons either as a form of punishment, for assessment, or as a means to protect their safety because adequate safety measures do not exist. Another reason that youth are put in solitary confinement is when they have been transferred to an adult jail or prison but the facility is not able to separate them from adult inmates by sight and sound, as required by law.[31]

The exact number of youth held in isolation, and for how long, is difficult to know for certain. These data are not routinely made public by the states. In select jurisdictions that have shared their solitary confinement practices, however, the results are troubling. In 2014, the Juvenile Law Center settled a lawsuit against New Jersey's Juvenile Justice Commission for keeping a teenage boy in isolation during 178 out of 225 days, even though he suffered from severe mental illness.[32] In Texas, state records show that in 2012, juveniles were placed in isolation more than 36,000 times.[33] And the adult jail in Polk County, Florida, was sued by the Southern Poverty Law Center in 2012 for keeping youth in solitary confinement for months at a time.[34] Finally, a Rhode Island federal district court described a juvenile facility that included a solitary confinement room "where boys were held for as long as a week, wearing only their underwear, and without toilet paper, sheets, blankets, or changes of clothes."[35] Similar examples, usually evident once litigation is initiated, exist in Ohio, California, New York City, Illinois, Mississippi, and Georgia.[36]

In 2012, the ACLU and Human Rights Watch authored a comprehensive report on the use of solitary confinement for adolescents.[37] In testimony before the U.S. Senate Judiciary Committee regarding their findings, one of the authors stated:

> The solitary confinement of children is a serious and widespread problem in the United States. Extended isolation of children can have a devastating impact inhibiting healthy growth, development and rehabilitation and causing serious

pain and suffering, or worse. All isolation practices are problematic; prolonged isolation is inconsistent with medical and correctional best practices and can violate both constitutional and international human rights law.[38]

Though solitary confinement has been a key tool within secure facilities since they were first established, it received national attention in December 2014 when New York's Department of Corrections announced it would eliminate the practice of solitary confinement for minors in its state prisons. In January 2015, administrators at the notorious Rikers Island, New York City's massive jail, announced that they, too, would end the use of "punitive segregation" for the youngest prisoners, those sixteen and younger. Shortly thereafter, administrators at Rikers Island extended this new policy to those aged seventeen and eighteen. Though prolonged isolation for any prisoner should not be tolerated, it is notable that the vast majority (85 percent)[39] of inmates at the Rikers Island facility are awaiting trial and have not been convicted of a crime; this is the case for juveniles as well. Numerous international and domestic bodies have urged the United States to discontinue to the use of solitary confinement for young inmates.

JUVENILE TRANSFER

Despite the significant scaling back of juvenile transfer laws discussed in chapter 6, thousands of youth continue to be processed in the adult criminal justice system every year. Exact estimates of the number of youth transferred are difficult to ascertain since only thirteen states publicly report the total number of transfers, and not all of these states reveal important demographic information or details on the processing and sentencing of transferred youth.[40] Some estimate that as many as two hundred thousand are tried as adults each year due to statutory age limits that disallow individuals under age eighteen to remain in the juvenile justice system.[41] In two states, adolescents are transferred to the adult court because the original juvenile court jurisdiction ends at age fifteen (New York and North Carolina), and in ten states original juvenile court jurisdiction ends at sixteen (Georgia, Illinois, Louisiana, Massachusetts, Michigan, Missouri, New Hampshire, South Carolina, Texas, and Wisconsin). An additional 55,000 juveniles are transferred to the adult system across 29 states because they have been charged with an offense that is not permitted within the juvenile court system.[42] Judicial waivers, permissible in 45 states, account for another 5,400 individuals transferred to adult court.[43] The use of prosecutorial discretion, available in 15 states, sends even more juveniles to adult court, though the exact figure is not available. In sum, young people can find themselves in either the adult system or the juvenile system depending on the state where they reside due to a bewildering array of responses by the criminal and juvenile justice systems.

Department of Justice figures from 2013 document that nearly 6,000 juveniles reside in prisons and jails, institutions designed and operated for adults.[44] As the cumulative result of youth receiving sentences in criminal court over the past few decades, there are 10,000 individuals serving life sentences for crimes committed before they were 18 years old, and approximately 2,500 of these were sentenced to life without the possibility of parole.[45]

Given all that is known about the problems with transferring youth to adult criminal justice systems, the pace of reform in this area has been too slow. The lack of any deterrent effects or public safety impacts are firmly established: as far back as 1996, researchers reported that children who were transferred to the adult system recidivated 30 percent more frequently than matched youth who were retained in the juvenile justice system.[46] Added to this is the consistent finding of heightened risk of physical and sexual assaults when youth are placed with adults. The Department of Justice identified that 7,400 prisoners under 18 were sexually assaulted in prison and jail in its 2014 study on inmate victimization.[47] And finally, youth are significantly more likely to commit suicide when housed alongside adults. The Department of Justice's *Deaths in Custody* report finds that 73.3 percent of all deaths among individuals under 18 in adult jails are because of suicide.[48] Among young inmates in adult prisons, the suicide rate is twice as high as the rate for older inmates.[49]

Aside from reports of abuse and suicide, programming for youth in adult facilities is substandard if it exists at all. According to Elizabeth Scott and Laurence Steinberg, the crucial educational, vocational, and social skill–building phase of adolescence is disrupted by the practice of transfer.[50] In some institutions, rehabilitation, vocational, or education programming is provided to young inmates but in others, depending on the system, state, or resources available, these might very well be denied. In Florida, fewer than 10 percent of transferred youth are provided with counseling or treatment services.[51] Among juveniles serving life without the possibility of parole, 62 percent of people do not participate in prison programs in large part due to state prison policies that prohibit their participation or due to limited program availability.

Progress in some states, such as successful legislation in Connecticut that, as of 2012, raised the age at which adolescents can be transferred to criminal court from sixteen to eighteen, serve as a model to the remaining states that have revised their statutes in accordance with documented proof that transferring youth to the adult system meets neither deterrent nor rehabilitative goals of the justice system.

COORDINATING CARE

Lack of coordination and collaboration across service agencies is one of the greatest barriers to effective responses to at-risk and delinquent youth.[52] Youth are frequently engaged in multiple child-oriented systems that are often disconnected from one another and over which they have no control.[53] At the same time, a young person may be involved in the education system, the mental health system, the foster care system, the child welfare system, and/or the juvenile justice system; these systems often operate in isolation from one another, putting youth at a disadvantage and sometimes in danger. In Washington's King County, for instance, it is estimated that 67 percent of the youth referred to the juvenile justice system also had some contact with the county's child welfare agency.[54] Even though youth cross over these various systems, staff working within them rarely do.[55] Because of their young age, decisions are frequently on behalf of so-called crossover or dual system youth without their input or that of their family. Added to this is the bias that youth sometimes experience because of their involvement in neighboring child-serving systems. Take, for instance, multivariate research findings from the Vera Institute that revealed that foster youth were 10 percent more likely to be detained before their court appearance than youth who were not involved in the foster care system, controlling for all other relevant factors.[56]

It is well documented that youth who commit crimes—especially violent and serious crimes—have frequently been victims of abuse and neglect themselves.[57] A well-known longitudinal study identified a 59 percent greater likelihood of arrest among juveniles who were abused or neglected.[58] The Department of Justice's *Defending Childhood* series, too, documents the cyclical effect of violence on families and communities.[59] Cathy Spatz-Widom, one of the nation's preeminent scholars on handling youth involved in multiple systems, warns that children with abuse and neglect histories who exhibit behavior problems have the greatest risk of receiving a juvenile and adult arrest record as well as engaging in violent criminal behavior.[60] Her suggestion is to intervene in the lives of these children as soon as possible with trauma-informed care so that their odds of involvement in the juvenile justice system are minimized.

Still, some youth will enter the system, and for these, a primary obligation of juvenile justice practitioners, advocates, researchers, and policy makers is to ensure that victimization is not repeated by the juvenile justice system. Consider the following account of a girl in multiple child-serving systems:

> Before being placed in the facility, she had been the victim of a serious sexual assault, had been placed in a psychiatric hospital, and had been suspended from school for fighting. The facility psychiatrist recommended that the youth receive psychotherapy in order to address her past trauma. Her single, simplistic treatment goal was: "Youth will identify one way that her behavior has consequences for her and for others" and listed the same treatment modalities as for any other youth at the facility. Several days after her treatment plan was completed, the youth attempted to hang herself with a shoelace. In a suicide risk evaluation following this incident, the youth asserted that "as long as she is feeling this bad, she will try to kill herself." Despite these signs of serious mental distress, her treatment plan remained unchanged following the suicide attempt.[61]

Currently, partnerships among neighboring systems of care are not enough systematically prioritized. Models and strategies exist that jurisdictions can adopt, such as those designed and advanced by the Robert F. Kennedy Children's Action Corps in its 2013 MacArthur-funded *Guidebook for Juvenile Justice and Child Welfare System Coordination and Integration.*[62] Efforts by these two entities are being made to coordinate the efforts of child welfare and juvenile justice for dual-system youth through interagency and intra-agency collaboration.

Parental Incarceration

Absence of a parent because of incarceration is such a common experience now that the topic of mass incarceration was covered in a 2013 episode of *Sesame Street.*[63] Parental incarceration affects approximately 2.2 million children who have a parent in prison or jail, a 529 percent increase from 350,000 in 1980.[64] By age fourteen, one in twenty-five white children and one in seven African American children born in 1990 had an incarcerated parent.[65] Fully one in two black boys of fathers who did not complete high school has experienced paternal imprisonment.[66]

America's experiment with mass incarceration did not attempt to anticipate the ripple effects of its consequences on families and communities. Donald Braman notes that the sharp rise in the use of imprisonment in the last twenty years has "in many ways missed the mark, injuring the families of prisoners often as much as and sometimes more than the criminal offenders themselves."[67] The extent of mass incarceration on children is only beginning to gather national attention as a source of trauma for children and an explanation for problem behavior, including delinquency.[68] Contrary to popular assumptions about incarcerated parents being uninvolved in the lives of their children before their imprisonment, research by Amanda Geller finds that parents who become incarcerated were typically in regular contact with their children: 42 percent of incarcerated fathers and 60 percent of incarcerated mothers lived with their children before they went to prison or jail, and 60 percent of fathers who did not live with their children still had regular visitation with them. "To a large extent, then," she says, "incarcerated parents were *parenting,* assuming the responsibilities associated with providing for and raising their children."[69]

In his ethnographic research on parental incarceration, Braman offers a particularly troubling account by a young boy who witnessed his father's arrest:

[The police] chased him in the house, and I was sitting there screaming, like, "Daddy! Daddy!" . . . The police came, and they pushed him down on the floor. He got up and pushed them off and ran through the front door, so I ran behind him . . . [T]hey came and pulled my father from under the car and started beating him. And I was standing there looking at them beating my father with night sticks, and they dragged him through the alley and put him in the paddy wagon.[70]

Among juveniles serving life sentences, more than one-quarter have had a parent in prison at some point in their lives, and 59.1 percent report having had a close relative who was or still is incarcerated.[71] While parental incarceration has been a known predictor of crime among their children for some time, the discussion of it as a source of trauma for youth is relatively recent.[72]

The documented effects on children of having a parent in prison are manifold; research documents both internalizing outcomes (e.g., depression, anxiety, social exclusion) and externalizing problems (e.g., fighting at school, drug use, school dropout) as a direct result of parental incarceration.[73] For instance, Terry Ann Craigie's research in this area finds that signs of trouble through externalizing behaviors such as aggression, violence, hostility, and destructive acts tend to emerge early in a child's life if they have a parent in prison.[74]

Research demonstrates that parental incarceration is a strong predictive factor in subsequent juvenile delinquency. A California study of incarcerated parents and their children detected that the "children were found to have experienced emotional problems, nightmares, fighting in school and a decline in academic performance as a result of being separated due to their mother's incarceration."[75] Studies elsewhere draw similar conclusions. For example, Roettger and Swisher take advantage of a large longitudinal data set of adolescents to young adults to examine the relationship between parental incarceration and juvenile offending. Their research finds that paternal incarceration is significantly associated with delinquency both in childhood and young adulthood, net of a combination of related factors including socioeconomic status, family structure, neighborhood characteristics, one's attachment to his or her father, other family processes, and peer friendships.[76] Data analyzed from the National Longitudinal Study of Adolescent Health show that a father's incarceration is strongly associated with externalizing behaviors including serious delinquency, marijuana use, hard drug use, and arrests in adolescence and adulthood.[77]

Race does not alter the strength of the relationship between parental incarceration and juvenile delinquency: black, white, and Hispanic boys are all similarly likely to engage in delinquency and be arrested if they have had an incarcerated father. Of importance here is the fact that, though these findings persist regardless of race, this does not suggest that all races are equally affected by parental incarceration. The burdens of a family member's incarceration fall disproportionately on black and Latino youth because parents in these two categories are much more likely to experience incarceration.

Christopher Uggen and Suzy McElrath write that in order to reduce the number of children affected by parental incarceration, sentencing reform on the adult side will have to take place.[78] However, steps can and should also be taken to address the emotional impact of having a parent in prison so that the risk of continuing in a parent's footsteps is minimized.

CONCLUSION

This chapter documents some of the most plaguing issues that remain in juvenile justice and impede reform. Some of these issues have been components of juvenile justice administration from the start, such as racial and ethnic disparities and the overuse of large institutions. Other problems, like parental incarceration and juvenile transfer, are the consequence of misguided crime policies in earlier decades. Without reforms in these areas—both in policy and practice—there is little chance of sustainable reform. As others have noted, by the time youth arrive at the doors of the juvenile justice system, they are the product of one or more systems that have already failed them, such as the education system, child welfare system, foster care system, or mental health system. Without making improvements in the areas discussed in this chapter, the juvenile justice system risks failing these youth as well.

Conclusion

In its short history the juvenile justice system has undergone a series of transformations, fluctuating dramatically in its philosophical basis for responses to youth who encounter legal trouble. In its earliest period, systems of congregate care were the preferred approach, adapted from existing institutions for adult offenders. Though they strived to be more humane, ultimately reform schools and houses of refuge served as little more than a warehouse for criminal and other unwanted youth. The development of a separate juvenile court marked the beginning of the concerted effort to insulate youth from the negative influence of adults. The system envisioned was likened to a compassionate and caring parent with a duty to redirect youth and provide the necessary supports. Procedural protections, established through case law in the 1960s and 1970s, resulted in substantial safeguards for youth in the ways they were treated in and by the system.

Yet in the latter part of the twentieth century, as juvenile crime experienced a troubling rise and political rhetoric reached a fevered pitch, accusations of being too soft on crime spread and, in response, the system reinvented itself again as one governed by accountability, punishment, and deterrence. The juvenile crime policies of this era showed an abandonment of established ideals, instead setting punitive sanctions in place, quickly shifting thousands of youth to the adult system where they received harsh sentences and no supports. Important distinctions between the juvenile justice system and the adult criminal justice system became blurred, and the methods by which law enforcement, prosecutors, and judges could apply tougher sanctions for youth eased.

A major component of the punitive shift in juvenile justice policies and practices experienced in the 1990s is explained by the fact that juvenile offenders were increasingly dehumanized through terms like "superpredator," which allowed lawmakers and the public to distance themselves from the punitive sanctions that were adopted. While race was always a dominant factor in the design and function of the juvenile justice system, it became openly hostile toward youth of color during this era.

Starting in the twenty-first century with the safety of several years of crime declines, the juvenile justice system reversed course again, making unprecedented changes to its structure and size. Jurisdictions around the country have now recommitted themselves to the purpose of supporting and diverting youth from unnecessary involvement in the justice system. Many systems of confinement have gotten smaller. Practitioners turn to a growing body of evidence of what works to prevent and respond to juvenile delinquency. And critical developments in science and medicine provide convincing evidence that kids are different in ways that merit unique treatment by the justice system. This treatment still demands accountability for wrong actions but, importantly, accommodates an adolescent's transitory stage of human development in deciding the appropriate response.

The current moment has great potential for juvenile justice to truly realize its vision. First, the reforms in youth justice since the start of the twenty-first century, and laid out in chapter 6, have been substantial. This is particularly true given the punitive era that preceded it. Juvenile crime has been declining for many years now and shows no sign of rising. In addition, the public supports rehabilitative solutions for youth offending: opinion polls present strong and consistent evidence that the public prefers rehabilitation over punishment. Moreover, citizens are willing to pay for rehabilitation even when it is more costly than incarceration.[1] The combination of these factors affords jurisdictions the latitude to challenge outdated practices and pursue more improvements.

Youth justice has not yet realized its original ideal, which was for it to serve as *parens patriae*, in the role of a caring and compassionate parent. A system that embodied this vision would consider the needs of the whole child rather than simply his or her delinquent behavior. Yet juvenile justice administration is still primarily defined by its ability to serve the safety needs of the public. Accordingly, it is governed by the dictates of custody and control. More than 160,000 young people are sentenced to correctional placements each year.[2] Recidivism rates as high as 60 percent in some places suggest that the tough on crime approach that demands incarceration does not work with children.[3] One scholar cites "an abundance of evidence thus suggests that juvenile incarceration is routinely failing to improve youths' lives"[4] and does nothing to predict recidivism. Switching to a more expansive view of youth—from one that looks only at the delinquent act he or she committed to a "whole-child" approach—would still consider the offense but do so in light of relevant individual and community factors. These factors might include the stability of one's family or community, school environment, learning disabilities, parental incarceration, mental health issues, access to counseling, exposure to violence, co-involvement in other systems, structural disadvantages, and other factors as appropriate.

Efforts to make a youth justice system that is suitable for children who need it should not be taken to mean that the juvenile justice system is an appropriate response to most acts of delinquency. Unlike the adult system, which has always used incarceration as a primary response to crime, the juvenile justice system was designed to divert the vast majority of youth from the immediate and long-lasting negative effects of incarceration. Today juvenile incarceration continues to be overused; among the 35,659 youth committed to secure placement in 2013, 61.8 percent have been adjudicated for nonviolent offenses.[5] Research shows that the vast majority of these cases are more effectively treated in the community where youth can benefit from evidence-based interventions while remaining connected to positive influences in their community, family, and school. The public benefits far more from an approach that favors broad prevention and early intervention strategies as well as evidence-based rehabilitation programs.

Adherence to the original design of an intervention is critical to success. Simply adopting an evidenced-based approach but not implementing it as was intended will not produce the desired outcomes and reduces the credibility of evidence-based programs more generally. One study that examined evaluations of evidence-based youth interventions conducted between 1996 and 2009 found that of the 141 studies that were examined, 120 failed to implement the intervention with fidelity.[6]

The detrimental juvenile crime policies of the 1990s can serve as a warning to the present environment; the tough on crime era shows how little is required to dismantle positive reforms given the right political climate and level of public panic. Recall that the field of corrections had not fully implemented rehabilitation before it was poorly evaluated and then harshly criticized. In an environment of rising violence and public fears, the notion of rehabilitation was easily rejected under the banner that "nothing works." As practitioners and advocates continue to reform the juvenile justice system, a question that must accompany this work is how to solidify reforms in the likely event of a rise in juvenile crime, which will undoubtedly cause some to question the whole-child approach. A shift in the political landscape or tightening of resources could easily lead to problems. To safeguard against another reversal it is essential to implement promising reforms as they are designed and continue to evaluate interventions that work to keep youth and communities safe.

The present moment offers both challenges and opportunities for improving the experiences of youth who encounter the law. To arrive at the ideal envisioned by those who designed the original juvenile justice system, the measures for success need to broaden beyond simply measuring whether the youth return to the system after release. Youth arrive at the doors of the justice system at a critically important time of adolescent development. The juvenile justice system can act as a catalyst toward positive youth development, or it can stand in the way, creating a scenario whereby repeated cycles through the system continue. With juvenile crime at remarkable lows, a strong evidence base on what works to rehabilitate youth, medical confirmation that adolescents are less culpable, and public support for rehabilitating youth rather than applying stiff penalties, the present moment offers a unique opportunity to continue reforms in the direction that the framers envisioned to create a system that is justly suitable for children.

Notes

INTRODUCTION

1. Douglas Evans, *Pioneers of Youth Justice Reform* (New York: John Jay College of Criminal Justice Research and Evaluation Center, 2012).

CHAPTER 1

1. Barry Feld, "Reforming Juvenile Justice," *American Prospect*, August 14, 2005.

2. Marc Mauer, *Race to Incarcerate* (New York: New Press, 2006).

3. Barry Feld, *Bad Kids: Race and the Transformation of the Juvenile Court* (New York: Oxford University Press, 1999).

4. Sanford Fox, "The Early History of the Court," *Future of Children* 6(3) (1996): 29–39.

5. "Punishing Children: Houses of Refuge and Juvenile Justice," *Prison Culture,* February 3, 2011, http://www.usprisonculture.com/blog/2011/02/03/punishing-children-houses-of-refuge-juvenile-justice/.

6. Barry Feld, *Bad Kids: Race and the Transformation of the Juvenile Court* (New York: Oxford University Press, 1999), 51.

7. Alexander Liazos, "Class Oppression: The Functions of Juvenile Justice," *Critical Sociology* 5(2) (1974): 8.

8. Sanford Fox, "The Early History of the Court," *Future of Children*, 6(3) (1996): 299–39. Note that in 1870, the Illinois Supreme Court ruled that youth could not be sent to the state's reform school if they had not been convicted of a crime and they had not been accorded with due process at trial. Two years later, the state reform school closed and all youth were processed in the adult criminal court system for the remainder of the nineteenth century.

9. Anthony Platt, *The Child Savers: The Invention of Delinquency* (New Brunswick: Rutgers University Press, 2009).

10. Alexander Liazos, "Class Oppression: The Functions of Juvenile Justice," *Critical Sociology* 5(2) (1974): 2–24.

11. Jerome Miller closed this institution in 1972 as part of his successful state-wide initiative to decarcerate all juveniles. Miller's influence on juvenile justice is discussed in depth in chapter 2.

12. Alexander Liazos, "Class Oppression: The Functions of Juvenile Justice," *Critical Sociology* 5(2) (1974): 2–24.

13. Anthony Platt, *The Child Savers: The Invention of Delinquency* (New Brunswick: Rutgers University Press, 2009), 102.

14. Utah State Juvenile Court, *Annual Report, 1978*, Salt Lake City, Utah State Juvenile Court.

15. Geoff Ward, *The Black Child-Savers: Racial Democracy and Juvenile Justice* (Chicago: University of Chicago Press, 2012), 74.

16. Geoff Ward, *The Black Child-Savers: Racial Democracy and Juvenile Justice* (Chicago: University of Chicago Press, 2012).

17. Geoff Ward, *The Black Child-Savers: Racial Democracy and Juvenile Justice* (Chicago: University of Chicago Press, 2012).

18. Geoff Ward, *The Black Child-Savers: Racial Democracy and Juvenile Justice* (Chicago: University of Chicago Press, 2012), 74.

19. Geoff Ward, *The Black Child-Savers: Racial Democracy and Juvenile Justice* (Chicago: University of Chicago Press, 2012).

20. John R. Sutton, "The Juvenile Court and Social Welfare: Dynamics of Progressive Reform," *Law and Society Review*, 19(1) (1985): 130.

21. Barry Feld, *Bad Kids: Race and the Transformation of the Juvenile Court* (New York: Oxford University Press, 1999), 37.

22. See, for example, Joseph M. Hawes, *Children in Urban Society* (New York: Oxford University Press, 1971).

23. Anthony Platt, *The Child Savers: The Invention of Delinquency* (New Brunswick: Rutgers University Press, 2009).

24. Kristin Finklea, *Juvenile Justice Legislative History and Current Legislative Issues* (Washington, DC: Congressional Research Service, 2012).

25. Alexander Liazos, "Class Oppression: The Functions of Juvenile Justice," *Critical Sociology* 5(2) (1974): 2–24.

26. Franklin Zimring, *American Juvenile Justice* (Oxford: Oxford University Publishing, 2005), 6.

27. Franklin Zimring, *American Juvenile Justice* (Oxford: Oxford University Publishing, 2005).

28. Anthony Platt, *The Child Savers: The Invention of Delinquency* (Chicago: University of Chicago Press, 1977).

29. David T. Tanenhaus, "The Evolution of Juvenile Courts in the Early Twentieth Century: Beyond the Myth of Immaculate Construction." In *A Century of Juvenile Justice,* ed. Margaret K. Rosenheim et al. (Chicago: University of Chicago Press, 2002), 42–73.

30. David T. Tanenhaus, "The Evolution of Juvenile Courts in the Early Twentieth Century: Beyond the Myth of Immaculate Construction." In *A Century of Juvenile Justice,* ed. Margaret K. Rosenheim et al. (Chicago: University of Chicago Press, 2002), 64.

31. David T. Tanenhaus, "The Evolution of Juvenile Courts in the Early Twentieth Century: Beyond the Myth of Immaculate Construction." In *A Century of Juvenile Justice,* ed. Margaret K. Rosenheim et al. (Chicago: University of Chicago Press, 2002).

32. Franklin Zimring, *American Juvenile Justice* (Oxford: Oxford University Publishing, 2005), 7.

33. Anthony Platt, *The Child Savers: The Invention of Delinquency* (New Brunswick: Rutgers University Press, 2009), 138.

34. John R. Sutton, "The Juvenile Court and Social Welfare: Dynamics of Progressive Reform," *Law and Society Review* 19(1) (1985): 107–45.

35. Anthony Platt, *The Child Savers: The Invention of Delinquency* (New Brunswick: Rutgers University Press, 2009), 138.

36. Randall Sheldon and Lynne Osborne, "'For Their Own Good': Class Interests and the Child Saving Movement in Memphis, Tennessee, 1900-1917," *Criminology* 27 (1989): 747–67, 759.

37. Katherine Lazarow, "The Continued Viability of New York's Juvenile Offender Act in Light of Recent National Developments," *New York Law School Review* 57 (2012): 595–635.

38. Julian Mack, "The State and the Child," *Harvard Law Review* 1 (1911): 676–81.

39. Franklin Zimring, *American Juvenile Justice* (Oxford: Oxford University Publishing, 2005), 9.

40. Sanford Fox, "The Early History of the Court," *Future of Children* 6(3) (1996): 29–39.

41. Charles Henderson, "Juvenile Courts: Problems of Administration," *Charities* 13 (1905): 340–41.

42. Paul Colomy and Martin Kretzmann, "Projects and Institution Building: Judge Ben B. Lindsey and the Juvenile Court Movement," *Social Problems,* 42(2) (1995): 191–215.

43. Ben B. Lindsey, "The Juvenile Laws of Colorado," *The Green Bag* (1906): 126–31, p. 127.

44. Paul Colomy and Martin Kretzmann, "Projects and Institution Building: Judge Ben B. Lindsey and the Juvenile Court Movement," *Social Problems,* 42(2) (1995): 191–215; Ben B. Lindsey, "The Juvenile Laws of Colorado," *The Green Bag* (1906): 126–31.

45. Paul Colomy and Martin Kretzmann, "Projects and Institution Building: Judge Ben B. Lindsey and the Juvenile Court Movement," *Social Problems,* 42(2) (1995): 191–215, 201.

46. Geoff Ward, *The Black Child-Savers: Racial Democracy and Juvenile Justice* (Chicago: University of Chicago Press, 2012).

47. Barry Feld, *Bad Kids: Race and the Transformation of the Juvenile Court* (New York: Oxford University Press, 1999).

48. John R. Sutton, "The Juvenile Court and Social Welfare: Dynamics of Progressive Reform," *Law and Society Review* 19(1) (1985): 107–45.

49. Anthony Platt, *The Child Savers: The Invention of Delinquency* (New Brunswick: Rutgers University Press, 2009).

50. Alexander Liazos, "Class Oppression: The Functions of Juvenile Justice," *Critical Sociology* 5(2) (1974): 2–24.

51. Alexander Liazos, "Class Oppression: The Functions of Juvenile Justice," *Critical Sociology* 5(2) (1974): 2–24.

52. Paul Colomy and Martin Kretzmann, "Projects and Institution Building: Judge Ben B. Lindsey and the Juvenile Court Movement," *Social Problems* 42(2) (1995): 191–215.

53. Randall Sheldon and Lynne Osborne, "'For Their Own Good': Class Interests and the Child Saving Movement in Memphis, Tennessee, 1900–1917," *Criminology* 27 (1989): 747–67.

54. The laws establishing juvenile courts did not affect conditions of confinement, however, though advocates fought for this before their passage. The Illinois Bar Association, for instance, championed for a thorough investigation of purported abuses during negotiations on the Illinois bill. In the end, only a juvenile court was created, but it was still a substantial step forward for juvenile justice.

55. Paul Lerman, "Twentieth Century Developments in America's Institutional Systems for Youth in Trouble." In *A Century of Juvenile Justice,* ed. Margaret K. Rosenheim et al. (2002): 74–110.

56. John R. Sutton, "The Juvenile Court and Social Welfare: Dynamics of Progressive Reform," *Law and Society Review* 19(1) (1985).

57. Anthony Platt, *The Child Savers: The Invention of Delinquency* (New Brunswick: Rutgers University Press, 2009), xliii.

58. For instance, see John Hagan and Jeffrey Leon, "Rediscovering Delinquency: Social History, Political Ideology and the Sociology of Law," *American Sociological Review* (42) (1977): 587–98; Randall Sheldon and Lynne Osborne, 1989. "'For Their Own Good': Class Interests and the Child Saving Movement in Memphis, Tennessee, 1900-1917," *Criminology* 27 (1989): 747–67; Steven L. Schlossman, *Love and the American Delinquent: The Theory and Practice of 'Progressive' Juvenile Justice* (Chicago: University of Chicago Press, 1977).

59. Geoff Ward, *The Black Child-Savers: Racial Democracy and Juvenile Justice* (Chicago: University of Chicago Press, 2012).

60. Geoff Ward, *The Black Child-Savers: Racial Democracy and Juvenile Justice* (Chicago: University of Chicago Press, 2012).

61. Anthony Platt, *The Child Savers: The Invention of Delinquency* (New Brunswick: Rutgers University Press, 2009).

62. Geoff Ward, *The Black Child-Savers: Racial Democracy and Juvenile Justice* (Chicago: University of Chicago Press, 2012); Anthony Platt, *The Child Savers: The Invention of Delinquency* (New Brunswick: Rutgers University Press, 2009).

63. Justin Picket, Ted Chiricos, and Marc Gertz, "The Racial Foundations of Whites' Support for Child Saving," *Social Science Research* 44 (2014): 44–59.

64. Geoff Ward, *The Black Child-Savers: Racial Democracy and Juvenile Justice* (Chicago: University of Chicago Press, 2012), 88.

65. Sanford Fox, "The Early History of the Court," *Future of Children* 6(3) (1996): 29–39.

66. Gerald P. Wittman, "Review of *Love and the American Delinquent*," *Juvenile and Family Court Judges*, 28(3) (1977): 1–2.

67. Steven L. Schlossman, *Love and the American Delinquent: The Theory and Practice of 'Progressive' Juvenile Justice* (Chicago: University of Chicago Press, 1977).

68. Alexander Liazos, "Class Oppression: The Functions of Juvenile Justice," *Critical Sociology* 5(2) (1974): 2–24.

69. Barry Feld, The Juvenile Court: Changes and Challenges: Update on Law-Related Education," *Juvenile Justice* 23(2) (2000): 10–14, 11.

70. Barry Feld, *Bad Kids: Race and the Transformation of the Juvenile Court* (New York: Oxford University Press, 1999), 52.

CHAPTER 2

1. Jason Barnosky, "The Violent Years: Responses to Juvenile Crime in the 1950s," *Northeastern Political Science Association* 38(3) (2006): 314–44, 320.

2. U.S. Department of Commerce and Labor, "The Children's Bureau." Available online: http://www.mchlibrary.info/history/chbu/20364.pdf).

3. Barry Krisberg, *Juvenile Justice: Redeeming Our Children* (Thousand Oaks: Sage, 2005).

4. Alexander Liazos, "Class Oppression: The Functions of Juvenile Justice," *Critical Sociology* 5 (1974): 2–24.

5. Barry Krisberg, Ira M. Schwartz, Paul Litsky, and James Austin, "The Watershed of Juvenile Justice Reform," *Crime and Delinquency* 32(1) (1986): 5–38.

6. Jason Barnosky, "The Violent Years: Responses to Juvenile Crime in the 1950s," *Northeastern Political Science Association* 38(3) (2006): 314–44.

7. *Morales v. Turman* 364 F. Supp 163 (1973).

8. *Morales v. Turman* 364 F. Supp 163 (1973).

9. Alexander Liazos, "Class Oppression: The Functions of Juvenile Justice," *Critical Sociology* 5(2) (1974): 2–24, 13.

10. Alexander Liazos, "Class Oppression: The Functions of Juvenile Justice," *Critical Sociology* 5 (1974): 2–24.

11. President's Commission on Law Enforcement and Administration of Justice, *The Challenge of Crime in a Free Society: A Report by the President's Commission on Law Enforcement and Administration of Justice* (Washington, DC: U.S. Government Printing Office, 1967), 64.

12. President's Commission on Law Enforcement and Administration of Justice, *The Challenge of Crime in a Free Society: A Report by the President's Commission on Law Enforcement and Administration of Justice* (Washington, DC: U.S. Government Printing Office, 1967).

13. Barry Krisberg, "Are You Now or Have You Ever Been a Sociologist?" *Journal of Criminal Law and Criminology* 82(1) (1991): 141–55.

14. Barry Krisberg, Ira M. Schwartz, Paul Litsky, and James Austin, "The Watershed of Juvenile Justice Reform," *Crime and Delinquency* 32(1) (1986): 5–38.

15. John Woods, New York's Juvenile Offender Law: An Overview and Analysis," *Fordham Urban Law Journal* 9(1) (1980): 1–50.

16. President's Commission on Law Enforcement and Administration of Justice, *The Challenge of Crime in a Free Society: A Report by the President's Commission on Law Enforcement and Administration of Justice* (Washington, DC: U.S. Government Printing Office, 1967).

17. Alexander Liazos, "Class Oppression: The Functions of Juvenile Justice," *Critical Sociology* 5 (1974): 2–24.

18. Kristen Finklea, *Juvenile Justice History and Current Legislative Issues* (Washington, DC: Congressional Research Services, 2012).

19. In 1988, the Disproportionate Minority Contact core requirement was added; this requirement was amended in 1992 to mandate states to address racial and ethnic disparities in their juvenile justice systems or risk loss of federal support.

20. Juvenile Justice and Delinquency Prevention Act, Public Law 93-415.

21. Testimony of Patricia A. Cruz, director of criminal justice, State of Michigan, before the Subcommittee on Human Resources, House Committee on Education and Labor, June 19, 1986.

22. Donna Bishop, Lonn Lanza-Kaduce, and Charles E. Frazier, "Juvenile Justice under Attack: An Analysis of the Causes and Impact of Recent Reforms," *University of Florida Journal of Law and Public Policy* 10 (1998): 129–156.

23. Edwin M. Schur, *Radical Non-Intervention: Rethinking the Delinquency Problem* (Englewood: Prentice Hall, 1973).

24. Richard A. Mendel, *Closing Massachusetts Training Schools: Reflections Forty Years Later* (Baltimore: Annie E. Casey Foundation, 2014).

25. Richard A. Mendel, *Closing Massachusetts Training Schools: Reflections Forty Years Later* (Baltimore: Annie E. Casey Foundation, 2014), 4.

26. Jerome Miller, *Last One Over the Wall: The Massachusetts Experiment in Closing Reform Schools*, 2nd ed. (Ohio: Ohio State University, 1998).

27. Jerome Miller, *Last One Over the Wall: The Massachusetts Experiment in Closing Reform Schools*, 2nd ed. (Ohio: Ohio State University, 1998).

28. Jerome Miller, *Last One Over the Wall: The Massachusetts Experiment in Closing Reform Schools*, 2nd ed. (Ohio: Ohio State University, 1998).

29. Ira Schwartz, *(In)Justice for Juveniles: Rethinking the Best Interests of the Child* (Lexington: Lexington Books, 1989).

30. Richard A. Mendel, *Closing Massachusetts Training Schools: Reflections Forty Years Later* (Baltimore: Annie E. Casey Foundation, 2014).

31. Richard A. Mendel, *Closing Massachusetts Training Schools: Reflections Forty Years Later* (Baltimore: Annie E. Casey Foundation, 2014).

32. Jerome Miller, *Last One Over the Wall: The Massachusetts Experiment in Closing Reform Schools.* 2nd ed. (Ohio: Ohio State University, 1998), 83.

33. Jerome Miller, *Last One Over the Wall: The Massachusetts Experiment in Closing Reform Schools.* 2nd ed. (Ohio: Ohio State University, 1998), 46.

34. Testimony of Ronald Stromberg before the Subcommittee on Human Resources, House Committee on Education and Labor, June 19, 1986; Utah State Juvenile Court, *Annual Report, 1978,* Salt Lake City, Administrative Office of the Juvenile Court, 1979.

35. Testimony of Ronald Stromberg before the Subcommittee on Human Resources, House Committee on Education and Labor, June 19, 1986.

36. Testimony of Ronald Stromberg before the Subcommittee on Human Resources, House Committee on Education and Labor, June 19, 1986; Douglas Evans, *Pioneers of Youth Justice Reform* (New York: John Jay College of Criminal Justice Research and Evaluation Center, 2012).

37. Ira Schwartz testimony, 1986.

38. Testimony of Ronald Stromberg before the Subcommittee on Human Resources, House Committee on Education and Labor, June 19, 1986.

39. Alexander Liazos, "Class Oppression: The Functions of Juvenile Justice," *Critical Sociology* 5(2) (1974): 2–24.

40. *In re Gault,* 387 U.S. 1, 20 (1967).

41. *In re Gault,* 387 U.S. 1, 20 (1967).

42. *In re Gault* 387 U.S. 1, 14, n.14 (1967).

43. *In re Winship,* 397 U.S. 358 (1970).

44. *McKeiver v. US,* 403 US 528 (1971).

45. *McKeiver v. US,* 403 US 528 (1971).

46. *Breed v. Jones,* 421 U.S. 529 (1975).

47. Barry Feld, "The Politics of Race and Juvenile Justice: The 'Due Process Revolution' and the Conservative Reaction." In *Race and Juvenile Justice,* eds. Everette B. Penn, Helen Taylor Greene, and Shaun L. Gabiddon (Durham: Carolina Academic Press, 2006), 196.

CHAPTER 3

1. In 1985, the rate was 7.68 per 100,000 and in 1993 the rate was 20.12 per 100,000.

2. Eric Lotke and Vincent Schiraldi, "An Analysis of Juvenile Homicides: Where They Occur and the Effectiveness of Adult Court Intervention" (Alexandria, VA: National Center on Institutions and Alternatives, July 16, 1996).

3. Benjamin Weiser, "Five Exonerated in Central Park Jogger Case Agree to Settle Suit for $40 Million," *New York Times,* June 19, 2014, http://www.nytimes.com/2014/06/20/nyregion/5-exonerated-in-central-park-jogger-case-are-to-settle-suit-for-40-million.html?hp&_r=1.

4. Richard J. Bonnie, Robert L. Johnson, Betty M. Chemers, and Julie A. Schuck, eds. *Reforming Juvenile Justice: A Developmental Approach* (Washington, DC: National Research Council of the National Academies, 2013).

5. Alfred Blumstein, "Violence by Young People: Why the Deadly Nexus?" *National Institute of Justice Journal* 229 (1995): 2–9.

6. Jeffrey Fagan and Deanna Wilkinson, "Guns, Youth Violence, and Social Identity." In *Youth Violence,* eds. Michael Tonry and Mark H. Moore (Chicago: University of Chicago Press, 1998), 106.

7. Alfred Blumstein, Frederick P. Rivara, and Richard Rosenfeld, "The Rise and Decline of Homicide—and Why," *American Journal of Public Health* 21 (2000): 505–41.

8. Barry Feld, "Race and the Jurisprudence of Juvenile Justice: A Tale in Two Parts, 1950-2000." In *Our Children Their Children: Confronting Racial and Ethnic Differences in American Juvenile Justice,* eds. Darnell F. Hawkins and Kimberly Kempf-Leonard (Chicago: University of Chicago Press, 2005).

9. Howard Snyder and Melissa Sickmund, *Juvenile Offenders and their Victims: A National Report* (Washington, DC: Office of Juvenile Justice and Delinquency Prevention, 1999).

10. Deanna Wilkinson and Jeffrey Fagan, "What Do We Know about Gun Use among Adolescents?" (Boulder: Center for the Study and Prevention of Violence, 2002).

11. Jeffrey Fagan and Deanna Wilkinson, "Guns, Youth Violence, and Social Identity." In *Youth Violence,* eds. Michael Tonry and Mark H. Moore (Chicago: University of Chicago Press, 1998), 105–88.

12. Jeffrey Fagan and Deanna Wilkinson, "Guns, Youth Violence, and Social Identity." In *Youth Violence,* eds. Michael Tonry and Mark H. Moore (Chicago: University of Chicago Press, 1998), 105–88.

13. Marc Mauer, *Race to Incarcerate* (New York: New Press, 2006), 61.

14. Marc Mauer, *Race to Incarcerate* (New York: New Press, 2006).

15. Alfred Blumstein, Frederick P. Rivara, and Richard Rosenfeld, "The Rise and Decline of Homicide—and Why," *American Journal of Public Health* 21 (2000): 505–41.

16. Alfred Blumstein, "Youth Violence, Guns, and the Illicit Drug Industry," *Journal of Criminal Law and Criminology,* 86(1) (1995): 10–36; Alfred Blumstein, Frederick P. Rivara, and Richard Rosenfeld, "The Rise and Decline of Homicide—and Why," *American Journal of Public Health* 21 (2000): 505–41.

17. Eric Lotke and Vincent Schiraldi, "An Analysis of Juvenile Homicides: Where They Occur and the Effectiveness of Adult Court Intervention" (Alexandria, VA: National Center on Institutions and Alternatives, July 16, 1996).

18. Graham C. Ousey and Michelle Campbell Augustine, "Young Guns: Examining Alternative Explanations of Juvenile Firearm Homicide Rates," *Criminology* 39(4) (2001): 938.

19. Graham C. Ousey and Michelle Campbell Augustine, "Young Guns: Examining Alternative Explanations of Juvenile Firearm Homicide Rates," *Criminology* 39(4) (2001): 933–68; Ramiro Martinez, Richard Rosenfeld, and Dennis Mares, "Social Disorganization, Drug Market Activity, and Neighborhood Violent Crime," *Urban Affairs Review* 43(6) (2004): 846–74; Graham C. Ousey and Matthew R.

Lee, "Investigating the Connections between Race, Illicit Drug Markets, and Lethal Violence, 1984–1997," *Journal of Research in Crime and Delinquency* 41(4) (2004): 352–83.

20. Eric Baumer, Janet L. Lauritsen, Richard Rosenfeld, and Richard Wright, "The Influence of Crack Cocaine on Robbery, Burglary, and Homicide Rates: A Cross-City, Longitudinal Analysis," *Journal of Research in Crime and Delinquency* 35(3) (1998): 316–40. Alfred Blumstein, "Youth Violence, Guns, and the Illicit Drug Industry," *Journal of Criminal Law and Criminology* 86 (1995): 10–36.

21. Deanna Wilkinson and Jeffrey Fagan, *What Do We Know about Gun Use among Adolescents?* (Boulder, Center for the Study and Prevention of Violence, 2002).

22. Jeffrey Fagan and Deanna Wilkinson, "Guns, Youth Violence, and Social Identity." In *Youth Violence,* eds. Michael Tonry and Mark H. Moore (Chicago: University of Chicago Press, 1998), 109.

23. A. M. Hoffman and R. W. Summers, eds., *Teen Violence: A Global View* (Westport: Guilford Press, 2001); Alfred Blumstein, *Why Is Crime Falling—Or Is It?* (Washington, DC: National Institute of Justice, 2001).

24. Jeffrey Fagan et al., *Brief of Jeffrey Fagan et al.,* Supreme Court of the United States, 10-9647, 10-9646, January 12, 2012.

25. Marc Mauer, *Race to Incarcerate* (New York: New Press, 2006).

26. Barbara C. Wallace, "Crack, Policy, and Advocacy: A Case Analysis Illustrating the Need to Monitor Emergent Public Health-Related Policy and Engage in Persistent Evidence-Based Advocacy," *Journal of Equity in Health* 3(1) (2014): 139–60.

27. Franklin Zimring, *American Youth Violence* (New York: Oxford University Press, 1998).

28. Franklin Zimring, "American Youth Violence: Implications for National Juvenile Justice Policy," *Update on Law Related Education: Juvenile Justice* 23(2) (2000): 8.

29. Lori Dorfman and Vincent Schiraldi, "Off Balance: Youth Race, and Crime in the News," *Building Blocks for Youth Initiative,* http://www.hawaii.edu/hivandaids/Off_Balance__Youth,_Race_and_Crime_in_the_News.pdf.

30. Federal Bureau of Investigation, *Crime in the United States* (Washington, DC: U.S. Government Printing Office, 1993), 287.

31. Eric Lotke, "Youth Homicide: Keeping Perspective on How Many Children Kill," *Valparaiso University Law Review* 31 (1997): 395–418; Franklin E. Zimring, "The 1990s Assault on Juvenile Justice: Notes from an Ideological Battleground," *Federal Sentencing Reporter* 11(5) (1999): 260–61.

32. "Al Regnery's Secret Life." *New Republic,* June 23, 1986. Available online: http://www.newrepublic.com/article/politics/al-regnerys-secret-life.

33. "Al Regnery's Secret Life." *New Republic,* June 23, 1986. Available online: http://www.newrepublic.com/article/politics/al-regnerys-secret-life.

34. National Advisory Committee for Juvenile Justice and Delinquency Prevention, *Serious Juvenile Crime: A Redirected Federal Effort* (Washington, DC: Office of Juvenile Justice and Delinquency Prevention, 1984).

35. National Advisory Committee for Juvenile Justice and Delinquency Prevention, *Serious Juvenile Crime: A Redirected Federal Effort* (Washington, DC: Office of Juvenile Justice and Delinquency Prevention, 1984), 4.

36. Alfred Regnery, "Getting Away with Murder: Why the Juvenile Justice System Needs an Overhaul," *Policy Review* 34 (1985): 65–68.

37. H. Snyder and J. Mulako-Wangota, Arrest Data Analysis Tool, accessed on February 13, 2015, at www.bjs.gov (Washington, DC: Bureau of Justice Statistics.).

38. James C. Howell, *Preventing and Reducing Juvenile Delinquency: A Comprehensive Framework* (Thousand Oaks: Sage, 2003); Michael Males, *The Scapegoat Generation: America's War on Adolescents* (Irvine: Common Courage Press, 1996); Howard Snyder and Melissa Sickmund, *Challenging the Myths* (Washington, DC: Office of Juvenile Justice and Delinquency Prevention, 2000).

39. John DiIulio, "The Coming of the Super-Predators," *Weekly Standard* 1(11) (November 27, 1995): 23.

40. William J. Bennett, John J. DiIulio, and John P. Walters, *Body Count* (New York: Simon and Schuster, 1996).

41. Franklin Zimring, *American Juvenile Justice* (Oxford: Oxford University Press, 2005).

42. Franklin Zimring, "Crying Wolf over Teen Demons; Crime: Projecting a New Crime Wave Serves Politicians, Even If It Has No Basis in Reality," *Los Angeles Times*, August 19, 1996.

43. Franklin Zimring, "Crying Wolf over Teen Demons; Crime: Projecting a New Crime Wave Serves Politicians, Even If It Has No Basis in Reality," *Los Angeles Times*, August 19, 1996.

44. Violent Youth Predator Act, introduced in the 104th Congress as HR 3565.

45. The Violent Youth Predator Act of 1996, Title II, Section 301 (a)(1)(2), 104th Congress, 1996.

46. Bill McCullom, testimony before the House Subcommittee on Early Childhood, Youth, and Families, Washington, DC, 1996.

47. Lori Dorfman and Vincent Schiraldi, "Off Balance: Youth Race, and Crime in the News," *Building Blocks for Youth Initiative*, http://www.hawaii.edu/hivandaids/Off_Balance__Youth,_Race_and_Crime_in_the_News.pdf.

48. Robert E. Shepherd, "Film at Eleven: The News Media and Juvenile Crime," *QLR* 18 (1999): 687–700.

49. Robert E. Shepherd, "Film at Eleven: The News Media and Juvenile Crime," *QLR* 18 (1999): 687–700.

50. Robert E. Shepherd, "Film at Eleven: The News Media and Juvenile Crime," *QLR* 18 (1999): 698.

51. Barry Feld, "Violent Youth and Public Policy: A Case Study of Juvenile Justice," *Minnesota Law Review* 79 (1995): 965–1128.

52. Franklin Zimring, "American Youth Violence: A Cautionary Tale." In *Choosing the Future for American Juvenile Justice*, eds. Franklin Zimring and David S. Tanenhaus (New York: New York University Press, 2014), 32.

53. Jeffrey Butts and Jeremy Travis, *The Rise and Fall of American Youth Violence: 1980 to 2000* (Washington, DC: Urban Institute, Justice Policy Center, 2002); Franklin Zimring, *American Youth Violence* (New York: Oxford University Press, 1998).

54. Alfred Blumstein, *Why Is Crime Falling—Or Is It?* (Washington, DC: National Institute of Justice, 2001).

55. Jeffrey Fagan et al., *Brief of Jeffrey Fagan et al.,* Supreme Court of the United States, 10-9647, 10-9646, January 12, 2012.

56. Franklin Zimring and Stephen Rushin, "Did Changes in Sanctions Reduce Juvenile Crime Rates?" *Ohio State Journal of Criminal Law* 11(1) (2013): 57–69.

57. Lawrence Winner, Lonn Lanza-Kaduce, Donna M. Bishop, and Charles E. Frazier, "The Transfer of Juveniles to Criminal Court: Reexamining Recidivism over the Long Term," *Crime and Delinquency* 548 (1997): 558–59; David L. Myers, "Excluding Violent Youths from Juvenile Court: The Effectiveness of Legislative Waiver." In *Criminal Justice: Recent Scholarship*, eds. Marilyn McShane and Frank P. Williams III (El Pason, TX: LFB Publishing Company, 2001); Eric L. Jensen and Linda K. Metsger, "A Test of the Deterrent Effect of Legislative Waiver on Violent Juvenile Crime," *Crime and Delinquency* 96 (1994): 102.

58. Jeffrey Fagan, "Separating the Men from the Boys: The Comparative Advantage of Juvenile Versus Criminal Court Sanctions on Recidivism Among Adolescent Felony Offenders." In *A Sourcebook: Serious, Violent, and Chronic Juvenile Offenders*, eds. James C. Howell, Barry Krisberg, J. David Hawkins and John J. Wilson (Thousand Oaks, CA: Sage, 1995): 238.

59. Donna Bishop, Lonn Lanza-Kaduce, and Charles E. Frazier, "Juvenile Justice Under Attack: An Analysis of the Causes and Impact of Recent Reforms," *University of Florida Journal of Law and Public Policy* 10: 129–56.

CHAPTER 4

1. Barry Feld, "Criminalizing the American Juvenile Court." In *Crime and Justice: An Annual Review of Research*, eds. Michael Tonry and N. Morris (Chicago: University of Chicago Press, 1986); Janet E. Ainsworth, "Youth Violence in a Unified Court: Response to Critics of Juvenile Court Abolition," *B.C. Law Review* 36 (1995): 927–51.

2. Robert E. Shepherd, "Film at Eleven: The News Media and Juvenile Crime," *Quinnipiac Law Review* 18 (1999): 687–700.

3. Rorie Sherman, "Juvenile Judges Say: Time to Get Tough," *National Law Journal* (August 8, 1994): 1.

4. Richard Redding, "Juveniles Transferred to Criminal Court: Legal Reform Proposals Based on Social Science Research," *Utah Law Review* (1997): 709–97.

5. Paul McNulty, "Natural Born Killers? Preventing the Coming Explosion of Teenage Crime," *Policy Review* 71 (1995): 84–87.

6. Alfred Regnery, "Getting Away with Murder: Why the Juvenile Justice System Needs an Overhaul," *Policy Review* 34 (1985): 65–68.

7. Franklin Zimring and Gordon Hawkins, *Incapacitation: Penal Confinement and the Restraint of Crime* (New York: Oxford University Press, 1995).

8. Jeffrey A. Butts, "Can We Do Without Juvenile Justice?" Washington, DC: Urban Institute.

9. Barry C. Feld, "Abolish the Juvenile Court: Youthfulness, Criminal Responsibility, and Sentencing Policy," *Journal of Criminal Law and Criminology* 88(1) (1998): 68–136, 81.

10. Paolo Annino, "Children in Florida Adult Prisons: A Call for a Moratorium," *Florida State University Law Review* 28(2) (2001): 471–90.

11. Barry C. Feld, "Abolish the Juvenile Court: Youthfulness, Criminal Responsibility, and Sentencing Policy," *Journal of Criminal Law and Criminology* 88(1) (1998): 68–136; 83 cites Linda F. Giardino, "Statutory Rhetoric: The Reality behind Juvenile Justice Policies in America," *Juvenile Law and Policy* 223 (1996).

12. Robert O. Dawson, "The Future of Juvenile Justice: Is It Time to Abolish the System?" *Journal of Criminal Law and Criminology*, 81(1) (1990): 136–55.

13. Barry C. Feld, "Abolish the Juvenile Court: Youthfulness, Criminal Responsibility, and Sentencing Policy," *Journal of Criminal Law and Criminology* 88(1) (1998): 68–136.

14. Barry C. Feld, "Abolish the Juvenile Court: Youthfulness, Criminal Responsibility, and Sentencing Policy," *Journal of Criminal Law and Criminology* 88(1) (1998): 68–136; Robert O. Dawson, "The Future of Juvenile Justice: Is It Time to Abolish the System?" *Journal of Criminal Law and Criminology* 81(1) (1990): 136–55.

15. Andrew Cohen, "Bill Clinton and Mass Incarceration," *Brennan Center for Social Justice,* October 2014.

16. US Senate Committee on the Judiciary, Confirmation hearings on federal appointments: hearings before the Committee on the Judiciary, United States Senate, One Hundred Third Congress, first session on confirmations of appointees to the federal judiciary (Washington, DC: Government Printing Office, 1995), 11.

17. Eligible crimes were 113(a), 113(b), 113(c), 1111, 1113, or the following crimes if the juvenile had a firearm: 2111, 2113, 2241(a), 2241(c).

18. U.S. Department of Justice, "Violent Crime Control and Law Enforcement Act of 1994" (Washington, DC, 1994). Fact Sheet. https://www.ncjrs.gov/txtfiles/billfs.txt.

19. H.R. 3355 became Public Law 103-322 on September 13, 1994.

20. Ronald Kramer and Raymond Michalowski, "The Iron Fist and the Velvet Tongue: Crime Control Policies in the Clinton Administration," *Social Justice* 22(2) (1995): 87–100.

21. "Classic Tough on Crime Debate," posted on February 25, 2014, http://www.c-span.org/video/?c4485190/classic-tough-crime-debate.

22. Lia Rodriguez, "Juvenile Legislation: Where's the Love in 'Tough Love,'" *Public Interest Law Section Reporter* 9(1) (2000): 11–12.

23. Mark Hollis, "Florida Toughest on Teen Criminals," *Sun Sentinel* (May 18, 2000). Available online: http://articles.sun-sentinel.com/2000-05-18/news/0005180020_1_ juvenile-crime-mandatory-minimum-sentences-jeb-bush.

24. Donna M. Bishop, Lonn Lanza-Kaduce, and Charles E. Frazier, "Juvenile Justice Under Attack: An Analysis of the Causes and Impact of Recent Reforms," *University of Florida Journal of Law and Public Policy* 10 (1998): 129–56.

25. Donna M. Bishop, Lonn Lanza-Kaduce, and Charles E. Frazier, "Juvenile Justice under Attack: An Analysis of the Causes and Impact of Recent Reforms," *University of Florida Journal of Law and Public Policy* 10 (1998): 129–56, 138.

26. Donna M. Bishop, Lonn Lanza-Kaduce, and Charles E. Frazier, "Juvenile Justice Under Attack: An Analysis of the Causes and Impact of Recent Reforms," *University of Florida Journal of Law and Public Policy* 10 (1998): 129–56.

27. Anne Stahl, "Cases Waived to Criminal Court, 1987-1996," U.S. Department of Justice, Office of Juvenile Justice and Delinquency Prevention Coalition, 1999.

28. Robert E. Shepherd Jr., "Film at Eleven: The News Media and Juvenile Crime," *Quinnipiac Law Review* 18 (1999): 687–700.

29. Melissa Sickmund, *Juvenile Offenders and Victims, 1997: Update on Violence* (Washington, DC: Office of Juvenile Justice and Delinquency Prevention Coalition, 1997).

30. Coordinating Council on Juvenile Justice, "Combating Violence and Delinquency: A National Juvenile Justice Action Plan: Summary" (Washington, DC: Office of Juvenile Justice and Delinquency Prevention, 1996). Available online: http://www. juvenilecouncil.gov/resource/jjplansm.pdf_summary.pdf.

31. Lonn Lanza-Kaduce, Charles Frazier, and Donna Bishop, "Juvenile Transfer in Florida: The Worst of the Worst?" *Journal of Law and Policy* 10 (1999): 277–312.

32. Lonn Lanza-Kaduce, Charles Frazier, and Donna Bishop, "Juvenile Transfer in Florida: The Worst of the Worst?" *Journal of Law and Policy* 10 (1999): 277–312.

33. Elizabeth E. Clarke, "A Case for Reinventing Juvenile Transfer: The Record of Transfer of Juvenile Offenders to Criminal Court in Cook County," *Juvenile and Family Court Journal* 47(4) (1996): 3–22.

34. Patrick Griffin, *Juvenile Transfer to Criminal Court Provisions by State, 2009* (Pittsburgh: National Center for Juvenile Justice, 2010).

35. Peter Katel, Melinda Liu, and Bob Cohn, "The Bust in Boot Camps," *Newsweek* 26 (1994).

36. Janet Reno, "Fighting Youth Violence: The Future Is Now," *Criminal Justice* 11 (1996): 33.

37. Darrick Jolliffe, David P. Farrington, and Philip Howard, "How Long Did it Last? A 10-Year Reconviction Follow-Up Study of High Intensity Training for Youth Offenders," *Journal of Experimental Criminology* 9 (4) (2013): 515–31.

38. M. Sickmund, T. J. Sladky, W. Kang, and C. Puzzanchera (2013). "Easy Access to the Census of Juveniles in Residential Placement," http://www.ojjdp.gov/ojstatbb/ ezacjrp/.

39. Benjamin Meade and Benjamin Steiner, "The Total Effect of Boot Camps That House Juveniles: A Systematic Review of the Evidence," *Journal of Criminal Justice* 38 (2010): 841–53.

40. Peter Greenwood, "Juvenile Crime and Juvenile Justice." In *Crime: Public Policies for Crime Control*, eds. James Q. Wilson and Joan Petersilia (Oakland: Institute for Contemporary Studies, 2002), 92.

41. Bruce Selcraig, "Camp Fear," *Mother Jones* (2000), http://www.motherjones.com/politics/2000/11/camp-fear.

42. Bruce Selcraig, "Camp Fear," *Mother Jones* (2000), http://www.motherjones.com/politics/2000/11/camp-fear.

43. State Juvenile Justice Facilities Findings Letter (1997). Available online: http://www.justice.gov/crt/about/spl/documents/gajuvfind.php.

44. Benjamin Meade and Benjamin Steiner, "The Total Effect of Boot Camps that House Juveniles: A Systematic Review of the Evidence," *Journal of Criminal Justice* 38(2010): 841–53; *Juvenile Boot Camps: Lessons Learned*. Available online: http://www.ncjrs.gov/txtfiles/fs-9636.txt.

45. David B. Wilson, Doris L. MacKenzie, and Fawn Ngo, "Effects of Correctional Boot Camps on Offending," *Campbell Collaborative Reviews* 6 (2005): 1–45.

46. Francis T. Cullen, "Rehabilitation and Treatment Programs," in *Crime: Public Policies for Crime Control*, eds. James Q. Wilson and Joan Petersilia (Oakland: Institute for Contemporary Studies, 2002), 284–85.

47. States defined as having mandatory JLWOP sentences upon conviction for homicide are Alabama, Arkansas, Florida, Louisiana, Massachusetts, Michigan, Mississippi, Montana, Nebraska, North Carolina, and Pennsylvania.

CHAPTER 5

1. Riya Saha Shah and Lauren A. Fine, *Failed Policies, Forfeited Futures: A Nationwide Scorecard on Juvenile Records* (Philadelphia: Juvenile Law Center, 2014).

2. Jon Gunnar Bernburg and Marvin D. Krohn, "Labeling, Life Chances, and Adult Crime: The Direct and Indirect Effects of Official Intervention in Adolescence on Crime in Early Adulthood," *Criminology* 41(4) (2003): 1287–1318.

3. Christopher Uggen, Sarah Shannan, and Jeff Manza, *State-Level Estimates of Felon Disenfranchisement, 2010* (Washington, DC: The Sentencing Project, 2012).

4. Michael Pinard, "The Logistical and Ethical Difficulties of Informing Juveniles about the Collateral Consequences of Adjudications," *Nevada Law Journal* 6 (2006): 1111–126.

5. Kristin Henning, "Eroding Confidentiality in Delinquency Proceedings: Should Schools and Public Housing Authorities Be Notified?" *New York University Law Review* 79 (2004), 520–611; Elizabeth Scott and Thomas Grisso, "The Evolution of Adolescence: A Developmental Perspective on Juvenile Justice Reform," *Journal of Law and Criminology* 137 (1997): 88.

6. Jon Gunnar Bernburg and Marvin D. Krohn, "Labeling, Life Chances, and Adult Crime: The Direct and Indirect Effects of Official Intervention in Adolescence on Crime in Early Adulthood," *Criminology* 41(4) (2003): 1287–318, 1290.

7. Franklin E. Zimring, *American Juvenile Justice* (Oxford: Oxford University Press, 2005).

8. Emily Bazelon, "Public Access to Juvenile and Family Court: Should the Courtroom Doors Be Open or Closed?" *Yale Law and Policy Review*, 18 (1999): 155–79.

9. Riya Saha Shah and Lauren A. Fine, *Failed Policies, Forfeited Futures: A Nationwide Scorecard on Juvenile Records* (Philadelphia: Juvenile Law Center, 2014).

10. Riya Saha Shah and Lauren A. Fine, *Failed Policies, Forfeited Futures: A Nationwide Scorecard on Juvenile Records* (Philadelphia: Juvenile Law Center, 2014).

11. *In re Gault*, 387 U.S. 1, 60 (1967).

12. Pennsylvania Juvenile Indigent Defense Action Network, Pennsylvania Collateral Consequences Checklist. Philadelphia, Models for Change (2010). Available online: http://www.pccd.pa.gov/Juvenile-Justice/Documents/Pennsylvania_Juvenile_Collateral_Consequences_Checklist.pdf.

13. Arthur R. Blum, "Disclosing the Identities of Juvenile Felons: Introducing Accountability to Juvenile Justice," *Loyola University of Chicago Law Journal* 27 (1996): 349–400.

14. National Criminal Justice Authority, *Juvenile Justice Reform Initiatives in the States, 1994–1996* (Washington, DC: Office of Juvenile Justice and Delinquency Prevention); National Conference on Juvenile Justice Records: Appropriate Criminal and Noncriminal Justice Uses, Proceedings of a BJS/SEARCH Conference, May 1997.

15. Sealing typically refers to placing court records in a separate repository that is not available to the public. Expungement refers to the process of destroying the court records and any history of court involvement in a particular case.

16. Riya Saha Shah and Lauren A. Fine, *Failed Policies, Forfeited Futures: A Nationwide Scorecard on Juvenile Records* (Philadelphia: Juvenile Law Center, 2014).

17. Robert Schwartz, *Keynote Address* (Presented at the Symposium on the Intersection of Juvenile Justice and Poverty, Washington, DC, Georgetown University Law Center, March 26, 2009); S. Simkins, *When Kids Get Arrested: What Every Adult Should Know* (New Jersey: Rutgers University Press, 2009).

18. Lynn A. Szymanski, *Sealing/Expungement/Destruction of Juvenile Court Records: Sealed Records That Can Be Unsealed or Inspected* (Philadelphia: National Center for Juvenile Justice, 2006).

19. Riya Saha Shah and Lauren A. Fine, *Failed Policies, Forfeited Futures: A Nationwide Scorecard on Juvenile Records* (Philadelphia: Juvenile Law Center, 2014).

20. NCGS § 7B-3200(c).

21. Washington Rev Code section 10.97.050 (2010).

22. Alfred Blumstein and Kiminori Nakamara, "Redemption in the Presence of Widespread Criminal Background Checks," *Criminology* 47(2): 327–59.

23. Christopher Gowen, Lisa Thurau, and Meghan Wood, "The ABA's Approach to Juvenile Justice Reform: Education, Eviction, and Employment: The Collateral Consequences of Juvenile Adjudication," *Duke Forum for Law and Social Change* 3 (2011): 187–203.

24. Office of the Surgeon General, *Youth Violence: A Report of the Surgeon General* (Washington, DC: Office of the Surgeon General, 2001).

25. L. Lochner and E. Moretti, "The Effect of Education on Crime: Evidence from Prison Inmates, Arrests, and Self Reports," *American Economic Review* 94(1) (2004): 155–89; see also R. Freeman, "Why Do So Many Young American Men Commit Crimes and What Might We Do about It?" *Journal of Economic Perspectives* 10(1) (1996): 25–42.

26. Paul Hirschfield, "Another Way Out: The Impact of Juvenile Arrests on High School Dropout," *Sociology of Education* 82 (2009): 368–93.

27. Jennifer Watson Marsh, *Juvenile Delinquency Adjudication, Collateral Consequences, and Expungement of Juvenile Records* (University of North Carolina Center for Civil Rights, n.d.).

28. Jessica Feireman, Marsha Levick, and Ami Mody, "The School-to-Prison Pipeline . . . and Back: Obstacles and Remedies for the Re-Enrollment of Adjudicated Youth," *New York Law School Law Review* 54 (2009–2010), 1115–29.

29. Jessica Feireman, Marsha Levick, and Ami Mody, "The School-to-Prison Pipeline . . . and Back: Obstacles and Remedies for the Re-Enrollment of Adjudicated Youth," *New York Law School Law Review* 54 (2009–2010), 1115–29.

30. Jessica Feireman, Marsha Levick, and Ami Mody, "The School-to-Prison Pipeline . . . and Back: Obstacles and Remedies for the Re-Enrollment of Adjudicated Youth," *New York Law School Law Review* 54 (2009–2010), 1115–29.

31. Jessica Feireman, Marsha Levick, and Ami Mody, "The School-to-Prison Pipeline . . . and Back: Obstacles and Remedies for the Re-Enrollment of Adjudicated Youth," *New York Law School Law Review* 54 (2009–2010), 1115–29.

32. Pat Arthur, "Issues Faced by Juveniles Leaving Custody: Breaking Down the Barriers" (San Francisco: National Center for Youth Law, 2007).

33. Thomas G. Blomberg, William D. Bales, Karen Mann, Alex R. Piquero, and Richard A. Berk, "Incarceration, Education, and Transition from Delinquency," *Journal of Criminal Justice* 39 (2011), 355–65.

34. Thomas G. Blomberg, William D. Bales, Karen Mann, Alex R. Piquero, and Richard A. Berk, "Incarceration, Education, and Transition from Delinquency," *Journal of Criminal Justice* 39 (2011): 355–65.

35. Henggeler and Schoenwald, "Evidence Based Interventions for Juvenile Offenders and Juvenile Justice Policies That Support Them," *Sharing Child and Youth Development Knowledge* 25(1) (2011): 1–20.

36. Thomas Blomberg, George Pesta, and Colby Valentine, "The Juvenile Justice No Child Left Behind Collaboration Project: Final Report" (Tallahassee: Florida State University, 2008).

37. Catherine Foley Geib, John F. Chapman, Amy H. D'Amaddio, and Elena L. Grigorenko, "The Education of Juveniles in Detention: Policy Considerations and Infrastructure Development," *Learning and Individual Differences* 21 (2011): 3–11.

38. Christopher Uggen and Melissa Thompson, "The Socioeconomic Determinants of Ill-Gotten Gains: Within-Person Changes in Drug Use and Illegal Earnings," *American Journal of Sociology* 109(1) (2003): 146; Shawn Bushway and Peter Reuter, "Labor Markets and Crime." In *Crime: Public Policies for Crime Control,* 3rd ed., eds. James Q. Wilson and Joan Petersilia (Oakland: Institute for Contemporary Studies Press, 2001).

39. Christopher Gowen, Lisa Thurau, and Meghan Wood, "The ABA's Approach to Juvenile Justice Reform: Education, Eviction, and Employment: The Collateral Consequences of Juvenile Adjudication," *Duke Forum for Law and Social Change* 3 (2011): 187–203.

40. Jeremy Travis, *But They All Come Back: Facing the Challenges of Prisoner Reentry* (Washington, DC: Urban Institute, 2005).

41. Robert Schwartz, *Keynote Address* (Presented at the Symposium on the Intersection of Juvenile Justice and Poverty, Washington, DC, Georgetown University Law Center, March 26, 2009).

42. Andrew Sum, Ishwar Khatiwada, Joseph McLaughlin, and Sheila Palma, *The Consequences of Dropping Out of High School: Joblessness and Jailing for High School Dropouts and the High Cost for Taxpayers* (Boston: Center for Labor Market Studies, Northeastern University, 2009).

43. Megan Kurleychek, Robert Brame, and Shawn Bushway, "Scarlet Letters and Recidivism: Does an Old Criminal Record Predict Future Offending?" *Criminology and Public Policy* 5(3) (2006): 483.

44. J. Hagan and B. McCarthy, "Homeless Youth and the Perilous Passage to Adulthood." In *On Your Own without a Net: The Transition to Adulthood for Vulnerable Populations,* eds. D. Wayne Osgood, E. Michael Foster, C. Flanagan, and G. R. Ruth (Chicago: University of Chicago Press, 2005).

45. R. Clark and M. J. Robertson, *Surviving for the Moment: A Report on Homeless Youth in San Francisco* (Berkeley: Alcohol Research Group, 1996); M. J. Robertson, *Homeless Youth in Hollywood: Patterns of Alcohol Use. Report to the National Institute on Alcohol Abuse and Alcoholism (No C51)* (Berkeley: Alcohol Research Group, 1989).

46. National Affordable Housing Act, Pub. L. No. 104–120, § 9(a)(2), 110 Stat. 836 (1996).

47. Dept. of H.U.D. v. Rucker 535 U.S. 125 (2002).

48. Wendy Kaplan and David Rossman, "Called 'Out' at Home: The One Strike Eviction Policy and Juvenile Court," *Duke Forum for Law and Social Change* 3 (2011): 109–138.

49. Wendy Kaplan and David Rossman, "Called 'Out' at Home: The One Strike Eviction Policy and Juvenile Court," *Duke Forum for Law and Social Change* (2011).

50. Elizabeth Garfinkle, "Coming of Age in America: The Misapplication of Sex-Offender Registration and Community Notification of Juveniles," *California Law Review* 91 (2003): 163.

51. Elizabeth Garfinkle, "Coming of Age in America: The Misapplication of Sex-Offender Registration and Community Notification of Juveniles," *California Law Review* 91 (2003): 163.

52. Elizabeth Garfinkle, "Coming of Age in America: The Misapplication of Sex-Offender Registration and Community Notification of Juveniles," *California Law Review* 91 (2003): 163.

53. Michael Caldwell et al., "Study Characteristics and Recidivism Base Rates in Juvenile Sex Offender Recidivism," *International Journal of Offender Therapy and Comparative Criminology* 54, 197–212; Franklin Zimring, *An American Travesty: Legal Responses to Adolescent Sexual Offending* (Chicago: University of Chicago Press, 2006);

54. North Carolina Department of Justice, Law Enforcement Liaison Section, *The North Carolina Sex Offender and Public Protection Registration Programs* (Raleigh: North Carolina Department of Public Safety, 2014). Available online: http://www.ncdoj.gov/sexoffenderpublication.aspx.

55. David Alire Garcia, "Juveniles Crowd Michigan Sex Offender Registry," February 10, 2010. Available online: http://michiganmessenger.com/34538/juveniles-well-represented-on-mich-sex-offender-registry.

56. David Alire Garcia, "Juveniles Crowd Michigan Sex Offender Registry," February 10, 2010. Aailable online: http://michiganmessenger.com/34538/juveniles-well-represented-on-mich-sex-offender-registry.

57. Pub. L. 109-248.

58. *J.B. v. York County*, http://jlc.org/blog/pennsylvania-supreme-court-rules-sex-offender-registration-unconstitutional-youth.

59. Brent B. Brenda and Connie L. Tollet, "A Study of Recidivism of Serious and Persistent Offenders among Adolescents," *Journal of Criminal Justice* 27(2): 111–26; Akiva M. Liberman, David S. Kirk, and Kideuk Kim, "Labeling Effects of First Juvenile Arrests: Secondary Deviance and Secondary Sanctioning," *Criminology* 52(3): 345–70; Raymond Paternoster, Carolyn Turpin-Petrosino, and Sarah Guckenburg, "Formal System Processing of Juveniles: Effects on Delinquency," *Campbell Systemic Reviews* (2010): 1–88.

60. Edwin M. Lemert, *Social Pathology: A Systemic Approach to the Theory of Sociopathic Behavior* (New York: McGraw Hill, 1951).

61. Stephanie Ann Wiley, Lee Ann Slocum, and Finn-Aage Esbensen, "The Unintended Consequences of Being Stopped or Arrested: An Exploration of the Labeling Mechanisms through Which Police Contact Leads to Subsequent Delinquency," *Criminology* 51(4) (2013): 927–96.

62. Robert Sampson and John Laub, "Life Course Desisters? Trajectories of Crime Among Delinquent Boys Followed to Age 70," *Criminology* 43: 905–13.

63. Akiva M. Liberman, David S. Kirk, and Kideuk Kim, "Labeling Effects of First Juvenile Arrests: Secondary Deviance and Secondary Sanctioning," *Criminology* 52(3): 363.

64. Devah Pager, *Marked: Race, Crime, and Finding Work in an Era of Mass Incarceration* (Chicago: University of Chicago Press, 2007).

65. Robert J. Sampson and John H. Laub, "A Life-Course Theory of Cumulative Disadvantage and the Stability of Delinquency." In *Developmental Theories of Crime and Delinquency*, ed. Terence P. Thornberry (New Brunswick: Transaction, 2004).

66. Jon Gunnar Bernburg and Marvin D. Krohn, "Labeling, Life Chances, and Adult Crime: The Direct and Indirect Effects of Official Intervention in Adolescence on Crime in Early Adulthood," *Criminology* 41(4) (2003): 1287–318.

67. Charles Puzzanchera, *Juvenile Arrests, 2011* (Washington, DC: Office of Juvenile Justice and Delinquency, 2014).

68. Sarah Hockenberry and Charles Puzzanchera, *Juvenile Court Statistics 2011* (Washington, DC: Office of Juvenile Justice and Delinquency Prevention, 2014).

69. Neelum Arya, *State Trends: Legislative Victories from 2005 to 2010: Removing Youth from the Adult Criminal Justice System* (Washington, DC: Campaign for Youth Justice, 2011).

70. Howard N. Snyder, "An Empirical Portrait of the Youth Reentry Population," *Youth Violence and Juvenile Justice* 2(1) (2004): 39.

71. Neelum Arya, *State Trends: Legislative Victories from 2005 to 2010: Removing Youth from the Adult Criminal Justice System* (Washington, DC: Campaign for Youth Justice, 2011).

72. "Cory Booker on How America's Criminal Justice System Destroys the American Dream," March 16, 2015, http://www.vox.com/2015/3/16/8205027/cory-booker-drug-war.

73. *State v. Hemp* 353 Wis.2d 146, 17.

74. Robert E. Shepherd, "Pleading Guilty in Delinquency Cases," *Criminal Justice Magazine* 16(3) (2001).

CHAPTER 6

1. James C. Howell, Barry C. Feld, Daniel P. Mears, David P. Farrington, Rolf Loeber, and David Petechuk, *Bulletin 5: Youth Offenders and an Effective Response in the Juvenile and Adult Court Systems: What Happens, What Should Happen, and What We Need to Know* (Washington, DC: Department of Justice, 2013).

2. Nell Bernstein, *Burning Down the House* (New York: The New Press, 2014).

3. Charles Puzzanchera, *Juvenile Arrests 2011* (Washington, DC: Office of Juvenile Justice and Delinquency Prevention, 2013).

4. Melissa Sickmund, T. J. Sladky, and W. Kang (2014). "Easy Access to Juvenile Court Statistics: 1985-2011." Available online: http://www.ojjdp.gov/ojstatbb/ezajcs/ Data source: National Center for Juvenile Justice (2014). *National Juvenile Court Data Archive: Juvenile court case records 1985-2011* [machine-readable data files]. Pittsburgh, PA: National Center for Juvenile Justice.

5. M. Sickmund, T. J. Sladky, W. Kang, and C. Puzzanchera, "Easy Access to the Census of Juveniles in Residential Placement," 2013. Available online: http://www.ojjdp.gov/ojstatbb/ezacjrp/. Unlike the adult system, which defines "secure facility" as either jail or prison, the juvenile justice system uses this term to apply to a broad number of possible structures, including foster homes, group homes, boot camps, residential treatment centers, and juvenile correctional facilities.

6. The four states that have not had drops in custody are Idaho, West Virginia, Nebraska, and North Dakota. CSG's Closer to Home Report, 2015, http://csgjustice-center.org/youth/publications/closer-to-home/.

7. Melissa Sickmund, T. J. Sladky, and W. Kang (2014). "Easy Access to Juvenile Court Statistics: 1985-2011." Available online: http://www.ojjdp.gov/ojstatbb/ezajcs/ Data source: National Center for Juvenile Justice. (2014). *National Juvenile Court Data Archive: Juvenile court case records 1985–2011* [machine-readable data files]. Pittsburgh, PA: National Center for Juvenile Justice.

8. U.S. Department of Justice Bureau of Justice Statistics, Prisoner Series and Jails at Midyear Series, 1985-2013.

9. Carmen Daugherty, *State Trends: Legislative Victories from 2011–2013: Removing Youth from the Adult Criminal Justice System* (Washington, DC: Campaign for Youth Justice, 2013).

10. David Farrington, "Age and Crime." In *Crime and Justice: An Annual Review of Research*, ed. Michael Tonry and N. Morris (Chicago: University of Chicago Press), 1986.

11. Richard J. Bonnie, Robert L. Johnson, Betty Chemers, and J. Schuck, *Reforming Juvenile Justice: A Developmental Approach* (Washington, DC: National Academies Press, 2013), p. 23.

12. Richard J. Bonnie, Robert L. Johnson, Betty Chemers, and J. Schuck, *Reforming Juvenile Justice: A Developmental Approach* (Washington, DC: National Academies Press, 2013), 20.

13. Elizabeth C. Scott and Laurence Steinberg, *Rethinking Juvenile Justice* (Boston: University of Harvard Press, 2008). The authors note that empirical adolescent research began in the 1970s but did not truly take hold until the 1980s.

14. Elizabeth Scott and Laurence Steinberg, *Rethinking Juvenile Justice* (Boston: Harvard University Press, 2008).

15. Laurence Steinberg and Elizabeth S. Scott, "Less Guilty by Reason of Adolescence: Developmental Immaturity, Diminished Responsibility, and the Juvenile Death Penalty," *American Psychologist* 58(12) (2003): 1010. Italics in the original.

16. Laurence Steinberg and K. C. Monahan, "Age Differences in Resistance to Peer Influence," *Developmental Psychology* 43 (2007): 1531–43.

17. Laurence Steinberg and Elizabeth S. Scott, "Less Guilty by Reason of Adolescence: Developmental Immaturity, Diminished Responsibility, and the Juvenile Death Penalty," *American Psychologist* 58(12) (2003): 1009–18.

18. Laurence Steinberg and Elizabeth S. Scott, "Less Guilty by Reason of Adolescence: Developmental Immaturity, Diminished Responsibility, and the Juvenile Death Penalty," *American Psychologist* 58(12) (2003): 1009–18.

19. James C. Howell, Barry C. Feld, Daniel P. Mears, David P. Farrington, Rolf Loeber, and David Petechuk, *Bulletin 5: Youth Offenders and an Effective Response in the Juvenile and Adult Court Systems: What Happens, What Should Happen, and What We Need to Know* (Washington, DC: Department of Justice, 2013).

20. Mississippi: 5; Arizona: 4; Louisiana: 4; North Carolina: 4; Florida: 3.

21. Roper at 569–70.

22. *Roper v. Simmons.*

23. Roper at 570.

24. *Graham v. Florida*, page 18.

25. *Graham v. Florida*, page 23.

26. *J. D. B. v. North Carolina*, 564 US–(2010).

27. *J. D. B. v. North Carolina*, 564 US–(2010).

28. Mark Soler, Dana Schoenberg, and Marc Schindler, "Juvenile Justice: Lessons for a New Era," *Georgetown Journal of Poverty Law and Policy* 26 (2009): 483–541.

29. Henggeler, S. *Multisystemic Therapy: MST 2012 and Beyond* (San Antonio: 2012 Blueprints Conference). Available online: http://www.blueprintsconference. com/presentations/T4-A.pdf.

30. Steven West and Keri K. O'Neal, "Project DARE Outcome Effectiveness Revisited," *American Journal of Public Health*, 94(6) (2004): 1027–29; Greg Berman and Aubrey Fox, *Lessons from the Battle Over D.A.R.E.: The Complicated Relationship Between Research and Practice* (Washington, DC: Bureau of Justice Assistance, 2009).

31. Robert Wood Johnson Foundation, *A New DARE Curriculum Gets Mixed Results* (Washington, DC: 2010). Available online: http://www.rwjf.org/content/dam/ farm/reports/program_results_reports/2010/rwjf70259.

32. Juvenile Justice Geography, Policy, Practice, and Statistics. http://www.jjgps. org/publications.

33. Jeffrey Butts and Daniel Mears, "Reviving Juvenile Justice," *Youth and Society* 33 (2) (December 2001): 189–94.

34. Anthony Petrosino, C. Turpin-Petrosino, M. Hollis-Peel, and J. G. Lavenberg, "Scared Straight and Other Juvenile Awareness Programs for Preventing Juvenile Delinquency: A Systematic Review," *Campbell Systematic Reviews* 5 (2013).

35. Office of the Surgeon General, *Youth Violence: A Report of the Surgeon General* (Washington, DC: US Centers for Disease Control, 2001).

36. Ohio Department of Youth Services website: http://www.dys.ohio.gov/DNN/ LinkClick.aspx?fileticket=i1abtQBjcLM%3D&tabid=78&mid=542.

37. Elizabeth S. Scott, "'Children Are Different': Constitutional Values and Justice Policy," *Ohio Journal of Criminal Law* 11(1): 71–105, 2013.

38. National Center for Juvenile Justice website: http://www.jjgps.org/ systems-integration.

39. Jasmine Tyler, Jason Zeidenberg, and Eric Lotke, *Cost-Effective Youth Corrections: Rationalizing the Fiscal Architecture of Juvenile Justice Systems* (Washington, DC: Justice Policy Institute, 2006).

40. T. J. Dishion, Joan McCord, and F. Poulin, "When Interventions Harm: Peer Groups and Problem Behavior," *American Psychologist* 54(9) (1999): 755–64.

41. J. Lin, *Exploring the Impact of Institutional Placement on Recidivism of Delinquent Youth* (Washington, DC: National Institute of Justice, 2007); Edward P. Mulvey, Laurence Steinberg, Alex R. Piquero, Michelle Besana, Jeffrey Fagan, Carol A. Schubert, and Elizabeth Cauffman, "Longitudinal Offending Trajectories among Serious Adolescent Offenders," *Development and Psychopathology* 22 (2010): 453–75.

42. Anna Aizer and Joseph J. Doyle Jr., "Juvenile Incarceration, Human Capital, and Future Crime: Evidence from Randomly Assigned Judges" *Quarterly Journal of Economics* (2015): 1–46,

43. Jasmine Tyler, Jason Zeidenberg, and Eric Lotke, *Cost-Effective Youth Corrections: Rationalizing the Fiscal Architecture of Juvenile Justice Systems* (Washington, DC: Justice Policy Institute, 2006).

44. Richard J. Bonnie, Robert L. Johnson, Betty Chemers, and J. Schuck, *Reforming Juvenile Justice: A Developmental Approach* (Washington, DC: National Academies Press, 2013), 418.

45. Amanda Petteruti, Marc Schindler, and Jason Zeidenberg, *Sticker Shock* (Washington, DC: Justice Policy Institute, 2015), http://www.justicepolicy.org/research/8477.

46. Missouri annual report: http://dss.mo.gov/re/dysar.htm.

47. Richard J. Bonnie, Robert L. Johnson, Betty Chemers, and J. Schuck, *Reforming Juvenile Justice: A Developmental Approach* (Washington, DC: National Academies Press, 2013), 424.

48. M. Moon, B. Applegate, and E. Latessa, "RECLAIM Ohio: A Politically Viable Alternative to Treating Youthful Felony Offenders," *Crime and Delinquency* 43(4) (1997): 438–56.

49. C. Lowenkamp and E. Latessa, *Reclaiming Texas Youth: Applying the Lessons from RECLAIM Ohio to Texas* (Austin: Texas Public Policy Foundation, 2009).

50. M. Moon, B. Applegate, and E. Latessa, "RECLAIM Ohio: A Politically Viable Alternative to Treating Youthful Felony Offenders," *Crime and Delinquency* 43(4) (1997): 438–56.

51. E. J. Latessa, M. G. Turner, M. M. Moon, and B. Applegate, *A Statewide Evaluation of the Reclaim Ohio Initiative* (Washington, DC: Bureau of Justice Assistance, 1998).

52. C. Lowenkamp and E. Latessa, *Reclaiming Texas Youth: Applying the Lessons from RECLAIM Ohio to Texas* (Austin: Texas Public Policy Foundation, 2009).

53. C. Lowenkamp and E. Latessa, *Evaluation of Ohio's RECLAIM Funded Programs, CCFs, and DYS Facilities* (Cincinnati: University of Cincinnati, 2005).

54. J. Travis, "Reflections on Juvenile Justice Reform in New York," *New York Law School Law Review* 56 (2011): 1317–28.

55. C. Lowenkamp, and E. Latessa, *Evaluation of Ohio's RECLAIM Funded Programs, CCFs, and DYS Facilities* (Cincinnati: University of Cincinnati, 2005).

56. J. Butts, *Transfer of Juveniles to Criminal Court Is Not Correlated with Falling Youth Violence* (New York: Research and Evaluation Center, John Jay College of Criminal Justice, 2012). Available online: http://johnjayresearch.org/wp-content/

uploads/2012/03/databit2012_05.pdf. Note: While many other states have also witnessed falling arrest rates for violent crime among their youth, the large drop in Ohio encourages confidence in handling eligible youth felony offenders in the community as an approach that is protective of public safety.

57. C. Lowenkamp and E. Latessa, *Evaluation of Ohio's RECLAIM Funded Programs, CCFs, and DYS Facilities* (Cincinnati: University of Cincinnati, 2005).

58. C. Lowenkamp and E. Latessa, *Evaluation of Ohio's RECLAIM Funded Programs, CCFs, and DYS Facilities* (Cincinnati: University of Cincinnati, 2005).

59. Amanda Petteruti, Marc Schindler, and Jason Zeidenberg, *Sticker Shock* (Washington, DC: Justice Policy Institute, 2015), http://www.justicepolicy.org/research/8477.

60. C. Lowenkamp and E. Latessa, *Evaluation of Ohio's RECLAIM Funded Programs, CCFs, and DYS Facilities* (Cincinnati: University of Cincinnati, 2005); J. Travis, "Reflections on Juvenile Justice Reform in New York," *New York Law School Law Review* 56 (2011): 1317–28.

61. C. Lowenkamp and E. Latessa, *Evaluation of Ohio's RECLAIM Funded Programs, CCFs, and DYS Facilities* (Cincinnati: University of Cincinnati, 2005). (Note that precise cost savings depends on youth risk levels.)

62. Department of Youth Services website: http://www.dys.ohio.gov/DNN/Link-Click.aspx?fileticket=i1abtQBjcLM%3D&tabid=78&mid=542.

63. Juvenile Law Center, *"Roper v. Simmons* Ten Years Later, Part 3: Juvenile Justice and Developmental Research in the Post-Roper Era." Posted online on JLC website, March 6, 2015: http://jlc.org/blog/roper-v-simmons-ten-years-later-recollec-tions-and-reflections-abolition-juvenile-death-penalt-1.

64. Mina Samuels, *Children in Confinement in Louisiana* (New York: Human Rights Watch, 1995).

65. U.S. Department of Justice findings letter, 1996, http://www.justice.gov/crt/about/spl/documents/lajuvfind2.php.

66. http://www.modelsforchange.net/about/States-for-change/Louisiana.html.

67. Rochelle Stanfield, *The JDAI Story: Building a Better Juvenile Detention System* (Baltimore: Annie E. Casey Foundation, 1999), 9.

68. Richard Mendel, *Two Decades of JDAI: From Demonstration Project to National Standard* (Baltimore: Annie E. Casey Foundation, 2009).

69. Richard Mendel, *Two Decades of JDAI: From Demonstration Project to National Standard.* (Baltimore: Annie E. Casey Foundation, 2009).

CHAPTER 7

1. Congressional Record, June 7, 1995, Senator Kohl, S7918, speaking on the Senate floor on the introduction of the Gun-Free Schools Act of 1994.

2. Anti-Drug Abuse Act, 1986; Sentencing Reform Act, 1984.

3. The act was originally passed with unanimous consent in 1990 but struck down by the Supreme Court for violating the Commerce Clause. The GFSA passed in 1994 corrected this flaw.

4. Congressional Record, June 7, 1995, Senator Kohl, S7918, speaking on the Senate floor on the introduction of the Gun-Free Schools Act of 1994. In 1993, the U.S. Supreme Court held in *U.S. v. Lopez* that the Gun-Free Schools Act violated the Commerce Clause of the Constitution because "possession of a gun in a local school zone was not economic activity that substantially affected interstate commerce." The Gun-Free Schools Act of 1994 was passed to correct this flaw.

5. Paul Hirschfield and Katarazyana Cerinska, "Beyond Fear," *Sociology Compass* 3(1) (2011): 1–12.

6. 20 U.S.C. Section 8921(b)(1).

7. 20 USC Section 8922(a)(1994), reenacted as 20 USC Section 7157(h)(2002).

8. U.S. Department of Education Implementation of GFSA reports. Available online: http://www2.ed.gov/about/offices/list/osdfs/gfsa.html.

9. Avarita L. Hanson, "Have Zero Tolerance School Discipline Policies Turned into a Nightmare? The American Dream's Promise of Equal Educational Opportunity Grounded in *Brown v. Board of Education*," *UC Davis Journal of Juvenile Law and Policy* 9(2) (2005): 289–379.

10. Kathleen M. Ceronne, "The Gun-Free Schools Act of 1994: Zero Tolerance Takes Aim at Procedural Due Process," *Pace Law Review* 20(1) (1999): 131–88.

11. Tobin McAndrews, "Zero Tolerance Policies," *ERIC Digest*, University of Oregon (2001).

12. Katayoon Majd, "Students of the Mass Incarceration Nation," *Howard Law Journal* 54(2) (2011).

13. MO REV. STAT. § 167.115, 164. (2000).

14. N.C.G.S. § 7B-3101 (a)(2); (a)(3); (a)(5).

15. Avarita L. Hanson, "Have Zero Tolerance School Discipline Policies Turned into a Nightmare? The American Dream's Promise of Equal Educational Opportunity Grounded in *Brown v. Board of Education*," *UC Davis Journal of Juvenile Law and Policy* 9(2) (2005): 289–379.

16. Advancement Project and The Civil Rights Project at Harvard University, "Opportunities Suspended: The Devastating Consequences of Zero Tolerance and School Discipline." Report from A National Summit on Zero Tolerance, June 15–16, 2000, Washington, DC.

17. U.S. Department of Education, Office of Safe and Healthy Students, *Report on the Implementation of the Gun-Free School Schools Act in the States and Outlying Areas for School Year 2010-11* (Washington, DC: U.S. Department of Education, 2013). Available online: https://www2.ed.gov/about/reports/annual/gfsa/gfsarptrevised4413.pdf.

18. Advancement Project and The Civil Rights Project at Harvard University, "Opportunities Suspended: The Devastating Consequences of Zero Tolerance and School Discipline." Report from A National Summit on Zero Tolerance, June 15–16, 2000, Washington, DC, page 14.

19. Youth United for Change, Advancement Project, "Zero Tolerance in Philadelphia: Denying Educational Opportunities and Creating a Pathway to Prison" (Washington, DC: Advancement Project, 2011).

20. Johanna Wald and Daniel J. Losen, "Defining and Redirecting a School-to-Prison Pipeline," *New Directions for Youth Development* 2003 (2003): 9–15.

21. Allison Ann Payne and Kelly Welch, "Modeling the Effects of Racial Threat on Punitive and Restorative School Discipline Practices," *Criminology* 48 (2010): 1019–62.

22. Maureen Carroll, "Educating Expelled Students After No Child Left Behind: Mending an Incentive Structure That Discourages Alternative Education and Reinstatement," *UCLA Law Review* 55 (2008): 1909–69.

23. Committee on the Judiciary, United States Senate, February 1977. "Challenge for the Third Century: Education in a Safe Environment—Final Report on the Nature and Prevention of School Violence and Vandalism." U.S. Government Printing Office, page 25.

24. Committee on the Judiciary, United States Senate, February 1977. "Challenge for the Third Century: Education in a Safe Environment—Final Report on the Nature and Prevention of School Violence and Vandalism." U.S. Government Printing Office, page 27.

25. American Psychological Association Zero Tolerance Task Force, "Are Zero Tolerance Policies Effective in the Schools? An Evidentiary Review and Recommendations," *American Psychologist* 63 (2008): 852–62.

26. Michael P. Krezmien, Peter E. Leone, Mark S. Zablocki, and Craig S. Wells, "Juvenile Court Referrals and the Public Schools: Nature and Extent of the Practice in Five States," *Journal of Contemporary Criminal Justice* 26(3) (2010): 273–93.

27. M. Mayer and Peter E. Leone, "School Violence and Disruption Revisited: Equity and Safety in the School House," *Focus on Exceptional Children* 40(1) (2007): 1–28.

28. The U.S. Congress renamed the decades-old Elementary and Secondary Schools Act as the No Child Left Behind (NCLB) Act during its reauthorization in 2001. It incorporated the Gun-Free Schools Act as well.

29. Linda Darling-Hammond, "Race, Inequality and Educational Accountability: The Irony of 'No Child Left Behind,'" *Race Ethnicity and Education* 10(3) (2007): 245–60.

30. Linda Darling-Hammond, "Race, Inequality and Educational Accountability: The Irony of 'No Child Left Behind,'" *Race Ethnicity and Education* 10(3) (2007): 245–60.

31. Advancement Project, Education Law Center-PA, FairTest, The Forum for Education and Democracy, Juvenile Law Center, and NAACP Legal Defense and Education Fund, Inc., *Federal Policy, ESEA Reauthorization, and the School-to-Prison Pipeline* (2011).

32. Advancement Project, Education Law Center-PA, FairTest, The Forum for Education and Democracy, Juvenile Law Center, and NAACP Legal Defense and Education Fund, Inc., *Federal Policy, ESEA Reauthorization, and the School-to-Prison Pipeline* (2011).

33. Linda Darling-Hammond, "Race, Inequality and Educational Accountability: The Irony of 'No Child Left Behind,'" *Race Ethnicity and Education* 10(3) (2007): 245–60.

34. *D. C., K. C., and K. J. v. School District of Philadelphia*, 879 A.2d 408 (2005).

35. National Center for Fair and Open Testing, "How Testing Feeds the School to Prison Pipeline," FairTes (2010) Washington, DC. Available online: http://www.fairtest.org/how-testing-feeds-schooltoprison-pipeline.

36. Russell Skiba and M. Karega Rausch, "Zero Tolerance, Suspension, and Questions of Equity and Effectiveness." In Carolyn M. Evertson and Carol S. Weinstein, eds., *Handbook of Classroom Management: Research, Practice, and Contemporary Issues* (Mahwah: Laurence Erlbaum Associates, 2006).

37. Miner Marchbanks et al., "More than a Drop in the Bucket: The Social and Economic Costs of Dropouts and Grade Retentions Associated with Exclusionary Discipline," *Journal of Applied Research on Children: Informing Policy for Children at Risk* 5(2): 1–36. Available online: www.digitalcommons.library.tmc.edu/childrenatrisk/vol5/iss2/17.

38. Miner Marchbanks et al., "More than a Drop in the Bucket: The Social and Economic Costs of Dropouts and Grade Retentions Associated with Exclusionary Discipline," *Journal of Applied Research on Children: Informing Policy for Children at Risk* 5(2): 1–36. Available online: www.digitalcommons.library.tmc.edu/childrenatrisk/vol5/iss2/17.

39. Gary Kleck, "Mass Shootings in Schools: The Worst Possible Case for Gun Control," *American Behavioral Scientist* (2009): 1447–64.

40. Glenn W. Muschert, "The Columbine Victims and the Myth of the Juvenile Superpredator," *Youth Violence and Juvenile Justice* 5(4) (2007): 351–66.

41. David Altheide, "The Columbine Shootings and the Discourse of Fear," *American Behavioral Scientist* 52(10) (2009): 1426–46, 1356.

42. U.S. Senate Bill 254, "Violent and Repeat Juvenile Offender Accountability and Rehabilitation Act of 1999." Available online: http://www.gpo.gov/fdsys/pkg/BILLS-106s254pcs/html/BILLS-106s254pcs.htm.

43. David Altheide, "The Columbine Shootings and the Discourse of Fear," *American Behavioral Scientist* 52(10) (2009): 1426–46.

44. Lynn Addington, "Cops and Cameras," *American Behavioral Scientist* 52(10) (2009): 1426–46.

45. Thomas A Birkland and Regina G. Lawrence, "Media Framing and Policy Change in Columbine," *American Behavioral Scientist* 52(10), 1405–25; David Altheide, "The Columbine Shootings and the Discourse of Fear," *American Behavioral Scientist* 52(10) (2009): 1426–46.

46. Thomas A Birkland and Regina G. Lawrence, "Media Framing and Policy Change in Columbine," *American Behavioral Scientist* 52(10): 1405–25.

47. Congressional Research Office, "School Resource Officers: Law Enforcement in Schools" (Washington, DC: Author, 2013).

48. Oddly, the bill never went through the usual channel of the Judiciary Committee, and there was never a single hearing on the bill; rather it was introduced directly on the Senate floor for debate and vote.

49. U.S. Senate Bill 254, "Violent and Repeat Juvenile Offender Accountability and Rehabilitation Act of 1999" Available online: https://www.congress.

gov/bill/106th-congress/senate-bill/254/amendments?q={%22search%22%3A[%
22s254%22]}.

50. Senator Patrick Leahy, May 12, 1999, Congressional Record. S5107. Available online: http://www.gpo.gov/fdsys/pkg/CREC-1999-05-12/pdf/CREC-1999-05-12-senate.pdf.

51. Donald P. Haider-Markel and Mark R. Joslyn, "Gun Policy, Opinion, Tragedy, and Blame Attribution: The Conditional Influence of Issue Frames," *Journal of Politics* 63(2) (2001): 537. A large 2007 meta-analysis shows little support for the argument that video games influence criminal behavior; J. Sherry, "Violent Video Games and Aggression: Why Can't We Find Links?" In R. Preiss, B. Gayle, N. Burrell, M. Allen, and J. Bryant, eds., *Mass Media Effects Research: Advances through Meta-Analysis* (Mahwah, NJ: Lawrence Erlbaum), 231–48.

52. Lynn Addington, "Cops and Cameras," *American Behavioral Scientist* 52(10) (2009): 1426–46.

53. Lynn Addington, "Cops and Cameras," *American Behavioral Scientist* 52(10) (2009): 1426–46.

54. Abigail Hankin, Marci Hertz, and Thomas Simon, "Impacts of Metal Detector Use in Schools: Insights from 15 Years of Research," *Journal of School Health* 81(2) (2011): 100–106.

55. American Psychological Association Zero Tolerance Task Force, "Are Zero Tolerance Policies Effective in the Schools? An Evidentiary Review and Recommendations," *American Psychologist* 63 (2008): 852–62; Lynn Addington, "Cops and Cameras," *American Behavioral Scientist* 52(10) (2009): 1426–46; Russell Skiba, "Zero Tolerance, Zero Evidence: An Analysis of School Disciplinary Practice," *Indiana Education Policy Center*, 7–8.

56. Lynn Addington, "Cops and Cameras," *American Behavioral Scientist* 52(10) (2009): 1426–46, 1435.

57. B. Gastic, "At What Price? Safe School Policies and Their Unintentional Consequences for At-Risk Students" (unpublished manuscript, presented at the Annual Meeting of the American Educational Research Association, April 2006); M. J. Mayer and P. E. Leone, "A Structural Analysis of School Violence and Disruption: Implications for Creating Safer Schools," *Education and Treatment of Children* 22, no. 3 (1999): 333–56.

58. Pedro Noguera, "Preventing and Producing Violence: A Critical Analysis of Responses to School Violence," *Harvard Educational Review* (Summer 1995): 189–213.

59. Loic Wacquant, "Deadly Symbiosis," in *Mass Imprisonment: Social Causes and Consequences* (Thousand Oaks: Sage, 2001), 95–134.

60. Youth United for Change, Advancement Project, "Zero Tolerance in Philadelphia: Denying Educational Opportunities and Creating a Pathway to Prison" (Washington, DC: Advancement Project, 2011).

61. Spencer C. Weiler and Martha Cray, "Police at School: A Brief History and Current Status of School Resource Officers," *Clearing House* 84(4) (2011): 160–63.

62. Jacob Kang-Brown, Jennifer Trone, Jennifer Fratello, and Tarika Daftary-Kapur, *A Generation Later: What We've Learned About Zero Tolerance in Schools* (New York: Vera Institute of Justice, December 2013).

63. Kerrin Wolf, "Arrest Decision Making by SRO Officers," *Youth Violence and Juvenile Justice* (2013).

64. Simone Robers, Jana Kemp, and Jennifer Truman, "Indicators of School Crime and Safety: 2012," *National Center for Education Statistics* (2013), Table 20.2 and 20.3.

65. Brentin Mock, "Good News in Mississippi: School-to-Prison Pipeline Closes," *Colorlines* (2013). http://colorlines.com/archives/2013/05/good_news_in_miss_school-to-prison_pipeline_closed.html.

66. U.S. Department of Justice, Press Release, "Justice Department Files Lawsuit in Mississippi to Protect the Constitutional Rights of Children," Washington, DC: U.S. Department of Justice. http://www.justice.gov/opa/pr/justice-department-files-lawsuit-mississippi-protect-constitutional-rights-children.

67. Consent decree: http://www.justice.gov/iso/opa/resources/8502013322112486 46502.pdf, page 32.

68. Julianne Hing, "What the DOJ Can't Do on School Discpline Reform," April 3, 2013, http://colorlines.com/archives/2013/04/what_the_doj_cant_do_on_school_discipline_reform_1.html.

69. Padres & jóvenes Unidos, "The Colorado School Discipline Report Card" (March 2014).

CHAPTER 8

1. Sarah Hockenberry and Charles Puzzanchera, *Juvenile Court Statistics 2011* (Washington, DC: Office of Juvenile Justice and Delinquency Prevention, 2014).

2. Sarah Hockenberry and Charles Puzzanchera, *Juvenile Court Statistics 2011* (Washington, DC: Office of Juvenile Justice and Delinquency Prevention, 2014).

3. M. Sickmund, T. J. Sladky, W. Kang, and C. Puzzanchera "Easy Access to the Census of Juveniles in Residential Placement" (2013). Available online: http://www.ojjdp.gov/ojstatbb/ezacjrp/.

4. Neelum Arya and Ian Augarten, *Critical Condition African American Youth in the Justice System* (Washington, DC: Campaign for Youth Justice, 2008).

5. Melissa Sickmund, Anthony Sladky, and Wei Kang, "Easy Access to Juvenile Court Statistics: 1985–2011" (2014). Available online: http://www.ojjdp.gov/ojstatbb/ ezajcs/ Data source: National Center for Juvenile Justice (2014). *National Juvenile Court Data Archive: Juvenile court case records 1985–2011* [machine-readable data files]. Pittsburgh, PA: National Center for Juvenile Justice.

6. Richard J. Bonnie, Robert L. Johnson, Betty M. Chemers, and Julie A. Schuck, eds. *Reforming Juvenile Justice: A Developmental Approach* (Washington, DC: National Research Council of the National Academies, 2013), p. 7.

7. Alice P. Green, *The Disproportionate Impact of the Juvenile Justice System on Children of Color in the Capital Region* (Albany: Center for Law and Justice, July 2012).

8. Richard J. Bonnie, Robert L. Johnson, Betty M. Chemers, and Julie A. Schuck, eds. *Reforming Juvenile Justice: A Developmental Approach* (Washington, DC: National Research Council of the National Academies, 2013).

9. Donna Bishop, "The Role of Race and Ethnicity in Juvenile Justice Processing." In *Our Children Their Children*, eds. Darnell F. Hawkins and Kimberly Kempf-Leonard (Chicago: University of Chicago Press, 2005).

10. Donna Bishop, "The Role of Race and Ethnicity in Juvenile Justice Processing." In *Our Children Their Children*, eds. Darnell F. Hawkins and Kimberly Kempf-Leonard (Chicago: University of Chicago Press, 2005).

11. Barry Feld, *Bad Kids: Race and the Transformation of the Juvenile* Court (Oxford: Oxford University Press, 1999); Geoff Ward, *The Black Child-Savers: Racial Democracy and Juvenile Justice* (Chicago: University of Chicago Press, 2012); Joshua Pickett and Ted Chiricos, "Controlling Other People's Children: Racialized Views of Delinquency and Whites' Punitive Attitudes toward Juvenile Offenders," *Criminology* 50(3) (2012): 673–710.

12. Nazgol Ghandnoosh, *Race and Punishment: Racial Perceptions of Crime and Support for Punitive Policies* (Washington, DC: The Sentencing Project, 2014).

13. Joshua Pickett, Ted Chiricos, and Marc Gertz, "The Racial Foundations of Whites' Support for Child Saving," *Social Science Research* 44 (2014): 44–59.

14. Joshua Pickett and Ted Chiricos, "Controlling Other People's Children: Racialized Views of Delinquency and Whites' Punitive Attitudes toward Juvenile Offenders," *Criminology* 50(3) (2012): 692.

15. George Bridges and Sarah Steen, "Racial Disparities in Official Assessments of Juvenile Offenders: Attributional Stereotypes as Mediating Mechanisms," *American Sociological Review* 63 (1998): 554–70.

16. James Bell, *Adoration of the Question: Reflections on the Failure to Reduce Racial and Ethnic Disparities in the Juvenile Justice System* (San Francisco: The W. Haywood Burns Institute, 2008).

17. Richard J. Bonnie, Robert L. Johnson, Betty M. Chemers, and Julie A. Schuck, eds. *Reforming Juvenile Justice: A Developmental Approach* (Washington, DC: National Research Council of the National Academies, 2013).

18. Marc Mauer, "Racial Impact Statements: Changing Policies to Address Disparities," *Criminal Justice* 23(4) (2009).

19. Sarah Hockenberry, Melissa Sickmund, and Anthony Sladky, *Juvenile Residential Facility Census, 2012: Selected Findings* (Washington, DC: Office of Juvenile Justice and Delinquency Prevention, 2015).

20. Sarah Hockenberry, Melissa Sickmund, and Anthony Sladky, *Juvenile Residential Facility Census, 2012: Selected Findings* (Washington, DC: Office of Juvenile Justice and Delinquency Prevention, 2015).

21. Nell Bernstein, *Burning Down the House* (New York: The New Press, 2014).

22. U.S. Department of Justice Civil Rights Division, December 1, 2011, Investigation of the Arthur G. Dozier School of Boys and the Jackson Juvenile Offender Center, Marianna, Florida. Page 4. Full report available online: www.justice.gov/crt/about/spl/documents/dozier_findltr_12-1-11.pdf.

23. Ben Montgomery, "More Bodies Found than Expected at the Dozier School," *Miami Herald* (January 4, 2012). Available online: http://www.miamiherald.com/news/state/florida/article5427669.html#/tabPane=tabs-b0710947-1-1.

24. Ben Montgomery, "USF Team Looks for Lost Graves at Closed Dozier School for Boys," *Tampa Bay Tribune* (May 19, 2012). Available online: http://www.tampabay.com/features/humaninterest/usf-team-looks-for-lost-graves-at-closed-dozier-school-for-boys/1230895.

25. Richard Mendel, *No Place for Kids* (Baltimore: Annie E. Casey Foundation, 2011), 5.

26. Sarah Hockenberry, Melissa Sickmund, and Anthony Sladky, *Juvenile Residential Facility Census, 2012: Selected Findings* (Washington, DC: Office of Juvenile Justice and Delinquency Prevention, 2015).

27. Annie E. Casey Foundation, *Juvenile Detention Facility Assessment: 2014 Update* (Baltimore: Annie E. Casey Foundation, 2014).

28. Robert Listenbee et al., *Report of the Attorney General's National Task Force on Children Exposed to Violence* (Washington, DC: U.S. Department of Justice).

29. Nell Bernstein, *Burning Down the House: The End of Juvenile Prison* (New York: The New Press, 2014), p. 131.

30. American Academy of Child and Adolescent Psychiatry, 2012 Policy Statements, Washington, DC, AACAP, 2012. Available online: http://www.aacap.org/aacap/Policy_Statements/2012/Solitary_Confinement_of_Juvenile_Offenders.aspx.

31. Prison Rape Elimination Act, P.L. 108-79 (2003).

32. http://www.jlc.org/blog/juvenile-law-center-negotiates-final-settlement-civil-rights-lawsuit-challenging-solitary-confi.

33. http://kut.org/post/texas-youth-placed-solitary-confinement-more-36000-times-last-year.

34. http://www.splcenter.org/sites/default/files/downloads/case/third_amended_complaint.pdf

35. Nell Bernstein, *Burning Down the House: The End of Juvenile Prison* (New York: The New Press, 2014), p. 130–31.

36. Nell Bernstein, *Burning Down the House: The End of Juvenile Prison* (New York: The New Press, 2014).

37. Ian Kysel, *Growing Up Locked Down: Youth in Solitary Confinement in Jails and Prisons Across the United States* (San Francisco: Human Rights Watch, 2012).

38. Ian Kysel, Testimony before the Senate Judiciary Subcommittee on the Constitution, Civil Rights, and Human Rights Hearing on Reassessing Solitary Confinement II: The Human Rights, Fiscal, and Public Safety Consequences, Tuesday, February 25, 2014, Washington, DC. Available online: http://www.law.georgetown.edu/academics/centers-institutes/human-rights-institute/opportunities/upload/Ian-Kysel-Solitary-Confinement-Hearing-Testimony-FINAL.pdf.

39. http://cironline.org/reports/teens-rikers-island-solitary-confinement-pushes-mental-limits-6130

40. Patrick Griffin, Sean Addie, Benjamin Adams and Kathy Firestine, *Trying Juveniles as Adults: An Analysis of State Transfer Laws and Reporting* (Washington, DC: Office of Juvenile Justice and Delinquency Prevention, 2011).

41. Jeffrey Butts and O. Mitchell, "Brick by Brick: Dismantling the Border between Juvenile and Adult Justice," *Criminal Justice* 2 (2000), 167–213; Howard Snyder and Melissa Sickmund, *Juvenile Offenders and Victims: 2006 National Report* (Pittsburgh: National Center for Juvenile Justice, 2006).

42. Patrick Griffin, Sean Addie, Benjamin Adams and Kathy Firestine, *Trying Juveniles as Adults: An Analysis of State Transfer Laws and Reporting* (Washington, DC: Office of Juvenile Justice and Delinquency Prevention, 2011).

43. Sarah Hockenberry and Charles Puzzanchera, *Delinquency Cases Waived to Criminal Court, 2011* (Washington, DC: Office of Juvenile Justice and Delinquency Prevention, 2014).

44. BJS Prisoner Series and Jails at Midyear series, 2013.

45. Ashley Nellis, *Life Goes On* (Washington, DC: The Sentencing Project).

46. Eric R. Lotke, "Youth Homicide: Keeping Perspective on How Many Children Kill," *Valparaiso University Law Review* 395, (1997): 395–418, article quoting Donna Bishop study 1996.

47. Allen Beck, Marcus Berzofsky, and Christopher Krebs, *Sexual Victimization in Prison and Jails Reported by Inmates, 2011-2012* (Washington, DC: Bureau of Justice Statistics).

48. Margaret E. Noonan, *Mortality in Local Jails and State Prisons, 2000–2012—Statistical Tables* (Washington, DC: Bureau of Justice Statistics, 2014).

49. Margaret E. Noonan, *Mortality in Local Jails and State Prisons, 2000–2012—Statistical Tables* (Washington, DC: Bureau of Justice Statistics, 2014).

50. Elizabeth Scott and Laurence Steinberg, *Rethinking Juvenile Justice* (Boston: Harvard University Press, 2008).

51. James C. Howell, *Juvenile Justice and Youth Violence* (Thousand Oaks: Sage, 1997).

52. Jeffrey Butts and Daniel Mears, "Reviving Juvenile Justice," *Youth and Society* 33(2) (2001): 169–98.

53. Richard J. Bonnie, Robert L. Johnson, Betty M. Chemers, and Julie A. Schuck, eds., *Reforming Juvenile Justice: A Developmental Approach* (Washington, DC: National Research Council of the National Academies, 2013), page 4.

54. Robert F. Kennedy National Resource for Juvenile Justice, "From Conversation to Collaboration: How Child Welfare and Juvenile Justice Agencies Can Work Together" (Beacon, MA: Author, n.d.).

55. Robert F. Kennedy National Resource for Juvenile Justice, "From Conversation to Collaboration: How Child Welfare and Juvenile Justice Agencies Can Work Together" (Beacon, MA: Author, n.d.).

56. Dylan Conger, *Reducing the Foster Care Bias in Juvenile Detention Decisions: The Impact of Project Confirm* (New York: Vera Institute for Justice).

57. Cathy Spatz Widom and M. G. Maxfield, *An Update on the "Cycle of Violence,"* (Washington, DC: National Institute of Justice: Research in Brief, 2001); Ashley Nellis, *The Lives of Juvenile Lifers* (Washington, DC: The Sentencing Project, 2012).

58. Cathy Spatz Widom and M. G. Maxfield, *An Update on the "Cycle of Violence"* (Washington, DC: National Institute of Justice: Research in Brief, 2001).

59. Robert Listenbee, *Report of the Attorney General's Task Force on Children Exposed to Violence* (Washington, DC: U.S. Department of Justice, 2012).

60. Cathy Spatz Widom and M. G. Maxfield, *An Update on the "Cycle of Violence"* (Washington, DC: National Institute of Justice: Research in Brief, 2001): 1–8.

61. Alice P. Green, *The Disproportionate Impact of the Juvenile Justice System on Children of Color in the Capital Region* (Albany: Center for Law and Justice, July 2012), page 4.

62. Janet K. Wiig and John A. Tuell, *Guidebook for Juvenile Justice and Child Welfare System Coordination and Integration: A Framework for Improved Outcomes*, 3rd ed., Robert F. Kennedy Children's Action Corps, MacArthur Foundation, 2013.

63. Sesame Workshop, "Little Children, Big Challenges: Incarceration," 2013.

64. Michael E. Roetger and Raymond R. Swisher, "Associations of Fathers' History of Incarceration with Sons' Delinquency and Arrest Among Black, White, and Hispanic Males in the United States," *Criminology* 49(4) (2011): 1109–47.

65. Chistopher Wildeman, "Parental Imprisonment, the Prison Boom, and the Concentration of Childhood Disadvantage," *Demography*, 46(2): 265–80.

66. Chistopher Wildeman, "Parental Imprisonment, the Prison Boom, and the Concentration of Childhood Disadvantage," *Demography*, 46(2): 265–80.

67. Donald Braman, "Families and Incarceration," in *Invisible Punishment: The Collateral Consequences of Mass Imprisonment,* eds. Marc Mauer and Meda Chesney-Lind (New York: The New Press, 2002), 118.

68. Megan Comfort, "Punishment Beyond the Legal Offender," *Annual Review of Law and Social Science* 3 (2007): 271–76; Chistopher Wildeman, "Parental Imprisonment, the Prison Boom, and the Concentration of Childhood Disadvantage," *Demography* 46(2): 265–80.

69. Christopher Uggen and Suzy McElrath, "Parental Incarceration: What We Know and Where We Need to Go," *Journal of Criminal Law and Criminology* 104(3) (2014): 597–604.

70. Donald Braman, "Families and Incarceration," in *Invisible Punishment, eds.* Marc Mauer and Meda Chesney-Lind (New York: The New Press, 2002): 117–35.

71. Ashley Nellis, *The Lives of Juvenile Lifers: Findings from a National Survey* (Washington, DC: The Sentencing Project, 2012).

72. Megan Comfort, "Punishment Beyond the Legal Offender," *Annual Review of Law and Social Science* 3 (2007): 271–76; Chistopher Wildeman, "Parental Imprisonment, the Prison Boom, and the Concentration of Childhood Disadvantage," *Demography* 46(2), 265–80.

73. For a review of the various internalizing and externalizing effects of parental incarceration on children that are documented in the literature, see Roettger and Swisher, 2011.

74. Terry Ann Craigie, "The Effect of Paternal Incarceration on Early Childhood Behavior Problems: A Racial Comparison," *Journal of Ethnicity in Criminal Justice* 9(3) (2011): 179–99.

75. Charlene Wear Simmons, "Children of Incarcerated Parents," Sacramento, California Research Bureau, 7(2): 1–11.

76. Michael E. Roettger and Raymond R. Swisher, "Associations of Fathers' History of Incarceration with Sons' Delinquency and Arrest among Black, White and Hispanic Males in the United States," *Criminology* 49(4) (2011): 1109–47.

77. Holly Foster and John Hagan, "The Mass Incarceration of Parents in America: Issues of Race/Ethnicity, Collateral Damage to Children, and Prisoner Reentry," *ANNALS of the American Academy of Political Science* 623 (2009): 179–94.

78. Christopher Uggen and Suzy McElrath, "Parental Incarceration: What We Know and Where We Need to Go," *Journal of Criminal Law and Criminology* 104(3) (2014): 597–604; see also Megan Comfort, "Punishment Beyond the Legal Offender," *Annual Review of Law and Social Science* 3 (2007): 275.

CONCLUSION

1. Alex Piquero and Laurence Steinberg, "Public Preferences for Rehabilitation Versus Incarceration for Juvenile Offenders," *Journal of Criminal Justice*, 38 (2010): 1–6.

2. C. Puzzanchera, B. Adams, and Melissa Sickmund, *Juvenile Court Statistics, 2011* (Washington, DC, Office of Juvenile Justice and Delinquency Prevention, 2014).

3. Laura S. Abrams and Ben Anderson-Nathe, *Compassionate Confinement: A Year in the Life of Unit C* (New Brunswick, NJ: Rutgers University Press, 2012).

4. Laura S. Abrams and Ben Anderson-Nathe, *Compassionate Confinement: A Year in the Life of Unit C* (New Brunswick, NJ: Rutgers University Press, 2012), 3.

5. Melissa Sickmund, A. Sladky, W. Kang, and C. Puzzanchera, "Easy Access to the Census of Juveniles in Residential Placement," 2013. Available online: http://www.ojjdp.gov/ojstatbb/ezacjrp/.

6. Michelle Evans-Chase and Huiquan Zhou, "A Systematic Review of the Juvenile Justice Intervention Literature: What It Can (and Cannot) Tell Us About What Works with Delinquent Youth," *Crime and Delinquency* 60(3) (2012): 451–70.

Bibliography

Abrams, Laura S., and Ben Anderson-Nathe, *Compassionate Confinement: A Year in the Life of Unit C* (New Brunswick, NJ: Rutgers University Press, 2012).

Addington, Lynn, "Cops and Cameras," *American Behavioral Scientist* 52(10) (2009): 1426–46.

Advancement Project and The Civil Rights Project at Harvard University, "Opportunities Suspended: The Devastating Consequences of Zero Tolerance and School Discipline." Report from A National Summit on Zero Tolerance, June 15–16, 2000, Washington, DC.

Advancement Project, Education Law Center-PA, FairTest, The Forum for Education and Democracy, Juvenile Law Center, and NAACP Legal Defense and Education Fund, Inc., *Federal Policy, ESEA Reauthorization, and the School-to-Prison Pipeline* (2011).

Ainsworth, Janet E., "Youth Violence in a Unified Court: Response to Critics of Juvenile Court Abolition," *B.C. Law Review* 927 (1995).

"Al Regnery's Secret Life." *New Republic*, June 23, 1986. Available online: http://www.newrepublic.com/article/politics/al-regnerys-secret-life.

Aizer, Anna, and Joseph J. Doyle, "Juvenile Incarceration, Human Capital, and Future Crime: Evidence from Randomly Assigned Judges," *Quarterly Journal of Economics* 130(2) (2015): 759–803.

Altheide, David, "The Columbine Shootings and the Discourse of Fear," *American Behavioral Scientist* 52(10) (2009): 1426–46, 1356.

American Academy of Child and Adolescent Psychiatry, 2012 Policy Statements, Washington, DC, AACAP, 2012. Available online: http://www.aacap.org/aacap/Policy_Statements/2012/Solitary_Confinement_of_Juvenile_Offenders.aspx.

American Psychological Association Zero Tolerance Task Force, "Are Zero Tolerance Policies Effective in the Schools? An Evidentiary Review and Recommendations," *American Psychologist* 63 (2008): 852–62.

Annie E. Casey Foundation, *Juvenile Detention Facility Assessment: 2014 Update* (Baltimore, MD: Annie E. Casey Foundation, 2014).

Annino, Paolo, "Children in Florida Adult Prisons: A Call for a Moratorium," *Florida State University Law Review* 28(2) (2001): 471–90.

Arthur, Pat, "Issues Faced by Juveniles Leaving Custody: Breaking Down the Barriers" (San Francisco: National Center for Youth Law, 2007).

Arya, Neelum, *State Trends: Legislative Victories from 2005 to 2010: Removing Youth from the Adult Criminal Justice System* (Washington, DC: Campaign for Youth Justice, 2011).

Arya, Neelum, and Ian Augarten, *Critical Condition African American Youth in the Justice System* (Washington, DC: Campaign for Youth Justice, 2008).

Barnosky, Jason, "The Violent Years: Responses to Juvenile Crime in the 1950s," *Northeastern Political Science Association* 38(3) (2006): 314–44.

Baumer, Eric, Janet L. Lauritsen, Richard Rosenfeld, and Richard Wright, "The Influence of Crack Cocaine on Robbery, Burglary, and Homicide Rates: A Cross-City, Longitudinal Analysis," *Journal of Research in Crime and Delinquency* 35(3) (1998): 316–40.

Bazelon, Emily, "Public Access to Juvenile and Family Court: Should the Courtroom Doors Be Open or Closed?" *Yale Law and Policy Review* 18 (1999): 155–79.

Allen Beck, Marcus Berzofsky, and Christopher Krebs, *Sexual Victimization in Prison and Jails Reported by Inmates, 2011-2012* (Washington, DC: Bureau of Justice Statistics).

Bell, James, *Adoration of the Question: Reflections on the Failure to Reduce Racial and Ethnic Disparities in the Juvenile Justice System* (San Francisco: The W. Haywood Burns Institute, 2008).

Bennett, William J., John J. DiIulio, and John P. Walters, *Body Count* (New York: Simon & Schuster, 1996).

Berman, Greg, and Aubrey Fox, *Lessons from the Battle over D.A.R.E.: The Complicated Relationship Between Research and Practice* (Washington, DC: Bureau of Justice Assistance, 2009).

Bernburg, Jon Gunnar, and Marvin D. Krohn, "Labeling, Life Chances, and Adult Crime: The Direct and Indirect Effects of Official Intervention in Adolescence on Crime in Early Adulthood," *Criminology* 41(4) (2003): 1287–318.

Bernstein, Nell, *Burning Down the House* (New York: The New Press, 2014).

Birkland, Thomas A., and Regina G. Lawrence, "Media Framing and Policy Change in Columbine," *American Behavioral Scientist* 52(10): 1405–25.

Bishop, Donna, "The Role of Race and Ethnicity in Juvenile Justice Processing." In *Our Children Their Children,* eds. Darnell F. Hawkins and Kimberly Kempf-Leonard (Chicago: University of Chicago Press, 2005).

Bishop, Donna, Lonn Lanza-Kaduce, and Charles E. Frazier, "Juvenile Justice under Attack: An Analysis of the Causes and Impact of Recent Reforms," *University of Florida Journal of Law and Public Policy* 10: 129–56.

Blomberg, Thomas G., William D. Bales, Karen Mann, Alex R. Piquero, and Richard A. Berk, "Incarceration, Education, and Transition from Delinquency," *Journal of Criminal Justice* 39 (2011): 355–65.

Blomberg, Thomas, George Pesta, and Colby Valentine, "The Juvenile Justice No Child Left Behind Collaboration Project: Final Report" (Tallahassee: Florida State University, 2008).

Blum, Arthur R., "Disclosing the Identities of Juvenile Felons: Introducing Accountability to Juvenile Justice," *Loyola University of Chicago Law Journal* 27 (1996): 349–400.

Blumstein, Alfred, "Violence by Young People: Why the Deadly Nexus?" *National Institute of Justice Journal* 229 (1995).

———, *Why Is Crime Falling—Or Is It?* (Washington, DC: National Institute of Justice, 2001).

———, "Youth Violence, Guns, and the Illicit Drug Industry," *Journal of Criminal Law and Criminology* 86(1) (1995): 10–36.

Blumstein, Alfred, and Kiminori Nakamara, "Redemption in the Presence of Widespread Criminal Background Checks," *Criminology* 47(2): 327–59.

Blumstein, Alfred, Frederick P. Rivara, and Richard Rosenfeld, "The Rise and Decline of Homicide—and Why," *American Journal of Public Health* 21 (2000): 505–41.

Bonnie, Richard J., Robert L. Johnson, Betty M. Chemers, and Julie A. Schuck, eds. *Reforming Juvenile Justice: A Developmental Approach* (Washington, DC: National Research Council of the National Academies, 2013).

Braman, Donald, "Families and Incarceration." In *Invisible Punishment: The Collateral Consequences of Mass Imprisonment*, eds. Marc Mauer and Meda Chesney-Lind (New York: The New Press, 2002): 118.

Brenda, B. B., and C. L. Tollet, "A Study of Recidivism of Serious and Persistent Offenders among Adolescents," *Journal of Criminal Justice* 27(2): 111–26.

Bridges, George, and Sarah Steen, "Racial Disparities in Official Assessments of Juvenile Offenders: Attributional Stereotypes as Mediating Mechanisms," *American Sociological Review* 63 (1998): 554–70.

Bushway, Shawn, and Peter Reuter, "Labor Markets and Crime." In *Crime: Public Policies for Crime Control*, 3rd ed., eds. James Q. Wilson and Joan Petersilia (Oakland, CA: Institute for Contemporary Studies Press, 2001).

Butts, Jeffrey, "Can We Do without Juvenile Justice?" (Washington, DC: Urban Institute).

———, *Transfer of Juveniles to Criminal Court Is Not Correlated with Falling Youth Violence* (New York: Research and Evaluation Center, John Jay College of Criminal Justice, 2012).

Butts, Jeffrey, and Daniel Mears, "Reviving Juvenile Justice," *Youth and Society* 33(2) (2001): 169–98.

Butts, Jeffrey, and O. Mitchell, "Brick by Brick: Dismantling the Border between Juvenile and Adult Justice," *Criminal Justice* 2 (2000): 167–213.

Butts, Jeffrey, and Jeremy Travis, *The Rise and Fall of American Youth Violence: 1980 to 2000* (Washington, DC: Urban Institute, Justice Policy Center, 2002).

Caldwell et al., Michael, "Study Characteristics and Recidivism Base Rates in Juvenile Sex Offender Recidivism," *International Journal of Offender Therapy and Comparative Criminology* 54: 197–212.

Carroll, Maureen, "Educating Expelled Students After No Child Left Behind: Mending an Incentive Structure That Discourages Alternative Education and Reinstatement," *UCLA Law Review* 55 (2008): 1909–69.

Ceronne, Kathleen M., "The Gun Free Schools Act of 1994: Zero Tolerance Takes Aim at Procedural Due Process," *Pace Law Review* 20(1) (1999): 131–88.

Clark, R., and M. J. Robertson, *Surviving for the Moment: A Report on Homeless Youth in San Francisco* (Berkeley: Alcohol Research Group, 1996).

Clarke, Elizabeth E., "A Case for Reinventing Juvenile Transfer: The Record of Transfer of Juvenile Offenders to Criminal Court in Cook County, Illinois," *Juvenile and Family Court Journal* 47(4) (1996): 3–22.

Cohen, Andrew, "Bill Clinton and Mass Incarceration" (Brennan Center for Social Justice, October 2014).

Colomy, Paul, and Martin Kretzmann, "Projects and Institution Building: Judge Ben B. Lindsey and the Juvenile Court Movement," *Social Problems* 42(2) (1995): 191–215.

Comfort, Megan, "Punishment Beyond the Legal Offender," *Annual Review of Law and Social Science* 3 (2007): 271–76.

Committee on the Judiciary, United States Senate, *Challenge for the Third Century: Education in a Safe Environment—Final Report on the Nature and Prevention of School Violence and Vandalism* (Washington, DC: U.S. Government Printing Office, 1977).

Conger, Dylan, *Reducing the Foster Care Bias in Juvenile Detention Decisions: The Impact of Project Confirm* (New York: Vera Institute for Justice).

Congressional Research Office, "School Resource Officers: Law Enforcement in Schools" (Washington DC: Author, 2013).

Craigie, Terry Ann, "The Effect of Paternal Incarceration on Early Childhood Behavior Problems: A Racial Comparison," *Journal of Ethnicity in Criminal Justice* 9(3) (2011): 179–99.

Cruz, Patricia A., director of criminal justice, State of Michigan, *Testimony before the Subcommittee on Human Resources, House Committee on Education and Labor,* June 19, 1986.

Cullen, Francis T., "Rehabilitation and Treatment Programs." In *Crime: Public Policies for Crime Control*, eds. James Q. Wilson and Joan Petersilia (Oakland, CA: Institute for Contemporary Studies, 2002), 284–85.

Darling-Hammond, Linda, "Race, Inequality and Educational Accountability: The Irony of 'No Child Left Behind,'" *Race Ethnicity and Education* 10(3) (2007): 245–60.

Carmen Daugherty, *State Trends: Legislative Victories from 2011–2013: Removing Youth from the Adult Criminal Justice System* (Washington, DC: Campaign for Youth Justice, 2013).

Dawson, Robert O., "The Future of Juvenile Justice: Is It Time to Abolish the System?" *Journal of Criminal Law and Criminology* 81(1) (1990): 136–55.

DiIulio, John, "The Coming of the Super-Predators," *Weekly Standard* 1(11) (November 27, 1995): 23–28.

Dishion, T. J., Joan McCord, and F. Poulin, "When Interventions Harm: Peer Groups and Problem Behavior," *American Psychologist* 54(9) (1999): 755–64.

Dorfman, Lori, and Vincent Schiraldi, "Off Balance: Youth, Race, and Crime in the News," *Building Blocks for Youth Initiative*, http://www.hawaii.edu/hivandaids/Off_Balance__Youth,_Race_and_Crime_in_the_News.pdf.

Evans, Douglas, *Pioneers of Youth Justice Reform* (New York: John Jay College of Criminal Justice Research and Evaluation Center, 2012).

Evans-Chase, Michelle, and Huiquan Zhou, "A Systematic Review of the Juvenile Justice Intervention Literature: What It Can (and Cannot) Tell Us About What Works with Delinquent Youth," *Crime and Delinquency* 60(3) (2012): 451–70.

Fagan, Jeffrey, "Separating the Men from the Boys: The Comparative Advantage of Juvenile Versus Criminal Court Sanctions on Recidivism Among Adolescent Felony Offenders." In *A Sourcebook: Serious, Violent, and Chronic Juvenile Offenders*, eds. James C. Howell, Barry Krisberg, J. David Hawkins, and John J. Wilson (Thousand Oaks, CA: Sage, 1995): 238.

Fagan et al., Jeffrey, *Brief of Jeffrey Fagan et al.*, Supreme Court of the United States, 10-9647, 10-9646, January 12, 2012.

Fagan, Jeffrey, and Deanna Wilkinson, "Guns, Youth Violence, and Social Identity." In *Youth Violence*, ed. Michael Tonry and Mark H. Moore (Chicago: University of Chicago Press, 1998), 105–18.

Farrington, David, "Age and Crime." In *Crime and Justice: An Annual Review of Research*, eds. Michael Tonry and N. Morris (Chicago: University of Chicago Press, 1986).

Federal Bureau of Investigation, *Crime in the United States* (Washington, DC: U.S. Government Printing Office, 1993), 287.

Feireman, Jessica, Marsha Levick, and Ami Mody, "The School-to-Prison Pipeline . . . and Back: Obstacles and Remedies for the Re-Enrollment of Adjudicated Youth," *New York Law School Law Review* 54 (2009–2010): 1115–29.

Feld, Barry, "Abolish the Juvenile Court: Youthfulness, Criminal Responsibility, and Sentencing Policy," *Journal of Criminal Law and Criminology* 88(1) (1998): 68–136, 81.

———, *Bad Kids: Race and the Transformation of the Juvenile Court* (New York: Oxford University Press, 1999).

———, "Criminalizing the American Juvenile Court." In *Crime and Justice: An Annual Review of Research*, eds. Michael Tonry and N. Morris (Chicago: University of Chicago Press, 1986).

———, "The Politics of Race and Juvenile Justice: The 'Due Process Revolution' and the Conservative Reaction." In *Race and Juvenile Justice*, eds. Everette B. Penn, Helen Taylor Greene, and Shaun L. Gabiddon (Durham, NC: Carolina Academic Press, 2006).

———, "Race and the Jurisprudence of Juvenile Justice: A Tale in Two Parts, 1950-2000." In *Our Children Their Children: Confronting Racial and Ethnic Differences in American Juvenile Justice*, ed. Darnell F. Hawkins and Kimberly Kempf-Leonard (Chicago: University of Chicago Press, 2005).

———, "Reforming Juvenile Justice," *American Prospect* (August 14, 2005).

——— "Violent Youth and Public Policy: A Case Study of Juvenile Justice," *Minnesota Law Review* 79 (1995): 965–1128.

Finklea, Kristin, *Juvenile Justice Legislative History and Current Legislative Issues* (Washington, DC: Congressional Research Service, 2012).

Fox, Sanford, "The Early History of the Court," *The Future of Children* 6(3) (1996): 29–39.

Foster, Holly, and John Hagan, "The Mass Incarceration of Parents in America: Issues of Race/Ethnicity, collateral Damage to Children, and Prisoner Reentry," *ANNALS of the American Academy of Political Science* 623 (2009): 179–94.

Freeman, R., "Why Do So Many Young American Men Commit Crimes and What Might We Do About It?" *Journal of Economic Perspectives* 10(1) (1996): 25–42.

Garcia, David Alire, "Juveniles Crowd Michigan Sex Offender Registry" (February 10, 2010). Available online: http://michiganmessenger.com/34538/juveniles-well-represented-on-mich-sex-offender-registry.

Garfinkle, Elizabeth, "Coming of Age in America: The Misapplication of Sex-Offender Registration and Community Notification of Juveniles," *California Law Review* 91 (2003): 163.

Gastic, B., "At What Price? Safe School Policies and Their Unintentional Consequences for At-Risk Students" (unpublished manuscript, presented at the Annual Meeting of the American Educational Research Association, April 2006).

Geib, Catherine Foley, John F. Chapman, Amy H. D'Amaddio, and Elena L. Grigorenko, "The Education of Juveniles in Detention: Policy Considerations and Infrastructure Development," *Learning and Individual Differences* 21 (2011): 3–11.

Ghandnoosh, Nazgol, *Race and Punishment: Racial Perceptions of Crime and Support for Punitive Policies* (Washington, DC: The Sentencing Project, 2014).

Christopher Gowen, Lisa Thurau, and Meghan Wood, "The ABA's Approach to Juvenile Justice Reform: Education, Eviction, and Employment: The Collateral Consequences of Juvenile Adjudication," *Duke Forum for Law and Social Change* 3 (2011): 187–203.

Green, Alice P., *The Disproportionate Impact of the Juvenile Justice System on Children of Color in the Capital Region* (Albany: Center for Law and Justice, July 2012), 4.

Greenwood, Peter, "Juvenile Crime and Juvenile Justice." In *Crime: Public Policies for Crime Control*, eds. James Q. Wilson and Joan Petersilia (Oakland, CA: Institute for Contemporary Studies, 2002), 92.

Griffin, Patrick, *Juvenile Transfer to Criminal Court Provisions by State, 2009* (Pittsburgh: National Center for Juvenile Justice, 2010).

Griffin, Patrick, Sean Addie, Benjamin Adams, and Kathy Firestine, *Trying Juveniles as Adults: An Analysis of State Transfer Laws and Reporting* (Washington, DC: Office of Juvenile Justice and Delinquency Prevention, 2011).

Hagan, John, and Jeffrey Leon, "Rediscovering Delinquency: Social History, Political Ideology and the Sociology of Law," *American Sociological Review* 42 (1977): 587–98.

Hagan, J., and B. McCarthy, "Homeless Youth and the Perilous Passage to Adulthood." In *On Your Own without a Net: The Transition to Adulthood for Vulnerable Populations,* eds. D. Wayne Osgood, E. Michael Foster, C. Flanagan, and G. R. Ruth (Chicago: University of Chicago Press, 2005).

Haider-Markel, Donald P., and Mark R. Joslyn, "Gun Policy, Opinion, Tragedy, and Blame Attribution: The Conditional Influence of Issue Frames," *Journal of Politics* 63(2) (2001): 537.

Hankin, Abigail, Marci Hertz, and Thomas Simon, "Impacts of Metal Detector Use in Schools: Insights from 15 Years of Research," *Journal of School Health* 81(2) (2011): 100–106.

Hanson, Avarita L., "Have Zero Tolerance School Discipline Policies Turned into a Nightmare? The American Dream's Promise of Equal Educational Opportunity Grounded in *Brown v Board of Education*," *UC Davis Journal of Juvenile Law and Policy* 9(2) (2005): 289–379.

Henderson, Charles, "Juvenile Courts: Problems of Administration," *Charities* 13 (1905): 340–41.

Henggeler, S., *Multisystemic Therapy: MST 2012 and Beyond.* (San Antonio: 2012 Blueprints Conference). Available online: http://www.blueprintsconference.com/presentations/T4-A.pdf.

Henggeler, S., and S. Schoenwald, "Evidence Based Interventions for Juvenile Offenders and Juvenile Justice Policies That Support Them," *Sharing Child and Youth Development Knowledge* 25(1) (2011): 1–20.

Henning, Kristin, "Eroding Confidentiality in Delinquency Proceedings: Should Schools and Public Housing Authorities Be Notified?" *New York University Law Review* 79 (2004): 520–611.

Hing, Julianne, "What the DOJ Can't Do on School Discipline Reform," April 3, 2013, http://colorlines.com/archives/2013/04/what_the_doj_cant_do_on_school_discipline_reform_1.html.

Hirschfield, Paul, "Another Way Out: The Impact of Juvenile Arrests on High School Dropout," *Sociology of Education* 82 (2009): 368–93.

Hirschfield, Paul, and Katarazyana Cerinska, "Beyond Fear," *Sociology Compass* 3(1) (2011): 1–12.

Hockenberry, Sarah, and Charles Puzzanchera, *Delinquency Cases Waived to Criminal Court, 2011* (Washington, DC: Office of Juvenile Justice and Delinquency Prevention, 2014).

Hockenberry, Sarah, and Charles Puzzanchera, *Juvenile Court Statistics 2011* (Washington, DC: Office of Juvenile Justice and Delinquency Prevention, 2014).

Hockenberry, Sarah, Melissa Sickmund, and Anthony Sladky, *Juvenile Residential Facility Census, 2012: Selected Findings* (Washington, DC: Office of Juvenile Justice and Delinquency Prevention, 2015).

Hoffman, A. M., and R. W. Summers, eds., *Teen Violence: A Global View* (Westport, CT: Greenwood Press, 2001).

Hollis, Mark, "Florida Toughest on Teen Criminals," *Sun Sentinel* (May 18, 2000). Available online: http://articles.sun-sentinel.com/2000-05-18/news/0005180020_1_juvenile-crime-mandatory-minimum-sentences-jeb-bush.

Howell, James C., *Juvenile Justice and Youth Violence* (Thousand Oaks, CA: Sage, 1997).

———, *Preventing and Reducing Juvenile Delinquency: A Comprehensive Framework* (Thousand Oaks, CA: Sage, 2003).

Howell, James C., Barry C. Feld, Daniel P Mears, David P. Farrington, Rolf Loeber, and David Petechuk, *Bulletin 5: Youth Offenders and an Effective Response in the Juvenile and Adult Court Systems: What Happens, What Should Happen, and What We Need to Know* (Washington, DC: Department of Justice, 2013).

Jensen, Eric L., and Linda K. Metsger, "A Test of the Deterrent Effect of Legislative Waiver on Violent Juvenile Crime," *Crime and Delinquency* 96 (1994): 102.

Jolliffe, Darrick, David P. Farrington, and Philip Howard, "How Long Did It Last? A 10-Year Reconviction Follow-Up Study of High Intensity Training for Youth Offenders," *Journal of Experimental Criminology* 9(4) (2013): 515–31.

Juvenile Law Center, "*Roper v. Simmons* Ten Years Later, Part 3: Juvenile Justice and Developmental Research in the Post-Roper Era." Posted online on JLC website, March 6, 2015: http://jlc.org/blog/roper-v-simmons-ten-years-later-recollections-and-reflections-abolition-juvenile-death-penalt-1.

Kang-Brown, Jacob, Jennifer Trone, Jennifer Fratello, and Tarika Daftary-Kapur, *A Generation Later: What We've Learned about Zero Tolerance in Schools* (New York: Vera Institute of Justice, December 2013).

Kaplan, Wendy, and David Rossman, "Called 'Out' at Home: The One Strike Eviction Policy and Juvenile Court," *Duke Forum for Law and Social Change* (2011).

Katel, Peter, Melinda Liu, and Bob Cohn, "The Bust in Boot Camps," *Newsweek* 26 (1994).

Robert F. Kennedy National Resource for Juvenile Justice, *From Conversation to Collaboration: How Child Welfare and Juvenile Justice Agencies Can Work Together* (Beacon, MA: Author, n.d.).

Kleck, Gary, "Mass Shootings in Schools: The Worst Possible Case for Gun Control," *American Behavioral Scientist* (2009): 1447–64.

Kramer, Ronald, and Raymond Michalowski, "The Iron Fist and the Velvet Tongue: Crime Control Policies in the Clinton Administration," *Social Justice* 22(2) (1995): 87–100.

Krezmien, Michael P., Peter E. Leone, Mark S. Zablocki, and Craig S. Wells, "Juvenile Court Referrals and the Public Schools: Nature and Extent of the Practice in Five States," *Journal of Contemporary Criminal Justice* 26(3) (2010): 273–93.

Krisberg, Barry, "Are You Now or Have You Ever Been a Sociologist?" *Journal of Criminal Law and Criminology* 82(1) (1991): 141–55.

———, *Juvenile Justice: Redeeming Our Children* (Thousand Oaks, CA: Sage, 2005).

Krisberg, Barry, Ira M. Schwartz, Paul Litsky, and James Austin, "The Watershed of Juvenile Justice Reform," *Crime and Delinquency* 32(1) (1986): 5–38.

Kurleychek, Megan, Robert Brame, and Shawn Bushway, "Scarlet Letters and Recidivism: Does an Old Criminal Record Predict Future Offending?" *Criminology and Public Policy* 5(3) (2006): 483.

Kysel, Ian, *Growing Up Locked Down: Youth in Solitary Confinement in Jails and Prisons Across the United States* (San Francisco, Human Rights Watch, 2012).

———, Testimony before the Senate Judiciary Subcommittee on the Constitution, Civil Rights, and Human Rights Hearing on Reassessing Solitary Confinement II: The Human Rights, Fiscal, and Public Safety Consequences, Tuesday, February 25, 2014, Washington, DC. Available online: http://www.law.georgetown. edu/academics/centers-institutes/human-rights-institute/opportunities/upload/Ian-Kysel-Solitary-Confinement-Hearing-Testimony-FINAL.pdf.

Lanza-Kaduce, Lonn, Charles Frazier, and Donna Bishop, "Juvenile Transfer in Florida: The Worst of the Worst?" *Journal of Law and Policy* 10 (1999): 277–312.

Latessa, E. J., M. G. Turner, M. M. Moon, and B. Applegate, *A Statewide Evaluation of the RECLAIM Ohio Initiative* (Washington, DC: Bureau of Justice Assistance, 1998).

Lazarow, Katherine, "The Continued Viability of New York's Juvenile Offender Act in Light of Recent National Developments," *New York Law School Review* 57 (2012): 595–635.

Lemert, Edwin M., *Social Pathology: A Systemic Approach to the Theory of Sociopathic Behavior* (New York: McGraw Hill, 1951).

Lerman, Paul, "Twentieth Century Developments in America's Institutional Systems for Youth in Trouble," in *A Century of Juvenile Justice,* ed. Margaret K. Rosenheim et al. (2002): 74–110.

Liazos, Alexander, "Class Oppression: The Functions of Juvenile Justice," *Critical Sociology* 5(2) (1974): 8.

Liberman, Akiva, M. David S. Kirk, and Kideuk Kim, "Labeling Effects of First Juvenile Arrests: Secondary Deviance and Secondary Sanctioning," *Criminology* 52(3): 345–70.

Lin, J., *Exploring the Impact of Institutional Placement on Recidivism of Delinquent Youth* (Washington, DC: National Institute of Justice, 2007).

Lindsey, Ben B., "The Juvenile Laws of Colorado," *The Green Bag* (1906): 126–31.

Listenbee, Robert, *Report of the Attorney General's Task Force on Children Exposed to Violence* (Washington, DC: U.S. Department of Justice, 2012).

Lochner, L., and E. Moretti, "The Effect of Education on Crime: Evidence from Prison Inmates, Arrests, and Self Reports," *American Economic Review* 94(1) (2004): 155–89.

Lopez, German, and Joe Posner, "Cory Booker on How America's Criminal Justice System Destroys the American Dream," March 16, 2015, http://www.vox. com/2015/3/16/8205027/cory-booker-drug-war.

Lotke, Eric, "Youth Homicide: Keeping Perspective on How Many Children Kill," *Valparaiso University Law Review* 31 (1997): 395–418.

Lotke, Eric, and Vincent Schiraldi, "An Analysis of Juvenile Homicides: Where They Occur and the Effectiveness of Adult Court Intervention" (Alexandria, VA: National Center on Institutions and Alternatives, July 16, 1996).

Lowenkamp, C., and E. Latessa, *Evaluation of Ohio's RECLAIM Funded Programs, CCFs, and DYS Facilities* (Cincinnati: University of Cincinnati, 2005).

Lowenkamp, C., and E. Latessa, *Reclaiming Texas Youth: Applying the Lessons from RECLAIM Ohio to Texas* (Austin: Texas Public Policy Foundation, 2009).

Mack, Julian, "The State and the Child," *Harvard Law Review* (1911).

Majd, Katayoon, "Students of the Mass Incarceration Nation," *Howard Law Journal* 54(2) (2011).

Males, Michael, *The Scapegoat Generation: America's War on Adolescents* (Monroe, ME: Common Courage Press, 1996).

Marchbanks et al., Miner, "More than a Drop in the Bucket: The Social and Economic Costs of Dropouts and Grade Retentions Associated with Exclusionary Discipline," *Journal of Applied Research on Children: Informing Policy for Children at Risk* 5(2): 1–36.

Marsh, Jennifer Watson, *Juvenile Delinquency Adjudication, Collateral Consequences, and Expungement of Juvenile Records* (University of North Carolina Center for Civil Rights, n.d.).

Martinez, Ramiro, Richard Rosenfeld, and Dennis Mares, "Social Disorganization, Drug Market Activity, and Neighborhood Violent Crime," *Urban Affairs Review* 43(6) (2004): 846–74.

Mauer, Marc, *Race to Incarcerate* (New York: New Press, 2006).

———, "Racial Impact Statements: Changing Policies to Address Disparities," *Criminal Justice* 23(4) (2009).

Mayer, M. J., and P. E. Leone, "School Violence and Disruption Revisited: Equity and Safety in the School House," *Focus on Exceptional Children* 40(1) (2007): 1–28.

Mayer, M. J., and P. E. Leone, "A Structural Analysis of School Violence and Disruption: Implications for Creating Safer Schools," *Education and Treatment of Children* 22(3) (1999): 333–56.

McAndrews, Tobin, "Zero Tolerance Policies," *ERIC Digest* (University of Oregon, 2001).

McCullom, Bill, Testimony before the House Subcommittee on Early Childhood, Youth, and Families, Washington, DC, 1996.

McGowen et al., supra note 20 citing Simon I. Singer and David McDowall, "Criminalizing Delinquency: The Deterrent Effects of the New York Juvenile Offender Law," *Law and Society Review* 22(521) (1988): 532–33.

McNulty, Paul, "Natural Born Killers? Preventing the Coming Explosion of Teenage Crime," *Policy Review* 71 (1995): 84–87.

Meade, Benjamin, and Benjamin Steiner, "The Total Effect of Boot Camps That House Juveniles: A Systematic Review of the Evidence," *Journal of Criminal Justice* 38 (2010): 841–53.

Mendel, Richard, *Closing Massachusetts Training Schools: Reflections Forty Years Later* (Baltimore: Annie E. Casey Foundation, 2014).

————, *No Place for Kids* (Baltimore: Annie E. Casey Foundation, 2011).

————, *Two Decades of JDAI: From Demonstration Project to National Standard* (Baltimore: Annie E. Casey Foundation, 2009).

Miller, Jerome, *Last One Over the Wall: The Massachusetts Experiment in Closing Reform Schools*, 2nd ed. (Ohio: Ohio State University, 1998).

Mock, Brentin, "Good News in Mississippi: School to-Prison Pipeline Closes," *Colorlines* (2013). http://colorlines.com/archives/2013/05/good_news_in_miss_school-to-prison_pipeline_closed.html.

Montgomery, Ben, "More Bodies Found than Expected at the Dozier School," *Miami Herald* (January 4, 2012). Available online: http://www.miamiherald.com/news/state/florida/article5427669.html#!tabPane=tabs-b0710947-1-1.

————, "USF Team Looks for Lost Graves at Closed Dozier School for Boys," *Tampa Bay Tribune* (May 19, 2012), Available online: http://www.tampabay.com/features/humaninterest/usf-team-looks-for-lost-graves-at-closed-dozier-school-for-boys/1230895.

Moon, M., B. Applegate, and E. Latessa, "RECLAIM Ohio: A Politically Viable Alternative to Treating Youthful Felony Offenders," *Crime and Delinquency* 43(4) (1997): 438–56.

Mulvey, Edward, Laurence Steinberg, Alex R. Piquero, Michelle Besana, Jeffrey Fagan, Carol Schubert, and Elizabeth Cauffman, "Longitudinal Offending Trajectories among Serious Adolescent Offenders," *Development and Psychopathology* 22 (2010): 453–75.

Muschert, Glenn W., "The Columbine Victims and the Myth of the Juvenile Superpredator," *Youth Violence and Juvenile Justice* 5(4) (2007): 351–66.

Myers, David L., *Excluding Violent Youths from Juvenile Court: The Effectiveness of Legislative Waiver*, LFB Scholarly Publishing (2001).

National Advisory Committee for Juvenile Justice and Delinquency Prevention, *Serious Juvenile Crime: A Redirected Federal Effort* (Washington, DC: Office of Juvenile Justice and Delinquency Prevention, 1984), 4.

National Conference on Juvenile Justice Records: Appropriate Criminal and Noncriminal Justice Uses, Proceedings of a BJS/SEARCH Conference, May 1997.

National Criminal Justice Authority, *Juvenile Justice Reform Initiatives in the States, 1994-1996* (Washington, DC: Office of Juvenile Justice and Delinquency Prevention).

Nellis, Ashley, *Life Goes On* (Washington, DC: The Sentencing Project).

————, *The Lives of Juvenile Lifers: Findings from a National Survey* (Washington, DC: The Sentencing Project, 2012).

Noguera, Pedro, "Preventing and Producing Violence: A Critical Analysis of Responses to School Violence," *Harvard Educational Review* (Summer 1995): 189–213.

Noonan, Margaret E., *Mortality in Local Jails and State Prisons, 2000-2012—Statistical Tables* (Washington, DC: Bureau of Justice Statistics, 2014).

North Carolina Department of Justice, Law Enforcement Liaison Section, *The North Carolina Sex Offender and Public Protection Registration Programs* (Raleigh: North Carolina Department of Public Safety, 2014). Available online: http://www. ncdoj.gov/sexoffenderpublication.aspx.Office of Juvenile Justice and Delinquency Prevention, *Juvenile Boot Camps: Lessons Learned*. Available online: http://www. ncjrs.gov/txtfiles/fs-9636.txt.

Office of the Surgeon General, *Youth Violence: A Report of the Surgeon General* (Washington: Office of the Surgeon General, 2001).

Ousey, Graham C., and Michelle Campbell Augustine, "Young Guns: Examining Alternative Explanations of Juvenile Firearm Homicide Rates," *Criminology* 39:4 (2001): 938.

Ousey, Graham C., and Matthew R. Lee, "Investigating the Connections between Race, Illicit Drug Markets, and Lethal Violence, 1984-1997," *Journal of Research in Crime and Delinquency* 41(4) (2004): 352–83.

Padres and jóvenes Unidos, "The Colorado School Discipline Report Card" (March 2014).

Pager, Devah, *Marked: Race, Crime, and Finding Work in an Era of Mass Incarceration* (Chicago: University of Chicago Press, 2007).

Raymond, Paternoster, Carolyn Turpin-Petrosino, and Sarah Guckenburg, "Formal System Processing of Juveniles: Effects on Delinquency," *Campbell Systemic Reviews* (2010): 1–88.

Payne Allison Ann, and Kelly Welch, "Modeling the Effects of Racial Threat on Punitive and Restorative School Discipline Practices," *Criminology* 48 (2010): 1019–62.

Petrosino, Anthony C., Turpin-Petrosino, M. Hollis-Peel, and J. G. Lavenberg, "Scared Straight and Other Juvenile Awareness Programs for Preventing Juvenile Delinquency: A Systematic Review," *Campbell Systematic Reviews* 5 (2013).

Petteruti, Amanda, Marc Schindler, and Jason Zeidenberg, *Sticker Shock* (Washington, DC: Justice Policy Institute, 2015).

Pickett, Joshua, and Ted Chiricos, "Controlling Other People's Children: Racialized Views of Delinquency and White's Punitive Attitudes toward Juvenile Offenders," *Criminology* 50(3) (2012): 673–710.

Pickett, Joshua, Ted Chiricos, and Marc Gertz, "The Racial Foundations of Whites' Support for Child Saving," *Social Science Research* 44 (2014): 44–59.

Pinard, Michael, "The Logistical and Ethical Difficulties of Informing Juveniles about the Collateral Consequences of Adjudications," *Nevada Law Journal* 6 (2006): 1111–26.

Piquero, Alex, and Laurence Steinberg, "Public Preferences for Rehabilitation Versus Incarceration for Juvenile Offenders," *Journal of Criminal Justice* 38 (2010): 1–6.

Platt, Anthony, *The Child Savers: The Invention of Delinquency* (New Brunswick, NJ: Rutgers University Press, 2009).

President's Commission on Law Enforcement and Administration of Justice, *The Challenge of Crime in a Free Society: A Report by the President's Commission on Law Enforcement and Administration of Justice* (Washington, DC: U.S. Government Printing Office, 1967).

Puzzanchera, Charles, *Juvenile Arrests, 2011* (Washington, DC: Office of Juvenile Justice and Delinquency, 2014).

Adams, Charles B., and Melissa Sickmund, *Juvenile Court Statistics, 2011* (Washington, DC: Office of Juvenile Justice and Delinquency Prevention, 2014).

Redding, Richard, "Juveniles Transferred to Criminal Court: Legal Reform Proposals Based on Social Science Research," *Utah Law Review* (1997): 709–97.

Regnery, Alfred, "Getting Away with Murder: Why the Juvenile Justice System Needs an Overhaul," *Policy Review* 34 (1985): 65–68.

Reno, Janet, "Fighting Youth Violence: The Future is Now," *Criminal Justice* 11 (1996): 33.

Robers, Simone, Jana Kemp, and Jennifer Truman, "Indicators of School Crime and Safety: 2012" (National Center for Education Statistics, 2013).

Robert Wood Johnson Foundation, *A New DARE Curriculum Gets Mixed Results* (Washington, DC: 2010). Available online: http://www.rwjf.org/content/dam/farm/reports/program_results_reports/2010/rwjf70259.

Robertson, M. J., *Homeless Youth in Hollywood: Patterns of Alcohol Use. Report to the National Institute on Alcohol Abuse and Alcoholism (No C51)* (Berkeley: Alcohol Research Group, 1989).

Rodriguez, Lia, "Juvenile Legislation: Where's the Love in 'Tough Love,'" *Public Interest Law Section Reporter* 9(1) (2000): 11–12.

Roetger, Michael E., and Raymond R. Swisher, "Associations of Fathers' History of Incarceration with Sons' Delinquency and Arrest Among Black, White, and Hispanic Males in the United States," *Criminology* 49(4) (2011): 1109–47.

Sampson, Robert, and John Laub, "Life Course Desisters? Trajectories of Crime Among Delinquent Boys Followed to Age 70," *Criminology* 43: 905–13.

Sampson, Robert J., and John H. Laub, "A Life-Course Theory of Cumulative Disadvantage and the Stability of Delinquency." In *Developmental Theories of Crime and Delinquency*, ed. Terence P. Thornberry (New Brunswick, NJ: Transaction, 2004).

Samuels, Mina, *Children in Confinement in Louisiana* (New York: Human Rights Watch, 1995).

Schlossman, Steven L., *Love and the American Delinquent: The Theory and Practice of 'Progressive' Juvenile Justice* (Chicago: University of Chicago Press, 1977).

Schur, Edwin M., *Radical Non-Intervention: Rethinking the Delinquency Problem* (Englewood: Prentice Hall, 1973).

Schwartz, Robert, *Keynote Address* (presented at the Symposium on the Intersection of Juvenile Justice and Poverty, Washington, DC, Georgetown University Law Center, March 26, 2009).

Shah Riya Saha, and Lauren A. Fine, *Failed Policies, Forfeited Futures: A Nationwide Scorecard on Juvenile Records* (Philadelphia: Juvenile Law Center, 2014).

Scott, Elizabeth S., "'Children Are Different': Constitutional Values and Justice Policy," *Ohio Journal of Criminal Law* 11(1) (2013): 71–105.

Scott, Elizabeth S., and Thomas Grisso, "The Evolution of Adolescence: A Developmental Perspective on Juvenile Justice Reform," *Journal of Criminal Law and Criminology* 137 (1997): 88.

Scott, Elizabeth S., and Laurence Steinberg, *Rethinking Juvenile Justice* (Boston: Harvard University Press, 2008).

Selcraig, Bruce, "Camp Fear," *Mother Jones* (2000), http://www.motherjones.com/politics/2000/11/camp-fear.

Sesame Workshop, "Little Children, Big Challenges: Incarceration," 2013.

Sheldon, Randall, and Lynne Osborne, "'For Their Own Good': Class Interests and the Child Saving Movement in Memphis, Tennessee, 1900–1917," *Criminology* 27 (1989): 747–67.

Shepherd, Robert E., "Film at Eleven: The News Media and Juvenile Crime," *Quinnipiac Law Review* 18 (1999): 687–700.

———, "Pleading Guilty in Delinquency Cases," *Criminal Justice Magazine* 16(3) (2001).

Sherman, Rorie, "Juvenile Judges Say: Time to Get Tough," *National Law Journal* (August 8, 1994): 1.

Sherry, J., "Violent Video Games and Aggression: Why Can't We Find Links?" In *Mass Media Effects Research: Advances through Meta-Analysis*, eds. R. Preiss, B. Gayle, N. Burrell, M. Allen, and J. Bryant (Mahwah, NJ: Lawrence Erlbaum, 2006), 231–48.

Sickmund, Melissa, *Juvenile Offenders and Victims, 1997: Update on Violence* (Washington, DC: Office of Juvenile Justice and Delinquency Prevention Coalition, 1997.

Sickmund, Melissa, A. Sladky, W. Kang, and C. Puzzanchera, "Easy Access to the Census of Juveniles in Residential Placement," 2013. Available online: http://www.ojjdp.gov/ojstatbb/ezacjrp/.

Sickmund, Melissa, M., A. Sladky,, and Kang, W. (2014). "Easy Access to Juvenile Court Statistics: 1985-2011." Available online: http://www.ojjdp.gov/ojstatbb/ezajcs/. Data source: *National Juvenile Court Data Archive: Juvenile court case records 1985-2011* [machine-readable data files]. Pittsburgh, PA: National Center for Juvenile Justice (2014).

Simkins, S. *When Kids Get Arrested: What Every Adult Should Know* (New Brunswick, NJ: Rutgers University Press, 2009).

Simmons, Charlene Wear, "Children of Incarcerated Parents," Sacramento, California Research Bureau, 7(2): 1–11.

Skiba, Russell, "Zero Tolerance, Zero Evidence: An Analysis of School Disciplinary Practice," *Indiana Education Policy Center*, 7–8.

Skiba, Russell, and M. Karega Rausch, "Zero Tolerance, Suspension, and Questions of Equity and Effectiveness." In *Handbook of Classroom Management: Research, Practice, and Contemporary Issues*, eds. Carolyn M. Evertson and Carol S. Weinstein (Mahwah, NJ: Laurence Erlbaum Associates, 2006).

Snyder, Howard N. "An Empirical Portrait of the Youth Reentry Population," *Youth Violence and Juvenile Justice* 2(1) (2004): 39.

Snyder, Howard, and Melissa Sickmund, *Juvenile Offenders and Victims: 2006 National Report* (Pittsburgh: National Center for Juvenile Justice, 2006.)

Snyder H., and J. Mulako-Wangota, Arrest Data Analysis Tool, accessed on February 13, 2015, at www.bjs.gov (Washington, DC: Bureau of Justice Statistics).

Snyder, Howard, and Melissa Sickmund, *Challenging the Myths* (Washington, DC: Office of Juvenile Justice and Delinquency Prevention, 2000).

Snyder, Howard, and Melissa Sickmund, *Juvenile Offenders and their Victims: A National Report* (Washington, DC: Office of Juvenile Justice and Delinquency Prevention, 1999).

Soler, Mark, Dana Schoenberg, and Marc Schindler, "Juvenile Justice: Lessons for a New Era," *Georgetown Journal of Poverty Law and Policy* 26 (2009): 483–541.

Spatz-Widom, Cathy, and M. G. Maxfield, *An Update on the "Cycle of Violence"* (Washington, DC: National Institute of Justice: Research in Brief, 2001) 1–8.

Stahl, Anne, "Cases Waived to Criminal Court, 1987-1996," U.S. Department of Justice, Office of Juvenile Justice and Delinquency Prevention Coalition, 1999.

Stanfield, Rochelle, *The JDAI Story: Building a Better Juvenile Detention System* (Baltimore: Annie E. Casey, 1999).

Steinberg, Laurence, and K. C. Monahan, "Age Differences in Resistance to Peer Influence," *Developmental Psychology* 43 (2007): 1531–43.

Steinberg, Laurence, and Elizabeth S. Scott, "Less Guilty by Reason of Adolescence: Developmental Immaturity, Diminished Responsibility, and the Juvenile Death Penalty," *American Psychologist* 58(12) (2003).

Sum, A., I. Khatiwada, J. McLaughlin, and S. Palma, *The Consequences of Dropping out of High School: Joblessness and Jailing for High School Dropouts and the High Cost for Taxpayers* (Boston: Center for Labor Market Studies, Northeastern University, 2009).

Sutton, John R., "The Juvenile Court and Social Welfare: Dynamics of Progressive Reform," *Law and Society Review* 19(1) (1985).

Szymanski, Lynn A., *Sealing/Expungement/Destruction of Juvenile Court Records: Sealed Records That Can Be Unsealed or Inspected* (Philadelphia: National Center for Juvenile Justice, 2006).

Tanenhaus, David T., "The Evolution of Juvenile Courts in the Early Twentieth Century: Beyond the Myth of Immaculate Construction." In *A Century of Juvenile Justice,* ed. Margaret K. Rosenheim et al. (Chicago: University of Chicago Press, 2002), 42–73.

Travis, Jeremy, *But They All Come Back: Facing the Challenges of Prisoner Reentry* (Washington, DC: Urban Institute, 2005).

———, "Reflections on Juvenile Justice Reform in New York," *New York Law School Law Review* 56 (2011): 1317–28.

Tyler, Jasmine, Jason Zeidenberg, and Eric Lotke, *Cost-Effective Youth Corrections: Rationalizing the Fiscal Architecture of Juvenile Justice Systems* (Washington, DC: Justice Policy Institute, 2006).

Uggen, Christopher, and Suzy McElrath, "Parental Incarceration: What We Know and Where We Need to Go," *Journal of Criminal Law and Criminology* 104(3) (2014): 597–604.

Uggen, Christopher, Sarah Shannan, and Jeff Manza, *State-Level Estimates of Felon Disenfranchisement, 2010* (Washington, DC: The Sentencing Project, 2012).

Uggen, Christopher, and Melissa Thompson, "The Socioeconomic Determinants of Ill-Gotten Gains: Within-Person Changes in Drug Use and Illegal Earnings," *American Journal of Sociology* 109(1) (2003): 146.

U.S. Department of Commerce and Labor, "The Children's Bureau." Available online: http://www.mchlibrary.info/history/chbu/20364.pdf.

U.S. Department of Education, Office of Safe and Healthy Students, *Report on the Implementation of the Gun Free School Zones Act Schools Act in the States and Outlying Areas for School Year 2010-11* (Washington, DC: U.S. Department of Education, 2013).

U.S. Department of Justice, "Violent Crime Control and Law Enforcement Act of 1994" (Washington, DC, 1994). Fact Sheet. https://www.ncjrs.gov/txtfiles/billfs.txt.

U.S. Department of Justice Civil Rights Division, December 1, 2011, Investigation of the Arthur G. Dozier School of Boys and the Jackson Juvenile Offender Center, Marianna, Florida. Page 4. Full report available online: www.justice.gov/crt/about/spl/documents/dozier_findltr_12-1-11.pdf.

U.S. Department of Justice, Press Release, "Justice Department Files Lawsuit in Mississippi to Protect the Constitutional Rights of Children" (Washington, DC: U.S. Department of Justice). http://www.justice.gov/opa/pr/justice-department-files-lawsuit-mississippi-protect-constitutional-rights-children.

U.S. Senate Committee on the Judiciary, Confirmation hearings on federal appointments: Hearings before the Committee on the Judiciary, United States Senate, One Hundred Third Congress, first session on confirmations of appointees to the federal judiciary (Washington, DC: Government Printing Office, 1995), 11.

U.S. Prison Culture, "Punishing Children: Houses of Refuge and Juvenile Justice," *Prison Culture* (February 3, 2011). http://www.usprisonculture.com/blog/2011/02/03/punishing-children-houses-of-refuge-juvenile-justice/.

Utah State Juvenile Court, *Annual Report, 1978*, Salt Lake City, Utah State Juvenile Court.

Wacquant, Loic, "Deadly Symbiosis," in *Mass Imprisonment: Social Causes and Consequences* (Thousand Oaks, CA: Sage, 2001), page 95–133.

Wallace, Barbara C., "Crack, Policy, and Advocacy: A Case Analysis Illustrating the Need to Monitor Emergent Public Health-Related Policy and Engage in Persistent Evidence-Based Advocacy," *Journal of Equity in Health* 3(1) (2014): 139–60.

Wald, Johanna, and Daniel J. Losen, "Defining and Redirecting a School-to-Prison Pipeline," *New Directions for Youth Development* 2003 (2003): 9–15.

Ward, Geoff, *The Black Child-Savers: Racial Democracy and Juvenile Justice* (Chicago: University of Chicago Press, 2012), 74.

Weiler, Spencer C., and Martha Cray, "Police at School: A Brief History and Current Status of School Resource Officers" *Clearing House* 84(4) (2011): 160–63.

Weiser, Benjamin, "Five Exonerated in Central Park Jogger Case Agree to Settle Suit for $40 Million" *New York Times* (June 19, 2014). http://www.nytimes.com/2014/06/20/nyregion/5-exonerated-in-central-park-jogger-case-are-to-settle-suit-for-40-million.html?hp&_r=1.

West, Steven, and Keri K. O'Neal, "Project DARE Outcome Effectiveness Revisited," *American Journal of Public Health* 94(6) (2004): 1027–29.

White, Henry George, Charles E. Frazier, and Lonn Lanza-Kaduce, "A Socio-Legal History of Florida's Juvenile Transfer Reforms," *University of Florida Journal of Law and Public Policy* 10 (1999): 249–76.

Wiig, Janet K., and John A. Tuell, *Guidebook for Juvenile Justice and Child Welfare System Coordination and Integration: A Framework for Improved Outcomes*, 3rd ed., Robert F. Kennedy Children's Action Corps, MacArthur Foundation, 2013.

Wildeman, Chistopher, "Parental Imprisonment, the Prison Boom, and the Concentration of Childhood Disadvantage," *Demography* 46(2): 265–80.

Wiley, Stephanie Ann, Lee Ann Slocum, and Finn-Aage Esbensen, "The Unintended Consequences of Being Stopped or Arrested: An Exploration of the Labeling Mechanisms Through Which Police Contact Leads to Subsequent Delinquency," *Criminology* 51(4) (2013): 927–96.

Wilkinson, Deanna, and Jeffrey Fagan, *What Do We Know about Gun Use among Adolescents?* (Boulder, CO: Center for the Study and Prevention of Violence, 2002).

Wilson, David B., Doris L. MacKenzie, and F. Mitchell, "Effects of Correctional Boot Camps on Offending," *Campbell Collaborative Reviews* 6 (2005).

Winner, Lawrence, Lonn Lanza-Kaduce, Donna M. Bishop, and Charles E. Frazier, "The Transfer of Juveniles to Criminal Court: Reexamining Recidivism Over the Long Term," *Crime and Delinquency* 548 (1997): 558–59.

Wittman, Gerald P., "Review of *Love and the American Delinquent*," Juvenile and Family Court Judges, 28(3) (1977): 1–2.

Wolf, Kerrin, "Arrest Decision Making by SRO Officers," *Youth Violence and Juvenile Justice* (2013).

Woods, John, "New York's Juvenile Offender Law: An Overview and Analysis," *Fordham Urban Law Journal* 9(1) (1980): 1–50.

Youth United for Change, Advancement Project, "Zero Tolerance in Philadelphia: Denying Educational Opportunities and Creating a Pathway to Prison" (Washington, DC: Advancement Project, 2011).

Zimring, Franklin, *American Juvenile Justice* (Oxford: Oxford University Publishing, 2005).

———, "American Youth Violence: A Cautionary Tale." In *Choosing the Future for American Juvenile Justice*, eds. Franklin Zimring and David S. Tanenhaus (New York: New York University Press, 2014), 32.

———, "American Youth Violence: Implications for National Juvenile Justice Policy," *Update on Law Related Education: Juvenile Justice* 23(2) (2000).

———, *An American Travesty: Legal Responses to Adolescent Sexual Offending* (Chicago: University of Chicago Press, 2006).

———, "Crying Wolf over Teen Demons; Crime: Projecting a New Crime Wave Serves Politicians, Even If It Has No Basis in Reality," *Los Angeles Times* (August 19, 1996).

———, "The 1990s Assault on Juvenile Justice: Notes from an Ideological Battleground," *Federal Sentencing Reporter* 11(5) (199): 260–61.

———, "Real Proportionality for the Young Offender: Notes on Immaturity, Capacity, and Diminished Responsibility." In *Youth on Trial: A Developmental Perspective on Juvenile Crime*, eds. T. Grisso and Robert Schwartz (Chicago: University of Chicago Press, 2000).

Zimring, Franklin, and Gordon Hawkins, *Incapacitation: Penal Confinement and the Restraint of Crime* (New York: Oxford University Press, 1995).

Zimring, Franklin, and Stephen Rushin, "Did Changes in Sanctions Reduce Juvenile Crime Rates?" *Ohio State Journal of Criminal Law* 11(1) (2013): 57–69.

Index

About the Author

Ashley Nellis, PhD, is a senior research analyst with The Sentencing Project. She has an academic and professional background in analyzing criminal justice policies and practices and has extensive experience in analyzing disparities among youth of color in the juvenile justice system. She leads The Sentencing Project's research and legislative activities in juvenile justice reform and serves on several youth-serving coalitions and working groups in the Washington, DC, area. She regularly delivers testimony, authors articles and other publications, and conducts research. Nellis is actively engaged in federal and state efforts to eliminate life without parole sentences for juveniles and to reconsider lengthy sentences for all prisoners. She is frequently interviewed by members of the media on a variety of juvenile justice–related topics.